THE BIPOLAR RUNNER

A Memoir

THE BIPOLAR RUNNER

A Memoir

JACQUI LOUISE SWALLOW

PEPPER PRESS

PEPPER PRESS

First published in 2024 by Pepper Press, an imprint of Fair Play Publishing
PO Box 4101, Balgowlah Heights, NSW 2093, Australia
www.fairplaypublishing.com.au

ISBN: 978-1-923236-11-0
ISBN: 978-1-923236-12-7 (ePub)

© Jacqui Louise Swallow

The moral rights of the author have been asserted.

All rights reserved. Except as permitted under the *Australian Copyright Act 1968* (for example, a fair dealing for the purposes of study, research, criticism or review), no part of this book may be reproduced, stored in a retrieval system, communicated or transmitted in any form or by any means without prior written permission from the Publisher.

This is a memoir based on a contemporaneous diary detailing the author's experience. It is not intended to, and does not, amount to advice which individuals should rely on. Organisations that can assist people seeking support and advice are listed on page 235.

Cover design and typesetting by Ismail Ogunbiyi.
Front cover photograph by Aua Kajewski.

All inquiries should be made to the Publisher via hello@fairplaypublishing.com.au

A catalogue record for this book is available from the National Library of Australia

For Daisy, my daughter and Daisy, my grandmother

CONTENTS

INTRODUCTION 1

THE DIARY: Sunday 4 June 2023 to Sunday 15 October 2023.........................7

EPILOGUE 231

ACKNOWLEDGEMENTS 233

ABOUT THE AUTHOR.. 235

INTRODUCTION

Before I start with the perhaps self-indulgent journal entries on the pathway to my first official marathon, I suppose I should introduce myself. My name's Jacqui, and there's nothing particularly interesting or noteworthy about me. I'm not a writer. I happen to suffer from bipolar disorder, and I happen to be a runner.

I've been getting into books about running lately, and I thought, *Hey, I'll google 'Bipolar Runner' and see what comes up*. Still, there was little information or inspiration for the bipolar runner.

I have a friend who is also a runner who says that just about every runner he knows has mental health issues, and generally, the more serious the runner, the more serious the mental health issues. Not that I'm saying running *causes* poor mental health—far from it. It's more that running is so beneficial for wellbeing that those who have stumbled upon it tend to throw themselves into it with such gusto that it becomes almost like a religion.

I was diagnosed with bipolar disorder in 2002, at the age of 19, during my first year of university, but there were signs that something wasn't quite right way earlier. When I was about nine years old, I lost a friend. When I say 'lost a friend,' I don't mean that my friend died; she just stopped being my friend. Most kids would find this upsetting, but my reaction was over the top. I cried myself to sleep every night for a year and ended up changing schools.

At 15, I experienced something of a nervous breakdown. I'm half-Mauritian on my mother's side, and for Mauritian girls, the 15th birthday is traditionally a big deal. Leading up to my birthday, I had this huge paranoia that no-one would come to my party and that no-one liked me. This was not true. There was a huge turnout.

On the night of my birthday party, I had a severe panic attack about people taking off their shoes and worrying that they wouldn't be able to find their shoes later. That night, I couldn't sleep, I was amped up, stressed, and hyper vigilant, hearing things and assuming everyone was awake and having fun without me when everyone was just asleep. My parents were extremely worried.

In the weeks that followed, I had panic attacks and floods of tears several times a day over nothing. I'd get overwhelmed by something at school, start crying uncontrollably, and be sent home.

I went to a bunch of psychiatrists and was tested for conditions like schizophrenia.

No one could figure out what was wrong, and in the end the verdict was that maybe I had generalised anxiety disorder. But they were not sure. And then one day I was magically fine. No drugs or anything. Whatever had been wrong with me just went away.

Then there was all the hypersexuality and promiscuity in my teens. Big red flag. It's normal for a teenager to be obsessed with sex, but I was like a bitch in heat! I'm surprised I did so well in year 11 and 12, with 99% of my attention directed at boys, and even the odd girl crush. I dated men in their 20s when I was only 17.

In the year leading up to my diagnosis, I had insomnia, often getting only one or two hours of sleep a night, and some nights, no sleep at all.

I don't know what pushed me over the edge—the sleep deprivation, the death of a close friend from high school, the second-hand bong smoke from my flatmates... probably a combination of all three, but I had another breakdown.

This time it was BAD. I had all these crazy, flighty, grandiose ideas of starting a dance school in my deceased friend's honour and having a yearly tap-dancing award named after him, having an exhibition of art made from fabric and buttons... I literally spent my life savings on buttons from Spotlight (which inspired the nickname 'Buttons' from a boyfriend to whom I told this story, many years later).

It got worse. I was auditioning for big drama schools like VCA, NIDA and WAAPA, and I was obsessed with the idea of becoming a famous actress. I envisioned myself starring in films directed by Jean-Pierre Jeunet and Tim Burton; of winning Oscars, Tonys and Golden Globes.

I felt sick after eating meat one day and immediately decided I had to become a Hare Krishna fanatic and a vegetarian. I followed a stranger home from the Hare Krishna restaurant because I was convinced that he was a guru in my spiritual journey.

I wandered around the city of Melbourne by myself and got lost one night because I felt as though different streets and parts of Fitzroy represented some deep meaning and connection to certain people in my life.

I ended up in the company of one of my brother's friends and they contacted my mother and sent me home. She was beside herself with worry for me and one night we had a big fight over the fact that I was having a bath in the middle of the night, in an attempt to relax and hopefully sleep. She was so emotionally exhausted from looking after me that she insisted I get out of the bath right away and go to bed. I flew off the handle at her.

My stepfather, who I adored, yelled at me over the way I was treating my mother, and I just fled. I just took off. I ran out of the house into the night with no shoes, no glasses, no wallet or phone and just kept walking/running. Where or why, I didn't know.

I had this vague idea (or concrete plan?) that I needed to get to Frankston Station (from Mornington) so that I could busk a cappella and get enough money for a train ticket, get to Melbourne, find the Hare Krishnas, and then they would support me in my mission to get to the Vatican and sing for the Pope!

I stopped at a gas station and looked in the mirror and was afraid of what I saw. My hair was a mess. My pupils were huge. I looked like a wild animal. Something was wrong. Eventually my parents found me at the top of Oliver's Hill in Frankston. I had made it all the way from Mornington by hiding every time I saw the headlights of a car.

I knew I was ill. Mentally ill. Seriously mentally ill. I called an ambulance. When the ambulance arrived my mum and Ivan assured the paramedics it was a false alarm and sent them away. I was furious. We had a huge argument. They finally conceded that if I wanted to go to the hospital so badly, they'd drive me.

We were in the car for ages when it finally dawned on me. They were driving around in circles, trying to convince me *not* to go to the hospital.

They knew the mental health system well, as health professionals, and were incredibly sceptical about the kind of treatment I'd get at the Frankston Hospital emergency room. Fair enough. But to a paranoid person this was a huge conspiracy and a violation of my rights. I demanded to be taken to the hospital right away. They relented.

After days of wandering around the ward thinking I was in Pentridge Prison, I was finally diagnosed with bipolar disorder and promptly put on Epilim.

This diagnosis had huge ramifications. Suddenly I wasn't the high-achieving superstar destined for fame. I was disabled. I was crazy. I was limited. I failed my first year of university and had to leave.

I eventually went back to university and did quite well, spending a semester on exchange in London and getting on the honour roll. Then I did a postgraduate course in teaching and got a job as a special education teacher, which didn't last long. I couldn't handle the stress. I tried (and failed) to become a professional artist, having one solo exhibition and selling a few pieces, but nothing sustainable.

I became a carer, then a teacher's aide. I got married and divorced within the space of two years.

My whole adult life has been spent grieving the loss of the person I always thought I was going to be—the world-famous actress/singer/dancer. The award-winning triple threat.

In reality, I should have been proud of myself. By 2020 I had undergraduate and postgraduate qualifications, and I had a steady job. I was finally in a healthy relationship. I was doing well.

Most people would refer to me as 'high-functioning.' I can work, have a partner, have a social life and maintain my physical health and self-care. I've learned to stop self-harming, have learned to manage suicidal ideation, and have stayed out of hospital for several years.

How do I do it? I take my medication. I keep regular appointments with my GP, my psychiatrist and my psychologist. I eat well, I get enough sleep, I exercise. And support. I get tonnes of support from my friends and family, who are always there for me.

But the magic balm for me is running. There have been times (many times) when I walk in the door after work crying my eyes out; then I just force myself to go through the motions of putting on my gym gear, and I just get out there. Every single time I come back feeling not only better but good, like I'm buzzing on the inside.

How did I get into running? Like most people with bipolar, I've always struggled with my weight.

I've been on everything from Epilim to Lithium to Olanzapine to Seroquel to Lamotrigine, and these meds cause weight gain. I was diagnosed at 19, a size 4 and weighing 42 kilos, and by the age of 36 I was a size 20 and weighed 85 kg, which, at 154 cm tall, wedged me into the 'obese' category.

I tried (on and off) several different things—cutting out carbs, cutting out sugar, cutting out fat, the Dukan diet, and going to the gym sporadically—but nothing seemed to stick. I'd catch glimpses of myself in shop windows and be disgusted—as if I didn't even recognise myself anymore. Even *that* wasn't enough of a kick up the arse to get me into gear.

The watershed moment that set everything in motion was watching the movie *Brittany Runs a Marathon*. It's a film about an obese party girl who takes up running, which changes her life and culminates in her running the New York Marathon.

No sooner had I turned off the TV than I'd signed up for a bunch of 5 km races.

The next step was to get out there and run! So I did. I put on the gym shoes I'd had for more than five years and attempted to run. I ran about a block, couldn't go any further, and went home. But ah! I wasn't discouraged—as that was exactly what had happened to Brittany in the film!

Then I got chatting with my runner cousin Emilie, who suggested something called the 'Couch to 5 K'— a running program designed for absolute beginners. I downloaded the app and started the eight-week walk-run program. By the end of it, I wasn't even close to 5 km, but I could run for 30 minutes without stopping.

I had caught the running bug!

As a child (before the bipolar diagnosis) I'd been something of a high-achiever, academically and in the arts, blitzing singing and dancing competitions and obliterating the competition. A typical type-A personality.

So this suited me to a T. There were always goals to work towards and conquer; my first 20-minute run, my first 30-minute run, and my first 5 km.

Through self-harm, anxiety attacks, insomnia, suicide attempts and hospitalisations, I kept running. Through fertility treatment, pregnancy, post-natal depression and the notoriously difficult first year as a parent, I kept running. I sometimes took little breaks, but I always came back to it.

Fast-forward to now, and I regularly run 5 km and 10 km distances and go to my local Parkrun every Saturday morning. I'm a size 10 and weigh 59 kilos, which puts me in the healthy Body Mass Index (BMI) category.

And now, I had decided to undertake my biggest challenge yet, the 2023 Melbourne Marathon in October 2023, raising funds for Beyond Blue in the process. It is a charity very close to my heart, as they literally saved my life after a suicide attempt in 2020.

The following pages are a journal of the 19-week program leading up to the Big Day—the challenges, the pitfalls, the ups and downs, and the Big Day itself, as well as the aftermath.

I hope that this book will inspire some other bipolar sufferers to take up running and for some other bipolar runners to see themselves reflected in these pages.

THE DIARY

Sunday, 4 June 2023
The Eve

Full disclosure: I'm drunk. I just threw up in the toilet. I haven't been this drunk in ages.

This morning I woke up not just tired—but exhausted. I don't know why. I got enough sleep. All I did yesterday was the Parkrun, and I walked it. I've been eating enough carbs (something I wasn't doing for ages to lose weight), so that's not the problem. I'm putting it down to one of those bipolar lows in energy, which people don't talk about. The public thinks it's all about moods.

I had asked my cousin Michelle to come and watch my gorgeous toddler, Daisy, while I went for my 11 km "long run", then I walked a kilometre home. Pretty good for someone who had no energy.

I came in the door feeling relatively satisfied, as I always do after a run, checked my Garmin watch, and then completed my post-run ritual with well-earned coconut water and a shower. I made myself look nice with a touch of makeup and my new leather jacket and headed out to karaoke.

My therapist said I should do something besides running to balance my life and nurture my creativity, so now, it's karaoke on Sunday afternoons. It's at a kid-friendly café-bar, which is good, as I can take Daisy.

I just had so much fun singing and catching up with friends. The time just flew by, and before we knew it, Caroline, a regular, was singing the last song of the night.

We were home early, as Chris is a baker and gets up at 3 a.m. Daisy woke up at 1 a.m. (as she is wont to do). I gave her a bottle and put her back to sleep. And that's when I threw up.

Naughty, Jacqui! Very naughty, Jacqui.

Monday, 5 June 2023
Week 1, Day 1
Rest Day

So hungover. Glad the auspicious first day of training begins with a 'rest day,' so I'm not required to do anything. Pretty ashamed of myself for drinking so much yesterday. What am I—20 years old?

I work three days a week as a teacher's aide in a primary school, and today was a work day. The day has been boring. I like to be on my feet, multitasking and solving problems, but today there was a lot of sitting around.

I had a 4:00 p.m. appointment at the gym to do something called an 'Evolt scan,' which scans you for fat mass, muscle mass, water weight, etc. Last time, I got a score of 7.7 out of 10, which is considered average, and my biological age came up as 39, which is the same as my chronological age. I was happy with that, as I'm sure a few years ago my biological age would have been in my 60s.

I was a bit nervous about today. Would I improve?

I got a score of 8 out of 10, which put me in the 'optimal' range, and hearing that word made my heart leap! It's such a great-sounding word. 'Optimal.' I even went so far as to Google its exact meaning, which is 'Best or favourable. Optimum.'

Tuesday, 6 June 2023
Week 1, Day 2
6 km Training Run

I woke up feeling tired, anxious, and tearful this morning. I was overwhelmed by the idea that I had two yard duties to do at work and a Zoom meeting. I hate Zoom meetings. I hate all technology. I don't think I'm a proper Gen Y / millennial at all.

The day went well, with no hiccups. As usual, I got worked up over nothing.

So my first proper run of the six-week training plan! Exciting! Scary! Normally my short runs are only 5 km, so 6 km is just that little bit extra.

According to the literature I've been reading, a training run should primarily stay in the heart rate 'Zone 3,' which is a little faster than the easy pace of a long run (Zone 2). I'm a bit wobbly on the whole science of heart rate zones because, according to my Garmin, I sit in Zone 2 even at a brisk walk. (There is no way could I work this stuff out with actual maths!) I'm pretty sure that's an indication that I'm extremely unfit.

In case you don't know what a Garmin is—it's a fancy sports watch that measures everything from heart rate to cadence (or steps per minute) and even analyses the quality of sleep you're getting.

I'm a creature of habit and routine. For my 5 km runs, I always run the exact same route, down the same streets to the 2.5 km mark, turning around and coming straight back.

Today, I decided to do pretty much the same thing, but starting at a different point and doing a little back-and-forth snake before ending in the usual way.

You would think that 6 km is only a little bit harder than 5 km. It turns out it's a lot harder. Why? I'm used to running 5 km at a fast pace, and anything further than that, I allow myself to run like a sloth. So 6 km of trying and putting in effort was a challenge.

And I didn't even mention the worst part. My Garmin died halfway through! When you run without your Garmin, is it even a run?

Wednesday, 7 June 2023
Week 1, Day 3
3 km 'Race Pace'

I was feeling kind of fresh and energised this morning! Work went well, I felt engaged and felt I was doing a good job for once.

I was kind of dreading the fast 3 km. I hate fast running. I am not a fast runner. I'm even a member of a running group on Facebook called the 'Slow Runner's Society.' Those are my people. My spirit animal is the sloth.

But by the end of the day, I'd turned my thinking around. If I can do 5 km mostly in Zone 5 (which I managed a few weeks ago), surely I can manage 3 km in Zone 4? Should be a walk in the park!

I got to daydreaming about race day—crossing the finish line and being cheered on by my family. They're so excited about this race and about supporting me. They're looking forward to it.

But then I had a thought.... What if they don't even *recognise* me amongst all the other runners and I just run straight past them, without the adoration and the fanfare? So now I've resolved to buy some super-bright (maybe pink?) running gear to wear on the day so that they can spot me in the crowd.

The 3 km run was easy and breezy. It's been forever since I ran anything less than 5 km, so 3 km felt like a naughty little treat—almost like I was cheating.

I'm conflicted by the training plan's definition of 'race pace,' though. My race pace is not the average marathoner's. My goal is just to finish the 42.195 km without stopping to walk. So it seems unnecessary to train at a somewhat fast pace (for me) when, on race day, I'll just be shuffling along at the back of the pack.

Thursday, 8 June
Week 1, Day 4
Rest Day

Working a three-day week means that Thursday is always the first official day of my extra-long weekend. It's also the morning I take Daisy to swimming lessons.

Historically, these mornings have not been easy. I'm not a morning person by any stretch of the imagination, and after three days of working I often just feel exhausted and have none of the spoons for anything.

I love the swimming lessons, but I have trouble getting ready and getting out the door. I have trouble changing Daisy's nappy, feeding her breakfast, packing the swimming bag, getting her into her swimming gear, and somehow managing to have my own breakfast and put on my own swimming gear.

But today wasn't one of those days. Maybe because Chris had the day off. It's always nice waking up together. As the partner of a baker, that doesn't happen very often.

Swimming was so much fun, as usual. The kids ran across a foam mat and jumped into our arms. They took turns going down a little mini waterslide, and they played with little water toys in the shallow end. Then swimming was over, and the rest of the day was pretty cruisy.

Friday, 9 June
Week 1, Day 5
6 km Training Run

It's another day off for Chris, so another day of waking up together! My fellow 'mum friend' Margaret and I had plans to meet up around late morning or midday, so we planned to get up around 5:30 a.m. and go for an early morning run. Ha!

As if. Instead, I slept in, and I went for a late morning run. Luckily, Margaret's baby, George, was sleeping, so she pushed back our plans until about 12:30 p.m. But I was stressed. Would I have enough time to go for my run, shower, get dressed, get my 'mum bag' together, and still meet Margaret and George on time?

This stuff is always on my mind. Fitting in running. Finding the time. Not losing track of all the other mum/friend/partner/daughter/teacher's-aide/housework stuff. The magical (and stressful) balancing act.

Once again, 6 km felt a lot harder than 5 km. But why? It's just one extra kilometre. If you've never run, or if you've always found running easy, you wouldn't know this, but a kilometre is a long way.

Saturday, 10 June 2023
Week 1, Day 6
45–60 Minutes of Strength Training

Woke up super excited for Parkrun.
Let me explain a little bit about what Parkrun is for those of you who don't know. Parkrun is a worldwide initiative that began in the UK in 2004 but has since spread to 22 countries. In just about every major town, on Saturday at 8 a.m., you'll find a large, enthusiastic group gathered in a local park getting ready to walk or run 5 km. It's run by volunteers (affectionately nicknamed

'Vollies') and is official and well-organised.

For years, I was deterred from going because I thought it was just a bunch of fast, competitive runners racing to achieve PBs (personal bests). There is an element of that, but plenty of people walk the whole thing, people take their dogs or prams, and there are even volunteer 'tail walkers' whose job is to walk behind everyone else so that no-one comes last.

This year, spurred on by my friend Margaret, I committed to turning up to the Dandenong Parkrun every week and even earned a special pin to commemorate my tenth Parkrun. That day, I was given a special tutu to wear on my run and had my picture taken. It was lots of fun.

This morning was a cold one, though thankfully not raining, so I was all rugged up in my puffer jacket. Today, Margaret was sick, so I walked with the tail walkers and had a nice chat about everything, from other Parkrun courses to netball to choir and volunteer work with domestic violence sufferers.

After Parkrun, the Vollies and a few other participants head to the café around the corner for a coffee, brunch, a chat, and a weekly ritual of general knowledge trivia, which I always fail at miserably.

I caught up with two of my new Parkrun friends, Stuart and Hung, who, as usual, made me feel welcome—as though I belonged. I'm yet to join the Vollie team, but I've been accepted as an honorary Vollie, as the 'Resident Librarian,' reading a different book on running every week and reviewing it in the group chat.

In the afternoon, it was time for my 'Strength Training,' which would last 45–60 minutes. I don't usually time my weight machine sessions, so I wasn't even sure if I'd have enough exercises to fill a 45-minute timeslot.

I needn't have worried. It got to the 60-minute mark, and I hadn't even used all the machines. I could have gone longer, but I was mindful of not pushing myself too hard; and that I had a beautiful little daughter waiting at home for me to spend some time with her.

Sunday, 11 June 2023
Week 1, Day 7
9 km Long Run

I woke up feeling incredibly tired and sore all over. I thought that gym soreness was supposed to kick in after two days, but according to my muscles, that's apparently a myth.

Going for a long run feeling like this was going to be a bit of a task. But I put on a playlist of my favourite songs and settled into an easy pace on a brand-new running route.

Towards the halfway mark I came to an overpass bridge, with the busy Monash Freeway traffic humming below. Being there automatically triggered a memory of a time when I came very close to jumping off such a bridge.

I had been suffering from extreme antenatal depression and was having intrusive thoughts that my unborn child would be better off dead than having me as a mother, and that everyone close to me would be better off if I was dead too.

I obsessively played out a scene in my head where I jumped off an overpass in front of a truck. With tears in my eyes, I slowly walked to the overpass nearest my house and stepped over the railing, prepared to jump, but I was jolted back to my senses by hearing the very real rushing of all the vehicles below.

I ended up sitting on the footpath of the bridge sobbing, and some strangers found me and sought medical help. That was the beginning of some very supportive interventions that put me back on the right track.

Even though my mind is now as far from that place as it possibly could be, I don't think I'll ever drive, run or walk across a bridge without making that dark association.

Today, the memory passed in and out of my mind with ease, without any sense of trauma. All I could feel was happiness about my life as it is and how far all that was behind me—in the past, where it belonged.

Monday, 12 June 2023
Week 2, Day 1
Rest Day

My muscles were still sore this morning but the pain had eased a little, thanks to a massage I had after yesterday's long run. It was the King's Birthday public holiday, so I didn't have to work.

I was keen to get to a 10:30 a.m. yoga class, so my mother-in-law looked after Daisy while I headed to the gym. I'd only recently started taking yoga classes but was already feeling a bit like a bona fide yogi, with all the residual flexibility from my dancing days.

Today's class knocked me straight off that lofty perch! I met with a new instructor I had never worked with before, and the whole class was like some kind of army cadet's drill—move this, stretch that, engage that, up, down, side to side, moving from pose to pose—faster than I could even mentally process!

I felt awkward and clumsy, like the slapstick lead actor of some candid camera comedy. I wobbled, slipped, lost my balance, and generally made a fool of myself. I was glad when it was over, but rather than being stressed and anxious about being such an obvious novice, I saw the humour in it and was able to laugh at myself. Maybe I'm starting to lose some of that lifelong control freak conditioning?

Tuesday, 13 June 2023
Week 2, Day 2
7 km Training Run

This morning, I simply didn't want to get out of bed. And when I say that, it's not like a 'normal' person saying it; it's a bipolar person saying it. This problem used to afflict me each morning with crippling paralysis.

The winters were the worst. I would peel the blanket back a few centimetres, then the sense of the cold air against my body would cause my chest to tighten in a vice-like grip. I'd retreat into the foetal position and often stay that way all day, only emerging to quickly dart to the toilet and back, as if too many seconds spent out of that cocoon would endanger my very life.

Today was not that bad, but it was still a battle. I rolled out of bed at the last possible second and gingerly dressed myself in my warmest, comfiest clothes and reluctantly faced the first day of my working week.

After work I checked my training plan and had to do a double-take. Seven kilometres? That was only two less than the previous weekend's long run! With my running speed (or lack thereof) it would be well and truly dark before my run was over. I'd never run in the dark before—it was a kind of phobia of mine. Under the cloak of darkness, female runners were surely susceptible to all the rapists and murderers lying in wait for some idiot like me to come jogging by.

But it turned out the looming darkness was the least of my worries. In my haste to get out there and get it done, I'd forgotten to put my contact lenses in, and of course Murphy's Law kicked in, and it started to rain.

There is nothing worse than running in the rain with glasses on. Huge droplets gather and hinder your vision; then, when you try to wipe them away, they spread into thick smears that turn everything into a complete blur.

I was completely freaked out! It was only my second time running in this part of my neighbourhood. How would I get home? Would I be able to read the street signs? My fears were realised when I became completely lost after making a wrong turn on the way home. I had no idea where I was, but I refused to stop running until I hit that 7 km mark.

At that point, I got out my phone, took off my glasses, and squinted at my Google Maps. I'd overshot the mark, and instead of a five-minute cool-down walk, I'd have to walk an extra 15 minutes to get to my warm, dry home, where I could strip out of my rain-soaked clothes and step into that inviting shower.

I'd never felt so relieved to walk in the door after a run.

Wednesday, 14 June
Week 2, Day 3
3 km Run—'Race Pace'

Today was 'medication box' packing day. We fill my medication dispenser once a week so that I only have access to a week's worth of medication at a time. The rest of it goes in a locked box that my partner Chris keeps, and only he has the key.

This ritual has become so automatic that I never stop to think about the reasons why we do it.

I have a history of overdosing. On more than one occasion, I've ended up in a coma for days, on life support.

The last time it happened, they had to intubate me, inserting a tube down my throat and pumping my stomach. I never knew this, but intubation is not without risks. The process caused me to have a build-up of fluid in my lungs, and I ended up with pneumonia for weeks on end.

The first couple of weeks were a living nightmare. I was so physically sick that I was severely delirious. I completely lost touch with reality.

Once I was out of intensive care I had to spend two weeks in a psychiatric ward.

Today's intense run was a chance to process and shake off those morbid thoughts and preoccupations. Running always clears my head.

Thursday, 15 June 2023
Week 2, Day 4
Rest Day

Today was an absolutely perfect day. Another Thursday off for Chris, so I didn't have to wake up alone.

Then swimming lessons. We'd changed to the 9 a.m. class, which was a small, intimate affair with just Margaret and me and two other parents. One of the other mothers, Jess, was new to the area with two babies to look after and no mum friends.

We all decided to meet up a few hours after swimming to go to the local shopping centre, have lunch, and then let the kids play in the little play area.

It was the sort of outing I'd envied during the long years that I had been childless. Just mumming around, doing mum things, talking to other mums about mum stuff, and gazing lovingly at our adorable little cherubs.

All those fertility issues and the long road to finally falling pregnant and giving birth to our miracle baby were finally over and in the past. I'd become something I never thought I'd be—a parent.

Friday, 16 June 2023
Week 2, Day 5
7 km Training Run

I was feeling enthusiastic about my run today. Running in a new part of town has shifted things a bit and made my runs more interesting and exciting. Seven km was intimidating at the start of the week, but to be honest, I killed it on Tuesday, so this afternoon I was pumped!

I tried to keep my steps light, and concentrated on opening up my stride (I'm a notorious shuffler), checking in on my body at regular intervals.

My mind is buzzing tonight, and I know it's going to be difficult to sleep. I didn't get much sleep last night either. I woke up early and I was feeling so creative and enthusiastic I couldn't get back to sleep.

I'm feeling excited because my short reviews on various running books, which I'd been sharing in the Parkrun group chat, had been posted on the official Parkrun website, meaning that I'm now officially a published writer! It's got me feeling so excited—I couldn't wait to tell everyone and share it on Facebook.

It's a funny thing, creativity and bipolar disorder. There's a bit of a cliché that we're all creative, and that we owe our creativity to the disorder. That somehow, one must be crazy in order to be creative.

There are many celebrities in the arts who suffer or suffered from bipolar disorder: Vincent Van Gogh, Carrie Fisher, Sia, Selena Gomez, Tim Burton, Demi Lovato, Kanye West, Ben Stiller, Sinead O'Connor and Jim Carrey.

There is also a debate as to whether medication hinders this creativity, which to me seems, at best, problematic and, at worst, dangerous.

For me, creative pursuits have often been a trigger. Often when I get inspired, I feel a surge of energy. I become obsessive, productive, irritable, restless and plagued by insomnia. I become overly confident and grandiose in my ambitions.

These behaviours are symptoms of a mental state known as hypomania, which often—but not always—can lead to a full-blown manic episode.

So tonight, I've taken a PRN med, and hopefully, I'll get some sleep and come back down to Earth a little.

Saturday, 17 June 2023
Week 2, Day 6
45-60 Minutes of Strength Training

This morning was Parkrun day again, which has now made Saturday my favourite day of the week!

Before Parkrun I'd want to lie in bed all morning on a Saturday, praying that Daisy would sleep in so that I could too. I'd reluctantly drag myself out of bed and go through the motions of our morning routine like a zombie.

But since Margaret and I introduced the weekly Parkrun ritual to our schedules, I'm excited to get up even earlier than I would on a work day. I wake up feeling enthusiastic!

It's not even about the 5 km run (which I'm walking at the moment because Saturday is sandwiched between training days). It's about that sense of community.

Today, Margaret was injured, but in her notable stubbornness, she was determined to come along to 'get her steps in.' I asked her, 'Are you limping?' She said yes. My response was, 'You're not coming then.' I was very firm.

So I looked around the small crowd gathered, ready for briefing, trying to spot someone with a big coat on. That's a sure-fire sign that the person has decided to walk instead of running. I spotted an older lady, introduced myself and asked if I could walk with her. She politely agreed.

She apologised and told me that she was very slow (not true) and that she can't manage to walk and talk at the same time (which also turned out to be not true). We had a great chat as we strode the 5 km course, talking about Serbian food, the languages we were teaching Daisy (French, English and Spanish) and also about work.

As usual, there was an enthusiastic crowd waiting at the finish line, cheering us on, and a cowbell ringing as we approached; I jogged the final few metres as the cheering grew louder and scanned my barcode to later receive an email with my official time.

Then we all went to the café for coffee, breakfast and trivia, and I popped into the nearby library to return a book and pick up one I'd placed on hold (both running books, of course). I had to keep my Parkrun website readers happy with more weekly reviews!

We had a lot going on today. A trip to the shopping centre with my mum, lunch with Chris's family, and after that I'd still have to find the time to get to the gym.

6:30 p.m. was the latest I could get to the gym and work out so that I could come home and watch Daisy after Chris's bedtime. My usual gym closes at 6 p.m. on a Saturday, but another gym covered by my membership recently announced it would now be open 24/7.

I'd never been there before, and I was pretty impressed when I walked in the door. Very modern—space-aged, almost. All the machines were brand new. I was tired, and I didn't want to be there, but I approached it all methodically, step by step, taking the process one machine at a time, without stressing over the bigger picture of the whole 45-60-minute session. I was listening to my favourite tunes, and it wasn't so bad. I do like the gym, but it's nowhere near as rewarding as running.

Sunday, 18 June 2023
Week 2, Day 7
12 km Long Run

This morning, I got to have a nice little sleep in; an actual—real—sleep in, without the guilt and negative self-talk.

Usually with any kind of sleep in, my 'inner monologue' would go something like this: *I'm a bad person. I'm a bad mother. I'm so lazy. I'm the worst person in the world. I'm totally incapable of being normal, living a normal life, and doing 'normal person' things. I'm worthless.*

And this would replay, over and over, as a loop in my head.

I haven't had a spiral of negative thinking like that in quite some time. I've generally been feeling pretty positive, and my self-esteem has been quite high.

Today, I was looking forward to my long run. I love easy, steady-paced runs. They take me away from the busy pace of life for an indulgent hour or two and allow me to revel in the solitude that appeals to my inner introvert.

Today I took a new route down the Eastlink trail. I'd walked and run parts of the trail before, but I've never traversed its entire length. Even today I got further than I ever have, but I still didn't get to the end. I'm looking forward to hopefully achieving that milestone next Sunday, on my 15 km-long run.

After I reached my turnaround point, my mind turned to karaoke. I decided to try a new song today, so I listened to it on repeat a few times, paying special attention to the words and the nuances of the melody. The time passed quickly, and before I knew it, I was back home, ready for a karaoke outing with my daughter, mum, brother and cousin.

I'm happy and proud to report that I didn't allow myself to get drunk this time. I stopped at two drinks and was pleased to get through the night without throwing up!

Monday, 19 June
Week 3, Day 1
Rest Day

Winter has come. I woke up to the sounds of the torrential rain I knew would eventually envelop Melbourne, but so far, the winter had been so mild it had lulled me into a false sense of security. *Oh, that's right. This is what winter is like.*

I did not want to get up. I pressed snooze, then turned my alarm off altogether, because I felt as though my snooze period was just way too short. The old me might have started crying, feeling totally overcome and calling in sick. In fact, I did momentarily consider it, but then looked at my watch and realised it was too late, and that I'd *have* to just drag myself out of bed.

I was proud of myself. I wasn't dreading work or feeling as though the day stretched ahead of me with unbearable effort required. I felt tired and unmotivated, but that wasn't accompanied by the thoughts or feelings of anxiety and depression, which was a big, positive psychological development for me.

Don't get me wrong, I didn't lightly float through the day like a ray of sunshine, but it was OK. Not good, not bad, but a very reasonable so-so.

Tuesday, 20 June 2023
Week 3, Day 2
8 km Training Run

I woke up in a good mood today. Chris was home, and for some reason that always makes it easier for me to get up.

I was looking forward to wearing a funky op-shop outfit I'd laid out the night before, and I felt stylish in my matching sea-green scarf, hat and pants.

There was a time when I was too depressed to even *think* about what to wear, as any kind of decisions about anything at all were overwhelming. I wore the same three outfits on rotation for a year.

Now, I love laying out my clothes and getting dressed in the morning. I colour-coordinate. I accessorise. I finally have my own unique style again!

Fashion used to be such a passion for me in my teens and twenties. I loved quirky, op-shop, retro and vintage pieces, and I prided myself on being an individual.

Somewhere along the line, I lost that. I grew out of all my nice clothes, and maybe subconsciously felt I needed a boring wardrobe to match my boring life.

That all changed one day when I was hanging out with Margaret. She made a passing comment (not about me) that wearing tracksuits was a sign that a person had 'given up on life.'

That observation resonated with me. She wasn't to know this, but I'd recently bought three tracksuits and had taken to living in them, even wearing them with Ugg boots to the shops, and on one occasion, even to the cinema.

Had I given up on life? I didn't want to be that person. So now I'm the girl who's always getting compliments on my shoes, my headband or my earrings.

Work was quite pleasant. I had a great meeting with my student's occupational therapist, who was very complimentary of our progress and offered some great ideas for moving forward.

All day I'd been looking forward to my training run. Eight km starting at 4:00 p.m. meant I'd probably be finishing just as it was getting dark, so I wanted to optimise my visibility for safety with regards to traffic. So, for the first time, I wore my top-to-toe, fluoro-pink running outfit that I'd bought during our last trip to Kmart. When I put it on, it was too much! And I loved it! I felt powerful! I felt like a boss! I felt like the rapper/singer Lizzo!

Speaking of Lizzo, as a celebratory post-half-marathon event (I'm doing a half-marathon race at the end of week six of my training), I'm going to see her in concert. I don't know what I'm more excited about, that or race day.

When people tell me that they don't know who Lizzo is, I'm shocked! Most people describe Lizzo as a rapper, but she also sings, dances and plays the flute. Lizzo is more than a person, she's a movement. She's a message. She embodies body positivity and self-love.

The run felt effortless, as though I was light-footed and strong. I threw in a few hills and managed to maintain my pace up some challenging inclines. Whenever I run up a hill, I make eye contact with passers-by with a self-confident grin on my face.

I know what you're thinking, random person. You're thinking, 'How is she doing that?' With my superpowers, that's how.

Wednesday, 21 June 2023
Week 3, Day 3
5 km—'Race Pace'

Today, I feel happy! Not manic, not depressed, not even a healthy 'OK.' Genuinely happy. It was my last day of work before two and a half weeks of holidays, and I'm so proud of myself for getting through half the working year and grateful that it's flown by so quickly.

Two years ago, I struggled to get through one day. Literally every session of the school day felt like hours, and I cried on the way to work every morning and as soon as I walked out the door every afternoon. Sometimes I even cried at work. I was constantly having to take deep breaths and pull myself together. I had so many sick days.

This year I feel proud of what I do. I'm so blessed to have such a great team around me: teachers, other education support workers, therapists and parents.

I had a big win today. One of my autistic students made a huge leap forward. He'd previously been reluctant to engage in any sort of physical activity, but today I found something that works, and that he enjoys throwing Velcro balls at a felt target. He spent nearly half an hour playing with them during our P.E. session, which he usually spends just wandering around and watching from the sidelines.

I also got asked to work on a new project that I'm excited about. They've appointed me as the facilitator of the school's playgroup program for two hours every Tuesday morning.

I love working with kids that age. Plus, my mother will be taking Daisy, and Margaret will be coming with George, so we'll all have more time together.

For today's 5 km 'race pace' run, I decided to go all out and aim for a personal best. My previous PB for a 5 km run was 34:36, with an average pace of 6:53 seconds. I'd been busting my arse all year to be able to maintain a pace of 7 min/km or under, and when I finally got there, I was over the moon.

With all the hard work and extra training I've been doing, I've been feeling fitter and stronger, so I thought, why not go for gold? Make today the day. I got dressed and set off like a rocket.

I usually feel my pace drop a little as I hit each kilometre, one by one, but today wasn't like that. My pace felt steady, but I looked at my watch and knew after 2 km that I wasn't going to get a PB.

But I pushed on. I thought, what if I could run the second half of my route even faster than the first half? A faster second half is called a 'negative split,' and runners rave about it.

Every time I started to falter, I just gave it more juice, and I felt like I was giving it my all for those last few km. I didn't end up getting a PB. My time was 36:50, with an average pace of 7:22 min/km. I looked at my Garmin data and expected to see a huge percentage of Zone 5 running, but it was mostly in Zone 4. Apparently, I have a lot more untapped potential lying dormant inside me.

Thursday, 22 June 2023
Week 3, Day 4
Rest Day

Today was mentally draining. After Daisy's swimming lessons we went to look at a potential kindergarten and a potential primary school. She's only 18 months old, but apparently, we already need to be thinking about all this stuff.

We looked at the fees for a private Catholic primary school, did the math, and decided it was within our budget. The staff strongly encouraged us to baptise Daisy to maximise her chances of getting in, so now there's that behemoth event to plan and worry about.

After all that, I had to have a bath and lie down. I shouldn't have to lie down during the day—I am not an old woman. I shouldn't have to have 'Nanna naps.' A part of the way my bipolar affects me is that I don't have much mental energy, and decision-making is challenging and exhausting. Particularly making important decisions about the future.

I literally had a nervous breakdown from the stress of looking for and buying our first home. And even looking at prams and car seats in Baby Bunting while I was pregnant gave me a huge anxiety attack, and I burst into tears. Too much to choose from, and the shop assistant might as well have been speaking Klingon, as I'd totally dissociated and zoned out, and it was all going in one ear and out the other. My mum had to take the reins on that one.

Kindergartens, schools, and churches, thinking ahead years in advance. It's all too much for my bipolar brain.

Friday, 23 June 2023
Week 3, Day 5
8 km Training Run

This morning, I felt like I had no energy to tackle a moderately paced 8 km run. It was a slow long run, maybe, but one that required real effort? That was a big ask.

It was 9.4 degrees, and I wondered how that would affect my heart rate. Would it take a while to speed up?

As I started running, I noticed my fingertips were freezing! I could see my breath forming little steamy puffs in front of my face. There was a light drizzle and thank God I'd remembered to wear my contact lenses and a cap to keep the rain off my face.

It was hard going. The brisk air woke me up a little and was somewhat energising, but 8 km is a long way to go when you're tired and pushing yourself. The first time I looked down at my watch I hadn't even hit 2 km.

I wasn't even a quarter of the way through, and I already wanted to turn around and go home. I took a similar route to my last 8 km run but without the hills. The aim was to get a slightly faster time.

I kept looking at my watch every 10 or 20 metres, praying to get to that magical halfway point soon. It was a psychological battle as much as a physical one.

By now, my body had warmed up, and I was sweating. Even my fingers felt nice and warm. I could still see my breath, though. Finally, I got to 4 km, and at least half of the run was behind me.

The way home was more forgiving. I counted down the kilometres and ticked off the landmarks with relief.

It felt great to press the 'Stop' button on my Garmin and then press 'Save.' Done and dusted. And yes, I beat my previous 8 km time.

Saturday, 24 June 2023
Week 3, Day 6 of Official Half-Marathon Training
45–60 Minutes of Strength Training

This morning, I was up before 7 a.m. I'm never up before 7 a.m., especially on a Saturday.

I was up so early because I needed to get to Parkrun by 7:30 a.m., and today was going to be my first time volunteering! I'm a true Vollie now!

My job was to give out barcode tokens at the finish line for people to scan, but the most important part of the job was cheering and shouting out words of encouragement to each participant as they approached the home stretch.

At the café afterwards, I found out that Stuart is going to be volunteering at my half-marathon, so we decided to car-pool. It'll be nice having someone with me on the drive there to calm my nerves.

Chris went out to play Dungeons and Dragons in the afternoon, so Margaret and I took the kids to a shopping centre to let them loose in the indoor play area. We also went to the chemist, the supermarket and the food court, which is not a lot, but it left me exhausted. When I got home, I needed to chill out with a cup of tea to recover while Chris did the cooking.

Then, after dinner, I couldn't put it off any longer. I had to go to the gym. I did not want to go to the gym. I wanted to stay home and watch Netflix. In fact, I need a bumper sticker that says, 'I'd rather be watching Netflix.'

Once I got to the gym, I decided to start with the leg press. The leg press is my favourite because it's nice and easy for me. My core and upper body are weak, but my legs are strong from all the running.

Tomorrow, I'll be running 15 km! It will be my longest run since before having Daisy. Maybe I'll finally get to the end of that Eastlink trail! Fifteen seems like a lot more than 12, so I have no idea how I'll go.

Sunday, 25 June 2023
Week 3, Day 7
Long Run—15 km

Did I wake up feeling energised, inspired and ready to go? Nope! I was tired; I just could not be bothered. But I hadn't missed a training session yet, and I wasn't about to start. I just had to get out there and get through it.

I didn't want to get out of my warm pyjamas and into my running gear, but, like a soldier with a uniform, or a knight with a suit of armour, I got kitted up and prepared for battle.

I stepped outside and it was freezing. Once I'd gone through my warm-up of walking, backwards running, ankle flicks, ankle and leg rotations etc. I was ready.

Because it was one of the longest distances of my training before the half marathon event, it was time to experiment with hydration and fuel. I wore my hydration vest, so I'd be able to sip on the go, and I tucked a muesli bar into the pocket of my hoodie so I could take little bites throughout my run.

All of my reading has emphasised the importance of regularly topping up my stores of carbohydrates. I was going to purchase some little sachets of carbohydrate gels that elite runners use, but I hadn't had the chance yet. That would be something for next week.

I expected to feel warm soon after I started my run, but the cold just gripped me and wouldn't let go for the first 5 km. There was an icy wind, and my face and ears were freezing. Running faster would have made a difference, but I wasn't about to expend too much energy too quickly and risk losing stamina for the duration of the run.

At the 5 km mark, I passed another runner going in the opposite direction, and suddenly there was a smile on my face, and I felt like I'd gotten some of my mojo back.

Suddenly I remembered I'd be exploring new parts of the trail I'd never seen before, and I began to feel excited again. How far would my run take me? What sights would I see?

I ran under bridges, past a creek, past a street of big brick houses, and I saw a sign indicating that I'd be approaching Wellington Road—a significant landmark I'd been striving to reach.

As I got closer and closer I began to hear the traffic slowly crescendo. It looked like the trail was about to end abruptly. But it suddenly curled sharply to the right and downhill, and I found myself jogging through an underpass decorated with colourful graffiti.

On the other side of Wellington Road, I was pleasantly surprised to be surrounded by proper bushland—tea trees, ferns, and gum trees. The dampness from the recent rain made me smell a subtle earthy scent all around me, and I felt at one with nature.

I started to see signposts pointing to Jells Park, a picturesque destination we'd frequently visited by car, and even those trips had seemed quite far.

I was so close to getting to Jells Park when I looked down at my watch and realised that I'd reached my turnaround point, so I bookmarked the spot for next week and began the homeward second half of my run.

As I headed home, I started to feel tired, bored, and lonely. I rarely felt that way running, but I realised those feelings were common for long-distance runners.

Then, with about 5 km to go, my headphones died, and suddenly, I had to contend with the relentless boredom of the Eastlink traffic, my laboured breathing, and my rhythmic footfalls.

I hated that last leg of the journey. It felt like I'd never get home to the burger and fries my partner had waiting for me—and all I could think about was how slow I was running and how my food would probably be cold by the time I got home!

A much fitter, much faster runner overtook me, and as she put more and more distance between us with her speed and ease of pace, I felt discouraged. A voice in my head said, "I'm not a runner. I'm not an athlete. I'm so unfit." Then I snapped out of it and focused on my vision board and my mantra, "I am strong! I am powerful! I AM an athlete! I am a machine."

I didn't know that other runner. I didn't know her story. Maybe instead of approaching the end of a 15 km run, she was at the start of a 5 km run. It didn't matter. I could only compare myself to myself. Three years ago, I couldn't even run a kilometre.

I got through the run, made it home, and felt very proud of myself—and my burger and chips were still warm. I savoured every bite.

Monday, 26 June
Week 4, Day 1
Rest Day

I slept in. After a huge night pub crawling from one karaoke event at a café to a second one at a bar—bringing the house down with virtuosic renditions of songs by Kate Bush and Bjork—I was understandably tired. I'd had a 'YOLO' (you only live once) moment while I was out, where I thought, 'What would Mum do?'

My mum is a notorious party animal and of course the answer was, 'Rage on!'. It was the school holidays! I'd just completed a 15 km run! It was time to celebrate and let my hair down.

And today was a time to rest. It was what my body wanted, and I deserved the break. I wasn't exhausted, I wasn't burnt out or hungover or depressed; I was just tired, and that was okay.

After lounging in the comfort of my bed while Chris handled Daisy's morning routine, we all had a nice shower, and I swathed myself in a warm, cosy tracksuit. No, Margaret, I haven't given up on life. Today was just a tracksuit kind of day.

In the evening Chris brought in some mail for me, and I instantly recognised the 'Sole Motive' logo (the company organising my half-marathon). I quickly tore the envelope open to find my race bib. Number 5791. JACQUI. WAVE D. I grinned from ear to ear.

Tuesday, 27 June 2023
Week 4, Day 2
8 km—Training Run

I never thought I'd say this, but I'm so bored with running! I'm used to running three times a week, for a total of about 20 km, but this week, I'll be running 37 km.

Maybe I'm just a little emotionally scarred by the headphones incident. Today would be different. I'd be using Chris's headphones, and I wouldn't have to run without music. I decided to vary my route slightly to end up in my old stomping ground, a little reserve in Noble Park, where I used to run every day when I was just starting out.

Being back in the place where it all started brought back many memories—those 60-second jogging intervals from week one of the Couch to 5 km, where I felt like I'd only pressed forward a few meters each time, running through Covid lockdown when running had been the highlight of my day, as it was the only time I was allowed to leave the house.

I also thought about how slow I used to be. My first 5 km, where I managed to run the whole thing, took me 47 minutes. We walk Parkrun faster than that most weeks now! Yep, I ran slower than a brisk walker!

In fact, there was a lady who always seemed to be out walking at the same time as my run. Our workouts seemed to be synchronised. I remember the embarrassment of her power walking past me each day as I plodded along.

One day... I thought. One day I'll be able to run faster than she walks. And in the end, I got there. It was a proud moment. For me, and for her, I think.

Today I overtook a few walkers, and even though it's easy for me now, it still makes me feel proud. I always see them ahead of me and speed up a little, wondering how long it will take me to catch up and run past.

The run was over in no time, and I achieved my goal of staying mostly in Zone 4. Eight km at a moderate pace, once daunting, had now become commonplace. After today, I'd only have three more 8 km training runs to go before my half-marathon.

The countdown has begun.

Wednesday, 28 June 2023
Week 4, Day 3
5 km—'Race Pace'

This morning, for the third day in a row, I woke up feeling tired and even a little depressed. It's a combination of things getting me down. It's the school holidays, so I don't have work to keep me busy. It's been days since I've seen Margaret, and we usually catch up a few times a week. My mum is on holiday in Mauritius, and I'm starting to miss her.

The worst thing is that I haven't had a car for weeks, as I had a slight bingle in the car park a few weeks ago, and it's being repaired, which means that I'm housebound. What I'd give to just get in the car and go to the shops, just to break up the day. And it's raining outside, so I can't even take Daisy out for a play.

Today I pumped myself up to run as fast as I could and try one more time for that elusive PB.

The first 2 km took just under 14 minutes, and then I felt a shift as I couldn't help but slow down. There was no chance of getting that PB. Often, in the past, I would get to the 3 km mark, realise I was running too slow to come in at under 35 minutes, and just give up and slow down to a jog. I would get disheartened and feel like there is no point.

But today I had to maintain a fast pace to keep up with my training, and I'd set myself a goal of staying in Zone 5 for most of my run. Before I even got to 4 km it was starting to feel like a battle.

Every time I'd feel the fatigue start to take over, I'd give myself a mental boost by imagining I was at the start of my run when it felt easy—and I would take off and fly with enthusiasm.

I wasn't going to beat my record, but I was still going to run as fast as I possibly could. The last 2 km I was pushing through by pure willpower. *Don't slow down. Don't slow down. You can do this!* I kept telling myself to work on my cadence—quick feet, quick steps.

I finished the run feeling like it had been a success. I checked my Garmin and was pleased to see that I had managed to stay in Zone 5 for 75% of my run. More than 27 minutes of my heart pumping at its maximum rate.

Thursday, 29 June 2023
Week 4, Day 4
Rest Day

As usual, we started the day with Daisy's swim class. This time, Chris's mum gave us a ride and took lots of videos. She'd never seen Daisy in the pool before, so she was so excited to watch her jumping in the water, kicking, paddling, and splashing.

Our swimming teacher has just won an award for Instructor of the Year for Victoria, so we're in very good hands. We already knew she was the best anyway. I'm sure she spends more money than she makes on toys for the kids to play and swim with. She sings, she plays games, she always keeps the kids entertained.

We did our usual post-swim routine of showers and lunch, and then I got a call from Margaret offering to take us to the shops. She has my baby seat in her car while my car's being fixed, so we can bundle up both the kids and go places together.

While we were there, I was keen to go to Rebel Sport to pick up some carbohydrate gels to use for fuel on my longer runs. I've never used them before, and I felt like this purchase was a sure-fire sign I was becoming a serious runner! No more muesli bars hidden in my pockets.

The reality and the enormity of this is finally setting in. This is going to be a big task. This is not going to be easy. There will be so much boredom. So much exhaustion. So many sore muscles, blisters and moments of feeling drained, with the thought that I won't be able to make it through dominating my mind. It'll be physically tough—but even more so mentally. I'd read somewhere that the top three inches of the body are the most important parts of the body in training and on race day.

Friday, 30 June 2023
Week 4, Day 5 of Official Half-Marathon Training
8 km Training Run

Last night, I went to bed exhausted, shut my eyes, and just couldn't get to sleep, so I just lay there with my mind ticking over. It was 2 a.m. before I thought, *This is ridiculous,* and took some sleep meds.

When I finally fell asleep, I had terrible nightmares. Nightmares about marathons! In the first one, I unknowingly had entered myself into a triathlon instead of a marathon and was in the middle of the sea for the swimming section when I remembered I'm not a particularly good swimmer. I also realised the tide was about to get stronger and take me in the opposite direction if I didn't get to the end of the swimming leg fast enough!

The second nightmare was equally strange. I'd just begun my marathon when I realised an old lady beside me had decided to jog the marathon while bouncing a basketball. She was having a lot of trouble, and I started trying to help her, but then we got to the halfway point, and I realised we were going so slowly that we'd both end up with a DNF (which stands for 'did not finish'). This must have been something to do with my recent reading about 'jogglers'—people who run marathons while juggling. Yes. That's a thing.

I woke up feeling as though I was made of lead. I had no energy. I zoned out through our morning routine like the walking dead. After a while, I realised

I'd have to face the reality of the day, so I decided to start by doing the dishes. And a funny thing happened. Suddenly I felt 'normal'—energised even. My head was clear and I felt able to get things done.

So then I kept doing adult things! I cleaned the stovetop. I meal-prepped a bunch of couscous with roast veggies and chicken—enough to feed an army. I did a load of washing and hung it out to dry. I put away the dishes and got into my active wear, ready to go off and run when Chris got home to take over Daisy duty.

I was feeling enthusiastic about a new running route. I had decided to go over a new overpass and head to the area where I'd run my first 5 and 10 km distances. I flew down a familiar hill where I'd once smashed my PB, with a time under 34 minutes (I still maintain that must have been a GPS glitch).

As I rounded a particular corner, after a little strip of shops, I remembered that part of the path had once been a significant landmark for me, where I'd finally gotten round the bend to the sounds of the song 'The Cup of Life' by Ricky Martin. I'd heard the lyrics, 'Go! Go! Go!' pumping in my brain as I pushed until I could run no more, hitting my very first 5 km.

When I got home, I checked my fundraising page, which I'd set up last night. My brain was already pumped full of endorphins from the run, and they spiked even further when I found I'd already raised over $100 for Beyond Blue, and it was only the first day after setting up the page!

Saturday, 1 July 2023
Week 4, Day 6
45–60 Minutes of Strength Training

Margaret and I skipped Parkrun this morning. We didn't feel like braving the rain, so we had breakfast at a café and schemed together a strategy for my fundraising campaign. Then we took some photos, and she whipped up an amazing promotional poster that we could put up in shops and email to organisations.

When I got home, I emailed all the local politicians in the area, as well as the local library and some other potential sponsors. It felt professional and official. It was exciting stuff. The templated fundraising page from the Melbourne Marathon has a default goal of $700, but Margaret suggested we think big, so we made a pact to shoot for the moon and aim to raise $10,000!

I also set up an Instagram account, especially for the Beyond Blue campaign, and began posting running related photos, quotes and even a video!

Then I couldn't avoid it any longer. The gym.

I'm just going to be negative and say it. I hate the gym. I pumped iron for exactly 45 minutes, no more, no less, then called Chris to ask him to pick me up.

With all this going on I was feeling agitated, stressed, irritable and frustrated. I was anxious to see how everything would play out and if I'd reach any of my goals.

I was obsessively checking Instagram, Facebook, my email, and my fundraising page. I couldn't leave my phone alone. I couldn't sit still. I started to do the dishes, but then stopped half-way because I was so distracted and couldn't focus.

These are all symptoms of hypomania, and anticipating a third night with very little sleep, I decided to take some PRN medication.

Sometimes, it's so hard to distinguish between hypomania and genuine excitement and motivation that falls within the realm of 'normal' human existence. We may be bipolar, but we're still allowed to be driven and ambitious. It isn't necessarily always a sign that our mental health is declining—but then again—sometimes it is. Where do you draw the line?

It's an internal debate we often face, and the people who care about us often don't know when to be concerned and when to be encouraging. I feel sorry for my family and friends who struggle with gauging how to do the right thing when it comes to supporting my well-being.

I am stress-eating, going through cups of herbal tea as fast as I can make them, and doing my best to relax while still giving Daisy the attention she needs and keeping her entertained.

Sometimes it's so hard, but I have my good days and bad days, like all of us.

Sunday, 2 July 2023
Week 4, Day 7
16 km Long Run

OK, so now it's time to be honest about something here. When I started writing this, I had no intention of running a marathon. It was going to be a six-week journal of my training and running of a half-marathon known as 'Run Melbourne' (which I'm still doing in two weeks). It was only when I read some books on running and marathons that I made the decision to bite the bullet and enter a full marathon. Then, I had to go back and change the start of my book and look at everything in terms of an 18-week plan and a much bigger commitment.

I never had any intention of fundraising. In a lot of ways, I'm extroverted, with karaoke and socialising, but when it comes to the idea of self-promotion and telling people I'm trying to raise money, I kind of feel terrified and freeze up.

But the Melbourne Marathon requires selecting a charity, and of course, I gravitated towards Beyond Blue, as mental health is so important to me, and they literally saved my life by calling an ambulance when I overdosed and ingested poison at my lowest point in 2020.

Today was my longest run before the big half-marathon race, my longest post-partum run. I was aiming to run as far as Jells Park, but at my turnaround point, I still hadn't made it there. It gives me something to look forward to in my serious marathon training.

I had the luxury of going slow, so I didn't necessarily need music to motivate me and get my heart rate up. So I decided to listen to an audiobook of one of my favourite motivational self-help books *Atomic Habits* by James Clear. I normally don't listen to many audiobooks, but I enjoyed it today.

One thing that resonates with me is the idea that an integral part of adopting positive habits is ingraining them into your identity and beliefs about yourself. 'I am a runner. That's who I am now.' I feel like I've adopted that belief now. Running is more than a hobby to me; it's an identity, a community, a lifestyle.

By the time I had four or five kilometres to go, I began to feel real discomfort and pain in my left shoulder. I was reminded of a quote in one of my marathon books that running a marathon is about accepting and embracing suffering. That's a loaded word. Suffering. I've faced discomfort and pain, but suffering? The idea of that is more than a little scary to me.

Monday, 3 July 2023
Week 5, Day 1
Rest Day

We were all up late last night, and Chris had the morning off, so the whole family had a sleep in. I woke up to an email from a journalist with the *Dandenong Star Journal* wanting to make an appointment for a phone interview and a photo-shoot to promote the Run Beyond Blue campaign. I was so excited that everything was already in motion and falling into place.

I replied with my availability during the week and did my phone interview straight after breakfast.

I only just had time to put on a touch of make-up and tidy up my hair when a photographer visited us and took some photos of me in my running gear, some action shots, and even one close-up of me with my shoes slung over my shoulder! Brooks sponsorship? Hint? Hint?

The photographer related how much he valued advocacy for mental health support, which made me feel that what I'm doing resonates with more people than I could imagine.

We have now raised over $400!

Tuesday, 4 July 2023
Week 5, Day 2
8 km Training Run

This morning I had to get to the pathologist early to get some fasting blood tests. I want to make sure all my basic levels of iron, etc., are at a healthy level before I take my training any further. I'm used to having blood taken, as some of the medications I've been on can affect liver or thyroid function, and these things must be closely monitored.

Pathology nurses can never seem to find my vein. I have small veins that like to hide, apparently. I waited patiently and clenched and pumped my fist repeatedly as she tapped and tapped on my inner arm until, finally, the elusive vein popped up, and she was able to insert the syringe. I never look. I don't like the sight of blood or needles. I'm not as bad as Chris, who has been known to faint in these scenarios! I was glad when it was over, and I was left pressing the little cotton ball against my puncture wound.

There was not much else on for today apart from my run. It was so, so cold, and I did not want to run. I wanted to sit in bed with a warm wheat bag on my feet and just read about running instead.

I motivated myself by remembering how lucky I am to be here. How lucky I am to be alive. How lucky I am to be able to run or even walk when so many can't. To be healthy and strong.

It's gotten to a point where these 8 km training runs have become quite easy. I don't even need to think or worry about it. I just lace up and go out and back, keeping my music upbeat and using it as a guide. Not so long ago, I was struggling with 6 km at a moderate pace. That seems like *ages* ago, but it's only been about a month. It just goes to show what sticking to a good training plan can do.

This morning, I received an email from the local newspaper in my hometown confirming that they'd like to run a feature on me (forgive the pun!). I sent them Margaret's poster and an overview of my journey, progress, trajectory, and goals.

I think being in the local San Remo rag will make my dad proud.

Wednesday, 5 July
Week 5, Day 3
5 km—'Race Pace'

I'm becoming increasingly obsessive about promoting this fundraising campaign. As soon as I woke up, I checked the *Dandenong Star Journal* website for my article. Nothing.

Then through the fog of a depressive fatigue I got Daisy and myself ready to leave the house, walking, with me pushing the pram, as I'm still waiting for my car to be fixed. I walked for over an hour, to three different strips of shops, looking for a place that stocks the *Dandenong Star Journal*. Nothing.

I was stressed and anxious. Even my Garmin watch told me I was stressed. It vibrated and came up with a little message saying my stress levels were higher than normal and suggesting I take some deep breaths. I messaged Chris and asked him to bring home some junk food so that I could munch away my anxiety.

I still needed to calm down, so I took a PRN med and crawled into bed. I had over an hour to rest and settle myself before 4:00 p.m., when I'd decided I would run. The PRN med made me tired and by 4 p.m. I was still only semi-conscious. I dragged myself out of bed and had the overwhelming thought loop of, *I can't do this*. I thought to myself, *I'm not built for speed. I feel like a canary trying to swim*.

I dismissed the idea of shooting for a personal best and decided to just get through the run. My first kilometre took over 7 minutes, so I was determined to try to maintain my pace, cadence, and heart rate and get a decent time.

I knew the fourth km was going to be hard, as that's when I hit the wall and it's at a point in my route that goes slightly uphill. I tackled it in little bursts. I'd lag, then pick up the pace, lose my rhythm, drift off and force myself to snap out of it and forge ahead.

I didn't give up. I didn't slow to a jog. I didn't walk. I made it.

My Garmin stats were good. My Garmin and I are friends now, after he/she/it checked in on me earlier in my time of need.

At home, I got some emails from the press: a journalist from the *Dandenong Star Journal* wanting to do some fact-checking and one from *The Sentinel Times* (one of my hometown papers) wanting to set up an interview and take some photos. It should be exciting for me, but with housework, training, and looking after Daisy, it's just another chore that drains me and saps my energy.

I felt so much self-doubt today. We still haven't hit the $500 mark, and I'm worried that all this media coverage will be a dead end, bearing no fruit and leaving us thousands of dollars short of our ambitious target.

Thursday, 6 July 2023
Week 5, Day 4 of Official Half-Marathon Training
Rest Day

Today has not been one of my better days in terms of executive functioning. Daisy and I both slept in. I texted Margaret that we wouldn't be making it to swimming. I think the phrase I used was, 'I'm wrecked.' The school holidays mess with my biological clock. Late nights, late mornings. It happens with Daisy too. She wakes up later, naps later, and stays up much too late.

This is the first time since Daisy started swimming that we've skipped a lesson. So I guess I decided not to be too hard on myself today. To give myself grace. A little rest as a form of self-care.

I didn't do the dishes today. That's a huge sign that things are going downhill. I knew right from the get-go that I wouldn't have it in me to cook, so I got some bolognese my mum had made from the freezer to thaw for dinner.

I've been so tired, exhausted, lethargic, unmotivated. And I've been stress-eating. For dinner I had pasta, then a quiche, two dim sims, then a toasted cheese and pesto sandwich.

I think it could be depression: the laziness, the overeating, the dirty dishes in the sink. It could also be a little niggling side-effect of the fact that I didn't get any exercise today. I'm used to being so active that inactivity feels weird. Where are those endorphins?

If this is me at my worst these days, it's a big step up.

There was one point in my life not so long ago, before I met Chris, where I lived in a constant state of anxiety. I experienced panic attacks over everything— what to wear, what to eat, what to say in a conversation. I had these sudden huge phobias of everything. Open spaces. Enclosed spaces. People. Being alone. The supermarket.

People talk about the state of anxiety, adrenaline and the fight-or-flight response, but there's a third response: freeze. I was a freezer. In these anxious states, the brain perceives everyday events and challenges as a literal threat to survival, and our most primal instincts kick in. Rapid, shallow breaths to conserve oxygen, the chest constricts, the heart rate rises, and the pupils dilate.

Something simple like, say, having to take a shower would incite the type of panic and hypervigilance an ordinary person might feel if they were awaiting news of a loved one in life-saving surgery. I felt that way all the time. Over nothing. So, for me, there are certainly worse things than having a messy kitchen for a couple of days and putting on a kilo or two from the odd cheeky snack binge.

Friday, 7 July 2023
Week 5, Day 5 of Official Half-Marathon Training
8 km Training Run

Another sleep in. Another morning of feeling like getting out of bed was going to be the most difficult thing in the world. Another morning of getting it together and getting it done anyway.

My cousin Michelle came over at about 10 a.m. to watch Daisy so that I could run, and I was still trying to properly wake up. I hadn't even had my cup of tea or my breakfast yet.

I summoned the energy to do the run—and do it right. I've established a bit of a benchmark for my three types of runs (easy, training and 'race pace') and how to tell if I'm putting in the right amount of effort without having to analyse my cadence or heart rate afterwards.

A simple matter of pace. All my easy runs seem to be at a pace of nine minutes per kilometre or slower; my training runs sit between eight and nine minutes, and my race pace runs are under eight minutes. I can glance at my Garmin watch at any point during my run, and my pace is clearly visible, so I can step it up if I start to lag. Today my average pace was 8:29, so I was right on track in terms of consistency.

When I got home, Michelle had stepped in and done the dishes, as well as bringing in the washing and folding it all. Just like Mum would have done. She apologised for one thing, though she hadn't folded my fitted sheet. 'I don't know how to do it properly,' she confessed. 'No one does!' I replied.

I may have previously mentioned that only 0.01% of people have run a marathon. I have a fair amount of confidence that I'll be able to cross the finish line, but I seriously doubt I'll ever be able to fold a fitted sheet. I wonder what percentage of people can do that? Less than 0.01%?

In the afternoon, I had a phone interview with a reporter from one of my hometown's local papers. I talked about how I never thought I'd be a runner and how, in high school, I'd do anything to get out of doing P.E.

Our fundraising campaign has reached over $700 now. I got an email from Beyond Blue, thanking me for my efforts and letting me know they would be sending me a Beyond Blue singlet (which I'm thinking about wearing on race day) to celebrate raising my first $50. I'll also be able to pick up a Beyond Blue Race Day Pack, which includes a sports cap (which I might also wear), a water bottle, a temporary tattoo, some blue zinc and a two-week gym pass. That will be my reward for raising over $500.

I also got an email with all my official race day info for the half-marathon I'll be running next weekend. The course map, timetable of wave start times, and information on the 'race village,' which will have entertainment, food and drinks, yoga, a massage tent and even an official group warm-up before the event. It also had information on road closures and where to park. Those are the logistics I'm most anxious about. And getting there on time. I'll be with Stuart, who starts volunteering at 6 a.m., so we'll work out a game plan together after Parkrun tomorrow.

Saturday, 8 July 2023
Week 5, Day 6
45-60 Minutes of Strength Training

This morning was my second time volunteering at Parkrun. Today, I was one of two tail walkers, and my partner was doing her 25th Parkrun milestone, so she got to wear a cute little purple tutu to celebrate!

At breakfast afterwards, I was proud of myself that I wasn't too shy to pipe up and ask for donations—which was fortunate, as one couple donated a generous amount.

Once home, with a bit of inspiration from some diagrams in a book on running training, I decided to do as much strength training as I could using free weights and my own body weight. I managed to do more than 45 minutes-worth at home, which meant I didn't have to go to the gym. I was glad this was possible for me, as my six-month gym membership is due to run out before the marathon.

Getting this done freed me up to spend the afternoon with Daisy, Margaret and George, and we took the kids to the park. They were both very tired and grumpy and screamed blue murder when it was time to take them off the swings and go home.

In the evening, I took the train into the city and met a friend who I hadn't seen in a long time. We were supposed to go to an indie cinema to watch a double feature of some B-grade horror movies, but our dinner took too long to arrive, and we missed the first movie.

Instead, we went to the cinema bar, where I got very buzzed on mimosas. We talked and laughed about our favourite movies and actors, and it was great to catch up after so long.

The movie we did see was hilarious, and it was in 3D. It was directed by Andy Warhol, so we knew it was going to be weird. It was about a mad scientist re-animating dead bodies and trying to get them to mate to create a superior race. It was very gory, visceral, and totally silly. The whole cinema laughed uproariously.

We ran into two other friends, Emily and Aya, and we all caught up afterwards for another drink (which was probably ill-advised on my part). We decided to ride-share home, which was fortuitous, as I hate public transport and would have felt a little uneasy and unsafe by myself on the train.

Sunday, 9 July 2023
Week 5, Day 7
11 km Long Run

This was the plan for my day: Michelle would arrive early in the morning to babysit Daisy while I went for my long run, then my dad would visit, and then in the afternoon, we'd go to karaoke with Emily and Aya.

The day did not go according to plan.

I woke up with a huge hangover! I felt seedy and totally dehydrated, as though I could barely move. There was no way I would be able to pull off an early morning long run in this state. I rolled over, picked up my phone (even this took some effort) and messaged Michelle to cancel. She found the whole situation very amusing.

Dad arrived earlier than expected, and Daisy and I were barely awake and out of bed. We hadn't even had breakfast.

I gingerly nibbled my way through a banana and fed Daisy her porridge. Then, while Dad played with Daisy, I downed copious amounts of water and coconut water to rehydrate, hoping that I'd be in a state to run in the afternoon.

I messaged Aya to say I was too hungover to go to karaoke, and funnily enough, both Aya and Emily were similarly afflicted.

When Chris came home, Dad had to go, and we had lunch—I heated some rice with chorizo and roast vegetables that I had made yesterday, which helped me feel a little bit better, but I was still in no fit state to go for an 11 km run.

Chris took one look at me and said, 'I think you should go and lie down.' I knew that wasn't a good idea. If I went to lie down, half an hour would turn into two hours, and getting up for a run would be near impossible.

Against my better judgement, I gave in to my exhaustion and went to lie down, telling Chris to drag me out of bed in half an hour.

When Chris came into the room, I was filled with dread. 'Please,' I begged, 'I just want to lie down for a little longer.' I wanted to lie down for at least another five hours, but I was desperate to get him off my case and resorted to childish pleading and bargaining.

Ultimately, he half-relented with a compromise to let me lie down for another 20 minutes.

After 20 minutes, my tiredness, whinging and complaining was even worse. Chris was steadfast in his mission to get me out and running. He kept repeating, 'You can do it. I know if you don't do it, you'll feel terrible.'

Over and over, I protested. 'I can't. I'm too tired. It's too cold. I'm sore all over. I'll do it tomorrow.' I tried to cover myself with the blanket and curl back into the foetal position, but Chris ripped the blanket off me and starfished himself all over the bed, taking up every inch of the mattress so that I physically had no space to lie down.

It got to a point where I was crying like a baby, and it took nearly an hour of this back-and-forth for him to convince me. I was so reluctant and worn down by the argument that I didn't have it in me to get dressed by myself. Chris got out my workout gear and helped me put on my socks and shoes.

This was not the first time Chris had to baby me in this way.

People with bipolar disorder and depression can have a lot of issues with self-care. Simple things like washing and brushing your hair, changing your clothes, brushing your teeth and showering can feel insurmountable.

With me, it was showering. When I was at my worst, I'd burst into tears at the very thought of having a shower. Chris would have to turn on the water, lay out my clothes, and physically help me undress. Often, I wouldn't even shower unless he came in with me for moral support.

Chris has the patience of a saint.

Today, getting dressed, putting in my contact lenses and putting on my hydration vest was the hardest part, but I also knew that 11 km was going to feel like 20.

I decided to endure it and plod on, holding tight to the thought that Chris had promised to cook dinner, and I could relax when I got home. I went at a snail's pace... probably even slower than a snail. It had been raining on and off all day, and it continued to do so throughout my run.

I allowed myself to feel a sense of relief and hope each time my watch buzzed, signalling another kilometre had gone by. When I got to kilometre 8, I realised I'd be able to finish the run without stopping to walk—or worse still—completely breaking down.

When I walked in the door, I was so grateful to Chris. He suggested I have a bath and read my book, but I knew if I got in, I'd never get out. Instead, I drank my coconut water, showered and glued myself to the couch with a good running book until dinner.

Monday, 10 July 2023
Week 6, Day 1
Rest Day

Today was my first day back at work after a two-and-a-half-week break. Getting out of bed was difficult, but I'd anticipated that. I had my clothes all laid out, and I just stumbled out of bed and got dressed and decided to have a shower after work.

It was so good to come back to work after the holidays without any sense of anxiety or dread. Before I went on maternity leave in 2021, I was suffering from extreme antenatal depression, and going back to work each day was hard enough; after a break, it was always hell, and it was difficult to adjust to the dramatic change in routine.

I enjoyed preparing maths and literacy work for my student, and we had an easy day to settle him back into the classroom.

After work, I checked my email, and Sahar from the *Dandenong Star Journal* said my article was now online and sent me the link. I was excited to read the article and share it with my friends on Facebook and my Facebook running groups. A woman in one of my groups thanked me for sharing my story and donated to my campaign.

Tuesday, 11 July 2023
Week 6, Day 2
5 km Training Run

The alarm went at six this morning, and there was no way I could get up. I have no idea how I will manage to leave the house at 5 a.m. for my half-marathon this Sunday. My actual wave start time is 7 a.m., but we have to be at the race village by 6 a.m., as that is when Stuart is starting his volunteering for the day. They also recommend you arrive an hour early on race day. I'm already starting to feel *so* nervous. The longest distance I've run since 2021 is 16 km, so I'm not sure where I will be able to pull that extra 5 km from!

This week is an easy training week. They call it tapering—when you dial back your training in the week or fortnight leading up to a big race, such as a half-marathon or marathon, to rest up, conserve energy, and prepare yourself. I'll also have to load up on carbohydrates this week to build up energy reserves.

Today after work, I called the auto repair place that still had my car. They confirmed it was ready and that we could pick it up at 4:30 p.m. I swung by the local shopping centre to pick up a few hard copies of the *Dandenong Star Journal* so I could see my article in print! I hadn't realised my story had made the front cover! I'm a cover girl!

When we got home it was already starting to get dark, but I was determined not to miss a day of training, so I set out for my 5 km run anyway.

It had been a while since I'd run 5 km at a moderate pace. I'd been pushing it in my last few 5 km runs—trying to get a PB, or at least close to it. I enjoyed myself for the first few kilometres, feeling like the run was nice and easy. But then, in my fourth kilometre, I felt a shift, and I thought this feels quite hard. Even something as simple as a little moderate 5 km takes a lot of effort, and it made me realise how hard I have to work at running all the time.

It doesn't come naturally to me at all.

A marathon or even a half-marathon is a big achievement for anyone— but for me, it's going to be huge! People are asking me if I have a specific goal in terms of pace or a finishing time, but my goal is just going to be to finish the race, even for my half-marathon this Sunday. Not too long ago my goals for running were mostly just to avoid developing diabetes or having a heart attack. To improve what was incredibly poor health and physical fitness.

During my 5 km runs I always pass the mental health ward of the Dandenong Hospital, where I've been admitted on several occasions. It always makes me wonder what the staff would think if they could see me now! Healthy. Mentally and physically. Would they recognise me? Would they be proud? Amazed?

A lot of people with mental health issues fear and dread being admitted. Movies and books like *One Flew Over the Cuckoo's Nest* and *Girl, Interrupted* spring to mind. They imagine confronting scenes of aggressive patients, feeling unsafe, and being mistreated by the hospital staff.

If you've never been inside a psychiatric ward, I'm here to reassure you it's not that bad. Every now and then, there'll be a bit of a scene going on where someone's disruptive, loud, or abusive to staff, but it's usually handled well, and the space you're in is always big enough that you can step away from the action and distance yourself until things calm down.

You don't get the sense that you're surrounded by 'crazy' people or that you're the only 'normal' one, or that you'll find no-one to connect with or relate to. The other patients are ordinary people—just like you and dealing with issues—just like you. A lot of them will have different problems going on in their lives—divorce, custody battles, family estrangement, unemployment, addiction, even homelessness, and sometimes hearing their stories will make you appreciate how lucky you are in the scheme of things.

You'll even find a sense of community and camaraderie amongst the patients. You're all in the same boat. You're all bored. You all want to unload and share your stories, and because of the boredom and monotony, most people are happy to listen to you and be a shoulder to cry on, as it helps pass the time and take your mind off your own problems.

You find yourselves bonding and getting together in little cliques and small groups, finding ways to pass the time. Mindful colouring or drawing. Playing card games. Uno is very popular. Endless cups of tea and coffee. Hunting down snacks because the medication almost invariably makes you hungry. There are perks. You don't have to cook. Hospital food is a lot better than you think it is. There is a comforting sense of routine, as everything happens at the same time every day.

Often, as a ward you'll pool money together and order pizza at night. Yes! They deliver pizza to psychiatric wards!

So when I jog past the hospital it's not a traumatic thing for me. The memories and feelings of being there are often fond ones. It's not such a bad place.

Wednesday, 12 July 2023
Week 6, Day 3
Rest Day

I slept in! By the time I woke up I only had 15 minutes to get dressed, have breakfast, pack my bag and head out the door. Somehow, I managed it! I wasn't late to work, I was early. I did some photocopying and prepared work for the first two sessions, and by the time the bell went I was ready for the school day.

In the staff room, I showed off my front page spread in the *Dandenong Star Journal*. It was a proud moment.

I got a chance to talk to another staff member who has done a couple of half-marathons, as well as the Great Ocean Road Marathon. He had some great advice. He injured himself with 5 km to go and got through it by just telling himself he had to get to each white post on the edge of the road—'I have to run that little bit further.' Over and over again.

Thursday, 13 July 2023
Week 6, Day 4
Easy 5 km Run

This morning, my alarm went off for us to get ready for swimming, and I pressed snooze. Margaret texted to say she had other plans and wouldn't be taking George to swimming lessons, and I thought, *What a perfect excuse not to go.* I planned to get up, but then I just climbed back into bed. Maybe if I slept for one hour, I could take Daisy to the 10 a.m. class, but both Daisy and I slept-in.

When she woke up and started crying, it was already 10 a.m. I'd missed both classes. I had failed to take my daughter to swimming two weeks in a row. Worse still, I saw texts from Margaret that had gone unanswered. She had changed her mind and gone to swimming after all and was concerned that I hadn't shown up. I felt so embarrassed.

There was a mountain of dishes. There was a load of washing to hang out, a load to bring in, and two more to wash. I felt like I didn't know where to start. I felt overwhelmed and was reduced to a quivering, blubbering mess. I texted Margaret that I felt like a bad mum, and she assured me I wasn't. I did the housework. I tried to have a cup of tea. Daisy kept trying to grab it. I tried to read. Daisy kept taking my book away.

When Chris came in the door, he knew something was wrong. I confessed that I hadn't taken Daisy to swimming. He'd already worked that out because the door was locked, and Daisy was still in her pyjamas. I expected him to be angry or disappointed. I don't know why. He never is. He was nothing but supportive.

He asked me if I wanted him to take over so that I could go for a run. I said I wanted to go into the bedroom, close the door, lie down and read a book. I needed to recharge before my run.

I read for a little while and then just had to close my eyes and roll over. I was too frazzled and brain-dead to make sense of the words. I lay like that for two hours, and by 4 p.m., I felt even more tired. I dragged myself out of bed, undressed, and pulled on my leggings and the rest of my running gear.

Before heading out the door, I checked my emails to see if there were any donations. There was an email from Beyond Blue, saying they'd read my article in the *Dandenong Star Journal*, thanking me for my fundraising efforts, and praising me for being open and vulnerable and fighting to reduce stigma. They said they wanted to do a story on me to inspire others.

I squealed with delight. It was just the boost I needed.

I listened to my favourite songs as I pounded the pavement and felt purposeful and motivated. Sure, I had no energy, but it was an easy run. Relaxing. A chance to have some alone time, de-compress and relax. I thought about how honoured I'd be to be an ambassador for Beyond Blue.

I was smiling, inside and out.

Friday, 14 July 2023
Week 6, Day 5
Rest Day

Another rest day! Last night was another late night. Daisy wouldn't go to sleep again, and I couldn't sleep either. My brain was ticking over about this Beyond Blue thing. I caught their attention! They believe I can make a difference! I was tired but couldn't switch my mind off, and I was awake past midnight.

All that meant was this morning was yet another sleep in for Daisy and for me. And a half an hour or so of walking around in a daze staring at the pile of dishes in what seemed like a *Groundhog Day* type of situation. Ahh, dishes.

The bane of my existence. And dinner. Cooking dinner.

But I handled it. I did the dishes, and Daisy wanted to go outside, so I quickly got her dressed and put some Ugg boots on—I'd slept in a tracksuit, which I was still wearing, and I left the house in these disguised pyjamas without a bra or undies on. I sat her in her little push tricycle and pushed her up and down the path outside our unit.

Then I got bored and decided to walk to the park, push Daisy on the swings for a while, and go down the slide a few times. The park was eerily quiet. It was just Daisy and me. I looked at my watch, and it had only been 20 minutes. It felt like an hour. I'm so used to us being at the park with Margaret and George that I felt like a piece of me was missing.

Margaret had texted me earlier, saying she was sick. Not having her around leaves such a void in my life.

Saturday, 15 July 2023
Week 6, Day 6
3 km Easy Run

Last night I couldn't sleep. I was so nervous and excited about Sunday, and I was beginning to realise fully what my involvement with Beyond Blue would entail. I was curious about these 'stories' of people with mental health issues and what they looked like, so I went on the Beyond Blue website to check it out.

I thought it might involve a quick phone interview and sending over a picture. Boy, was I wrong! I discovered the 'stories' are full-on, documentary-style short videos with stellar production values. I would have to speak on camera about my experiences and be filmed going about my everyday life! It was going to be a very big deal!

Surprisingly, after all that tossing and turning with my mind ticking over, I woke up quite easily, feeling ready for Parkrun. I didn't lie in bed, inwardly groaning like a teenager on a school day; I just got dressed and ate my breakfast.

It was my third time volunteering at Parkrun, and by now, I knew the drill. I felt like an old pro. Breakfast involved a lot of excitement for my half-marathon, tips and encouragement.

As I departed, Prue said to me, 'You'll be fine. You've done the training.' And I have. To the letter. I feel quite ready. I think I'll be fine for the race if I can just get some sleep and manage to wake up on time!

In the afternoon, the tiredness from my sleepless night finally hit me. Again, I made the mistake of having 'a little lie down' and ended up feeling even more tired. I still had one last 3 km run to do. Surely I could skip it? Wouldn't I be better off well rested for my big day, instead of worn out from one quick last-minute run? But I had trusted and had faith in my training plan all this time, and I wasn't about to abandon it.

I realised the effect of this one last run was primarily psychological. One last chance to get out there, reflect, and clear my head. To get my head in the game.

My run was not that bad. I listened to my eBook again and took it easy. One and a half km out, 1.5 km back. A couple of little hills that I did without pushing myself too much. Not enough to sap any of my energy for tomorrow.

I watched part of a comedy with Chris on Netflix and we ordered chips and brisket. It was a pleasant evening. I had made the decision to take some sleep meds and go to bed at 7:30 p.m., knowing full well I wouldn't be able to fall asleep for at least another two hours. I was dreading tomorrow's 4:30 a.m. start, but the actual run? Not so much.

Sunday, 16 July 2023
Week 6, Day 7
HALF-MARATHON!!!

The second my alarm went off I felt happy and excited! I knew it was going to be a great day. I jumped right out of bed and had a shower. I had laid out my clothes and packed my bag in advance and felt super organised. I didn't have much of an appetite, but I needed to fuel up, so I had two pieces of toast with peanut butter.

At 5 a.m., Stuart arrived right on schedule. We bundled into the car with all our gear and brought up the car park that Stuart had carefully chosen and booked on the GPS. It was a straightforward drive into the city, and I was so glad I had Stuart's company. We mostly talked about things other than the half-marathon, which suited me. It was good to take my mind off it and not obsess about it.

Arriving at the race village was like Christmas morning! I love race villages! All the tents and marquees, the catering vans, being surrounded by people who were all united in the exact same mission and goal, the air thick with nerves, excitement and anticipation. I put on my hydration vest, my bum bag full of gels and my phone, and pinned my race number to my chest. Then I waited for a nice hot coffee and munched on a banana for a little boost.

I chatted to lots of people, some doing their very first half-marathon, some seasoned veterans, and I felt so happy—and so ready. Runners are such nice people! I don't think you'll ever find a more inclusive, more welcoming atmosphere than the start line of a race. I was chatting to a lovely gentleman about how ready I was, saying, 'I have all the essentials. I've got my gels; I've got my phone ... wait! I forgot my headphones!!' I raced back to the bag drop, grabbed my headphones and raced back to the start line—in plenty of time for my wave's start time. I warmed up by jogging, jumping and marching on the spot.

The faster runners shuffled to the front. We were packed in like sardines, and wave by wave, each group started off, and we were jostled that little bit further forward until it was finally our turn.

It was still dark, pleasantly brisk but not too cold, and the city of Melbourne, all lit up, stretched out before us in all its glory.

We finally set off, and I began trotting along like it was just another long run, but this time I was accompanied by thousands of people!

My mind was buzzing. Was I running too fast? Was I being swept up in the crowd? All my running books had warned me about this. It's the mistake that almost every long-distance runner makes. I didn't feel overly exerted, so I just trusted my body and pushed on; many people passed me, and others hung behind.

The first clear thought I remembered having was at the 1 km marker, *How has it only been one kilometre??? It feels like we've come such a long way! This is going to be a long race!* As we all jogged along, I got compliments about my fluoro pink get up. 'Are you Runner Barbie? You look fantastic!'. Each compliment gave me a boost and made me smile.

It wasn't long before we reached the first drink station. I had plenty of water in my pack, but suddenly I questioned whether it would be enough. *Better grab a cup.* Trying to drink from a cup while running was a disaster. I lost all co-ordination, nearly slowed to a walk and couldn't get any in my mouth. Then I remembered a tip from one of my books: squeeze the cup mostly shut so there was a small opening. I did manage one gulp but decided then and there to skip the rest of the drink stations.

While we were running through the Docklands, we passed a public toilet. There was a queue of runners lined-up who had stopped entirely, suddenly realising they needed to 'go.' I felt grateful not to be in that situation but suddenly had another anxious thought. *Would I make it? Would there be other toilets? Why didn't I go right before the race?? All the books said to go right before the race!!!*

When we hit 7 km I grinned and felt a surge of adrenaline and dopamine. We were a third of the way through, and I still had plenty of energy.

At 11 km, I got another powerful hit. We were more than halfway. I felt like I was smashing it.

At 13 km I felt confident. Eight km to go. I'd run tonnes of 8 km training runs in my training. People always say, 'trust your training.' I trusted it completely. This was going to be a walk in the park!

Somewhere around the 15 km mark I started to feel tired. Why did I feel tired? I'd run 16 km in my training!

We were running through the Botanical Gardens, past the Shrine of Remembrance, and it felt like a real celebration. I tried to enjoy the scenery and take it all in.

Sixteen km. No man's land. Unchartered territory. That last 5 km I would have to somehow pull out of my arse! But I didn't feel worried—it was encouraging. I'd run 5 km thousands of times before. The 5 km run was my bread and butter. I'd started many a 5 km run feeling worse than this.

I don't know when exactly this happened in the race—because it bowled me over and completely took me by surprise—but suddenly, a surge of sprinters came zooming past, nearly knocking us over! *Where had these people come from? Were they elite athletes who had already run the course and were coming back for a second round? How rude!* It was ages before I realised these sprinters were doing the 5 and 10 km races, which had started much later than ours.

At 18 km I hit the wall.

Everybody talks about 'The Wall.' *How the hell would I keep going?* I was exhausted and I still had 3 km to go. That felt like such a long way. That was all of yesterday's run! My legs were like robot legs—on autopilot. I don't know how they were still moving, but I was glad they were. I was reminded of the song from *Finding Nemo*. 'Just keep swimming, just keep swimming, just keep swimming and swimming and swimming.'

After what seemed like an age, we hit the home stretch. I saw a big sign saying, 'Only 500 metres to go!' And then they did something mean to us. Torturous. They ended the race with a hill!

How could they?!! Every inch of my body was telling me to stop running and walk up that hill, but my mind was stronger. *You can do this girl, you got this! You've run up hills before.*

There was an amazing, loud, booming, drumming sound filling the air with something purely primal, driving us on. A huge drumming troupe was greeting us as we approached the finish line, surging us up that God-damned hill! Hundreds of spectators were squished against the barriers, with signs and pom-poms, cheering and waving and whooping. I scanned the crowed for Margaret, looking in both directions. I couldn't see her! I crossed the finish line with my arms raised up in victory!

It was an amazing feeling.

I was on a high. I was on top of the world!

Somehow my legs kept pumping and taking me past the Gatorade station, where I gulped down two cups. I walked right past the volunteers who were giving out medals; I didn't even notice them. My brain was mush. The first thing I did was call Margaret. 'I did it!'

'What?!! We were right there at the finish line! We didn't see you!' There was a huge crowd, so we agreed to meet at the Beyond Blue tent and there was a lot of fussing over me, congratulations and hugs, with her, her husband Steve, and George.

Then I remembered to get my medal (how could I have forgotten?) and my bag from the bag drop. I'd promised to get in an ice bath at the ASICS tent, and Margaret filmed me getting in and screaming. It felt great though! After that George was getting a little fussy, so they took off, but not before Margaret handed me a much-needed protein bar.

I put my name down for a massage and wolfed down a chicken burger and soft drink while I waited. They were going to concentrate on my legs, but I insisted my shoulders were worse, so they targeted my left shoulder and worked wonders.

After that I noticed there was a lounge area where people seemed to be lying back with big, inflated boots encasing their legs, looking very relaxed. I enquired about it and was told they were called 'recovery boots' and were used by elite athletes, and they worked by applying pressure all around the legs and feet for a period of about ten minutes. I put my name down for that as well, and after a short wait it was my turn and it felt like absolute heaven! I was treating myself to the whole works!

I texted Stuart to check if he'd still be finishing up his volunteer work at about 6 p.m. He said his finish time would be much earlier, so I decided to wait for him and walk down to the nearest pub for a beer. It was quite a long walk, and I was surprised my legs could handle it, but that beer felt *so* well-earned. The only problem was that it felt a little bit anti-climactic, sitting there by myself with no-one to celebrate with.

So I went to a nearby table and politely introduced myself to some nice people who allowed me to sit with them. They were suitably impressed by my medal, and it was nice not to be on my own. After a couple of drinks, it was time to meet Stuart back at the race village and head home. On the way I picked up Epsom salts, cupcakes and a bottle of champagne.

It was a night for celebration.

Monday, 17 July
Week 7, Day 1
7 km 'Race Pace'

I forgot to mention the blisters! I have a recurring, ongoing blister issue on the ball of my right foot. It comes and goes, and usually flares up when I'm running long distances. It doesn't usually give me much trouble, as the skin there is so thick. I could feel it building up during the race yesterday and was not surprised to see afterwards that it was bad and needed lancing. The jury is out on whether you should or shouldn't pop blisters, but I love gross stuff, so that's the real reason why I do it!

Today at work, I had a huge win! The student I work with sometimes plays with Legos, but he never makes anything. He usually just methodically sorts the pieces by colour and shape and presses similar pieces together. It's a very autistic thing to do—it's common for people on the spectrum to prefer lining up or organising toys rather than playing with them.

Today, I started making a little colourful peacock. Instead of trying to get him to follow the instructions or find the right piece, I'd get the piece and model exactly where it had to go, then hand him the piece, and he pressed it in. He managed to stay focused on this task until we'd built the whole thing together. When we were finished, he was proud of himself, and I gave him a high five and got him to show the teacher.

It was supposed to be a rest day today. In my training plan, rest days are always scheduled after long runs, but as I'm going to see Lizzo tomorrow night, I made up my mind that if I was feeling okay, I'd go for a run, so I did not miss a training session.

You wouldn't believe it, but I felt fine! Not tired, not sore, much the same as I'd feel after any average long run, but I was still worried about today's run. The longest I've ever run at race pace is 5 km, so to jump straight up to 7 km feels like I'm being thrown in at the deep end a little bit. I figured I would just try my best, and if I couldn't keep up a sub-eight-minute pace, I wouldn't beat myself up about it.

I still hadn't got used to looking at my watch as I ran without getting distracted and slowing down—so it was a bit bumpy and up and down. It was hard to keep up the pace. I felt so unfit!

There were a few seconds here and there when I was running a little over the eight-minute pace, but each time, I pushed as hard as I could, upping my cadence, trying to bounce more, or opening up my stride. Every time, I managed to nudge myself up to a speed I was happy with—and when I looked at my stats after the run, I had an average pace of 7:43.

Speaking of pace, when I looked at my stats after the half-marathon, I was blown away! My fastest kilometre was 7:12, and my slowest kilometre was 8:24! I'd managed to run every kilometre well under nine minutes! It's something about that race-day atmosphere and the motivation to try to keep up with everyone else.

I'm feeling so psyched for Lizzo tomorrow night! I feel like I've earned this amazing night out, and I can't wait to see my idol in concert.

Tuesday, 18 July 2023
Week 7, Day 2
Lizzo!

Today was a great day at work. Obviously, I woke up in a good mood, knowing that tonight I was going to see Lizzo, but Tuesdays are always pretty good. It's the day I run the playgroup at school, and therefore, it's the day I get to see Daisy for an extra two hours and watch her play with other gorgeous little toddlers.

Now that Mum was back from Mauritius, she was able to bring Daisy into school, and I was proud for her to see where I work and to watch me in action. There were only three kids at playgroup today, so I had the chance to interact with them and play with them all.

They all have such different little personalities. One little girl loves music and dancing and knows all the actions to all the kids' songs. A little boy who was new today was shy, but eventually, he joined in with some building blocks and drawing. Daisy was in a giggly, silly mood, playing Peek-a-boo inside a little cubby house and chuckling every time I popped my head up inside the window.

After work, I only had time to pop in at home, get changed, put in my contact lenses and slap on some makeup. I managed to give Daisy, Chris and Mum a quick kiss and a cuddle, then I raced out the door to beat the peak-hour traffic on my way to pick up my friends.

Driving into the city was awful! I always feel a little stressed driving anywhere outside my local area, and in the city, it's particularly stressful, with trams, hook turns, and so many places where right turns and U-turns are not allowed. There was an accident on our route to the car park my friend had booked, so we ended up driving around in circles in the city and getting totally lost.... We got there in the end after much frustration, and luckily, we still had plenty of time to eat dinner and get to the concert on time.

When Lizzo walked out onto the stage, I got emotional. *She's here! She's in Melbourne!*

I think Lizzo is probably the most beautiful woman in the world. She's big, curvy, and sexy, and she owns it. She is the world's biggest weapon in the fight against fatphobia, even posting tasteful, untouched nude images of herself online in all her big, black, beautiful glory. She's an inspiration and a positive influence on women and girls all over the world.

She came out in a sexy red and black PVC corset-style dress, and her backup dancers were all in skimpy little black PVC jumpsuits, wearing red harnesses on top.

Her backup dancers are all plus-sized, and they're amazing. So fit and athletic, jumping around manically for two hours, proving you don't have to look like an Instagram model to be able to dance with stamina and electric energy.

I couldn't say what my favourite song was, but there are a couple of lyrics that resonate with me. In 'Fitness' she proclaims: 'Independent, athletic, I've been sweating, doing calisthenics. Booty-licious? Mind your business! I've been workin', workin' on my fitness!' In 'Soul-mate' the chorus resounds with: 'Cos I'm my own soul-mate, I know how to love me, I know that I'm always gonna hold me down. Yeah I'm my own soul-mate! No I'm never lonely! I know I'm a queen but I don't need no crown, look up in the mirror, like damn! She the one!'

Lizzo got me through a lot of tough times. When I was suffering from postnatal depression, I woke up every morning feeling depressed, unmotivated and exhausted. I felt so guilty for feeling this way, and I had no self-esteem. Then I discovered Lizzo.

She had a reality show on Amazon Prime called *Watch Out For the Big Grrrls* in which she chooses unknown plus-sized dancers from all over America to audition for her by learning all the choreography for her concerts and performing different dance challenges each week—but also confidence and self-esteem challenges, like nude photo shoots and make-overs.

Instead of eliminating a different person each week in the style of reality TV competition, she just sent girls home at any time when they were struggling with stamina or the choreography or if they were struggling to fit in with the other girls and build a sense of camaraderie. She seemed so nice and nurturing, and every one of those girls was an inspiration.

The show made me think about Daisy and the example I'm setting, and I decided to work on my confidence and self-esteem. I read self-help books and filled out self-esteem workbooks like *I'm Awesome—Here's Why* and *Dear Me, I Love You*.

I also decided to face each morning with bravery and courage and turn the day around using healthy coping strategies. When I was feeling low and tired, I'd have a shower using a nice citrus body wash, put in eye drops to help me feel more awake, and drink a Berocca, with vitamin B, for energy.

Then, I'd turn Lizzo right up loud and dance and sing along while I began to tackle the housework. I always started with the dishes or making the bed. Just getting those things done made me feel like I had started the day right and I'd achieved something. The infectious positivity of Lizzo's lyrics began to rub off on me and sink in on a deeper level, helping me see myself as a powerful woman.

I even used one of her songs as my alarm to wake up in the morning, 'I do my hair toss, check my nails, Baby, how you feelin'? Feeling good as hell!' It helped me to wake up feeling good as hell.

At the concert, the way she interacted with the audience was amazing. She took the time to carefully read every sign her fans had made, thank them for their support and tell them, 'I love you, you're beautiful.' She even got the cameras to film every sign and put them up on the big screen.

She talked to her fans and asked them their names, offering them a microphone to have little conversations. She also looked through the crowd and acknowledged all the amazing outfits people were wearing. 'I see you! You look great!' The cameras followed everyone she mentioned, and she allowed so many people to feel special.

I think everyone walked out of that concert feeling amazing, happy, and energised.

Wednesday, 19 July 2023
Week 7, Day 3
8 km Training Run

I came home around 12:30 a.m. last night and couldn't get to sleep straight away. In the morning, I pressed snooze twice, then forced myself to get up. Work was fine, I was relaxed about being there and I got a lot done.

At the end of the work day, I was feeling tired and sore in the shoulders, especially that pesky left shoulder. All I wanted to do was get a massage. Instead, I drove home, greeted Daisy and Chris with a kiss and procrastinated getting into my gym gear. I didn't want to go for a run.

They say that what goes up must come down, and after my race and the Lizzo concert, I have nothing immediate to look forward to, just months of hard, dedicated training, with little time for a life outside of running.

I was feeling discouraged. My hometown paper hasn't run my story yet, and I'm still waiting to hear from Beyond Blue about the story they wanted to do on me. I felt stagnant. I was thinking, *What's the point?* I haven't had many donations lately —they had slowed down to a trickle, and I'm not even close to the $2,000 mark. What if the donations stop, and I've already reached the peak of my fundraising? What was I even doing all this for?

I'd planned to run at 4 p.m., but by the time I steeled myself up to get out of the house into the cold it was already 4:45 p.m. Another run that was going to finish after dark. I didn't know what to listen to and settled on Lizzo, and as I ran, I revisited my recent concert experience in my head.

It was a tough run. Not all days are good. I was starting to get sick of my 'new' route, and I was nervous about the number of cars on the road. A couple of times, I had to run on the spot to allow cars to pass.

The further I ran, the more my left shoulder hurt. I thought, *I've just got to push through the pain. Remember, a marathon is all about suffering.*

Thursday, 20 July 2023
Week 7, Day 4
Rest Day

I am so stressed and tense right now. I feel like an arsehole for saying this, but sometimes being a mum is just so hard. Daisy hardly eats anything, so that stresses us out, and she's such a night owl. Before bed, I just want to read, write, scroll social media or watch TV, but by the time Daisy goes to bed, I'm just so tired! And if I try to do those things while she's still awake, she just climbs all over me and makes it impossible.

If I'm reading, she snatches the book out of my hand. If I put a book down within reach of her, she pulls out my bookmark. She tries to steal my phone and has a tantrum when I try to take it back—same with remotes. If I try to have a snack and a drink, she tries to snatch that out of my hands too! She stole the top half of my sandwich before, and I kept having to move my drink out of her reach. If I try to sit at the table with my laptop, she comes over and starts reaching up for me and either says 'up' or 'Mum' repeatedly until I pick her up. Usually, I let her watch a couple of songs on YouTube before putting her down, but it's not long before she's bothering me again.

My shoulders are sore. I have a hot wheat bag around my neck, but it's not helping. I got a massage today, but that didn't help either. I'm just so tense.

Friday, 21 July 2023
Week 7, Day 5
8 km Training Run

At last, Daisy and I could have a sleep in. Both of us got to lie in bed until 9:30 a.m. I was groggy and foggy and just out of it this morning. My mind was just mush, and I was panicking about how I'd manage to do the housework, meet my friends, take back that hoodie, go for my run, then get ready to go out and manage to have the energy to drink, dance and socialise 'til the wee hours of the morning.

Sometimes it's all just too much.

I decided to go through the motions of my little pick-me-up strategies, drinking Berocca, and listening to Lizzo while I did the dishes, but I was still feeling flaky and forgot the other mums and I were meant to be meeting at a specific time and place at 11 a.m. Usually, we play these things by ear and work around when the kids are eating and sleeping. At 10:30 a.m. I still hadn't hung the washing out, and Daisy and I weren't even dressed.

In the end, I had to shove some things in my bag, throw on some clothes and head out the door. I needed to exchange a hoodie that I had bought, but it would have to wait.

We had a nice lunch at a Mexican place, and I had a fancy taco and some nachos. We tried to give the kids chips and corn, but as usual, Daisy didn't want to eat anything. Then we went to the park, and Daisy went up to some strangers and stole their chips. I was mortified! The people were nice about it and said they were finished anyway and gave Daisy the rest of their chips to eat!

This whole time, I was looking at my watch, conscious of the time, and hoping I could get away by 2 or 2:30 p.m. to get to the shops and then get my run in. We said our goodbyes right on schedule, and Margaret helped me find my way back to my car.

Sorting out the hoodie exchange was quick and painless, and we were back home in no time. Daisy was still asleep, but I woke her up getting her out of the car.

Running was just another chore. Something to get done. It's just become second nature to me now. Like having a shower or brushing my teeth. Part of my routine. Part of my schedule. And having a very exact training plan that I'm following means no excuses. No 'I'm tired today, I'll do it tomorrow.' I make it a priority—just like my job. No ifs, no buts.

I got home in plenty of time to shower and get ready, but I didn't have time to cook dinner as well, so we got take-away. Chris's dad soon arrived to babysit Daisy, and we were out the door for a night out.

I had a great time. It turns out drunk people are generous, and I spent the night hustling and got around $1,000 in donations! Every time someone scanned the QR code, I let out a little squeal and jumped up and down on the spot. We got home around 1 a.m. exhausted and just fell into bed. It had been a long day.

Saturday, 22 July 2023
Week 7, Day 6
Rest Day

After very little sleep I had to drag myself out of bed at 7 a.m. to get to Parkrun. I was volunteering again, tail walking this time. My fellow Vollies commiserated with me over the fact that soon, my long runs would be longer than half-marathons. 'That's when you know it's getting serious.'

While I was having breakfast with the Parkrun crew, Margaret called and suggested we take the kids to the park to take advantage of the nice weather. I was feeling worn out but decided it was much better for Daisy to be outside playing and spending time with her friend George than sitting at home in front of Cocomelon while Mummy collapses into a heap and tries to recharge her fried body and mind.

The park was nice at first, but it turned into a bit of a disaster when Daisy kept falling down the steps leading up to the slide. It only happened twice, but that was enough. After the second tumble, she even had a very slight nosebleed and was upset (as was I!), so I decided to take her home.

Today was not meant to be a rest day. Today was meant to be for strength training. I wanted to go to the gym after lunch, but Chris went to play board games with some friends, so I stayed home with Daisy. As soon as she went down for a nap, I did the same. I was exhausted. Chris got home while she was still asleep, so I stayed in bed until about 4:30 p.m. I would have lain there for hours longer, but I had to get up and make dinner.

Luckily, it was an easy one-pot recipe, and I just went through the motions on autopilot. We sat on the couch to eat and watched TV. We tried to give Daisy some of our food but didn't have much success. I was totally spent. I wrapped a blanket around myself like a cocoon and just curled up on the couch like a vegetable.

The plan was to do some weights, planks, and other strength training after dinner, but there was just no way. Instead of skipping the workout altogether, I decided to postpone it until Monday, which is usually a rest day.

Tomorrow it's a 15 km run, then lunch and seeing the *Barbie* movie with friends, then visiting relatives. No rest for the wicked.

Sunday, 23 July 2023
Week 7, Day 7
15 km Long Run

I woke up just before 7 a.m. and turned my alarm off before it had a chance to make that annoying sound and make me feel bad about still being in bed. That was still much too early for me. Why had I agreed to meet our friends for lunch at 11:30 a.m. before we went to see the *Barbie* movie? Why had I cursed myself to get out of bed at a ridiculous hour for a Sunday and run 15 kilometres?? Why was I doing anything at all on a Sunday besides going for my run, eating, and occasionally migrating from the couch to the toilet and back?

I stayed in bed until 8 a.m. and resigned myself to the fact that I'd probably finish my run way too late for a lunch date. I thought maybe setting some boundaries and cancelling would be healthy.

I can't do it all. I like to think I'm the 'woman who can do it all,' but I'm just the woman who can do most of it—under the proviso that I unravel several times a week.

Some runs are harder than others, and this one was a doozy. I was spent after just 2 km. My audiobook taunted me with a lengthy chapter on genetic predisposition and not setting yourself up for failure by choosing a path that doesn't play to your natural strengths. Running does not play to my natural strengths. I'm heavy. I have short legs. I'm physically very weak. I have asthma. It was a very discouraging diatribe to have to endure.

The next chapter was much more up my alley. The premise was that the secret to success and to maintaining effective habits is the ability to endure and 'fall in love' with boredom. Long runs can be the very definition of boredom. After seven weeks of training, they are both boring and lonely. And I'm the queen of sucking it up and doing it anyway. That is my superpower. My absolute mastery of boredom is what will get me through and get me across the finish line.

Last weekend, I ran a 21 km half-marathon, so I don't know why 15 km was so hard. Once I reached my turnaround point, I felt a slight psychological boost, but home still felt like a long way away. My audiobook finished, and I switched to a very eclectic, mish-mash playlist. I tried the technique of breaking my run up into manageable chunks: tree to tree, post to post, sign to sign.

It wasn't until I got to back to the start of the trail and on the street again that I started to feel some optimism and positivity. It was nearly over. I'd achieved what I set out to do. I'd put in the work and done my training like a good girl. And I wasn't running that late! I got in the door at 10:30 a.m., and by 11:45 a.m. we managed to make it to the restaurant before the others! Success!

The Barbie movie was everything I hoped it would be and more. It hit me right in the sweet spot of my sense of humour. I was in hysterics, laughing out loud, and so were my friends. It was such a great experience to share and bond over.

Monday, 24 July 2023
Week 8, Day 1
45-60 Minutes of Strength Training

Last night, Daisy was a nightmare! She woke up at 2 a.m. and wouldn't go back to sleep until 6 a.m.! That was when I called in sick, and then Daisy and I both slept in until 9 a.m. Calling in sick might sound a bit lazy, lame or extreme, but sleep is extremely important for people with bipolar disorder. Lack of sleep is one of the most common factors in triggering a manic episode.

The last time I had a manic episode, which was a few years ago, I spent all my money and couldn't afford to fill my car with petrol. Then, I drove my car to all these different places with a completely empty tank and ended up stranded on the side of the road. This happened three times in one week! I would call Chris to come to my rescue with a can of petrol and a funnel, then get angry and snappy at him for taking too long or not doing it right. I was awful to him, and he didn't deserve it.

The worst of it was when I finally realised I was manic and called 000. At the time I was in Hungry Jack's. They said the ambulances were all busy, but they'd send a taxi to take me to the hospital. While I was waiting for the taxi to arrive, I changed my mind and decided to drive to Chris's mum's house, where I knew I'd be well looked after. My head was so messed up that I missed the turn-off to her house, but I kept driving and got completely lost. I had also lost my phone, so I couldn't even look at Google maps and re-orient myself. I left my car on the side of the road in the middle of nowhere and decided it was a good idea to flag down a stranger's car and ask for a ride to the nearest GP, where, hopefully, they would prescribe me an antipsychotic. In my mind, I'd be able to take one pill, go to sleep and wake up fine. To be fair, this had happened once before.

The guy who picked me up was dodgy. He asked me on a date, and I politely declined. He dropped me off at a GP near Southland Shopping Centre, and of course, when I saw the GP, he wasn't comfortable prescribing an antipsychotic to a patient he'd never met before. Then I walked to the shopping centre, without my phone, and without any way to contact anyone. It was early and none of the shops were open yet. My body was tired even though my mind was ticking at 100 miles per hour.

I had this crazy idea that if I waited outside a bookshop until it opened, I could go in, find a book written by one of my author acquaintances, find the publisher's name, and call up the publisher. The publisher would then call the author, and they could organise for someone to come and pick me up. I had never even met these authors in real life. They were friends of friends who I'd added on Facebook. It was a convoluted plan that made no sense.

Some security guards noticed me hanging around outside the bookshop and asked me what I was doing. When I explained my whole story, they realised something was not right, and they called the police to come and handle the situation. I told the police I was manic, had lost my phone, and that I had no idea where my car was. They offered to call an ambulance and accompany me to the hospital, and I was so relieved that I was finally going to get some help. My mum and Chris had to drive around for ages until they finally found my car. My phone was under the passenger seat.

All of this was precipitated by a bout of extreme insomnia—so that's why I protect my sleep at all costs.

Even after the sleep in I was extremely tired and felt like there was no way I would get anything done today. All I had the energy for was drinking cups of tea while scrolling through Facebook. Then, a funny thing happened. A friend posted a meme to my Facebook page that was like a role-playing game card, called the *Executive Functioning Chicken*. It stated: 'This card grants you the ability to stop scrolling and complete one task you've been putting off.'

It worked! I walked over to the kitchen sink, turned on the hot water, waited for it to heat up, and tackled the dishes one by one. I'm not going to lie; I was crying as I did them, but I managed. Then, knowing the chicken only granted one task, I returned to the couch and my phone.

At least the day wasn't a total write-off. A more functional me would have put some clothes away and done some meal-prepping, but I was struggling to even stay awake and silently pleading for Daisy to go down for a nap. I felt like there was no chance I would get my strength training done, and that made me feel so guilty and useless. I'd never missed a training session yet and a skipped session felt like a massive failure.

I was so relieved when Chris came home early from work. He showered, and we all had lunch; then I took some medication before lying down for a while. I have trouble sleeping during the day, no matter how tired I am, so I wasn't sure I'd be able to have a proper nap, but I ended up sleeping soundly for a few hours.

I woke up still feeling tired and felt like I'd never summon the energy to hit the gym. Then Chris cooked dinner, and I started to feel a little more awake, and decided to get in my gym clothes and go.

When I got to the gym, I booked in for a personal training session and another 'Evolt' scan for the following Monday, then used the machines. I tried doing five lots of 20 reps on most machines and managed well. I hate core exercises, but I managed five sets of 40 Russian twists.

I was only there for 45 minutes, but technically I had done it! I had officially completed the training session from my 18-week plan!

Even after waking up feeling like it would be impossible!

Tuesday, 25 July 2023
Week 8, Day 2
7 km 'Race Pace'

Today was my third morning running the playgroup. I got to school early and turned on the heater and made sure I had everything ready. I hunted down some trucks and cars (I'm still figuring out where everything is) as some of the feedback from last week was that we didn't have enough 'boy's toys.'

I waited and waited for ages. It starts at 9:00 a.m., but Mum and Daisy didn't arrive until 9:30 a.m., and only one other girl came at about 10:00 a.m. A mother from last week showed up with her little boy, but he cried when she brought him inside, so they left straight away. Margaret texted me to say she needed to get some things done, and she and George wouldn't be coming.

Daisy and the other little girl played a little bit together, a little bit in parallel also, enjoying the toys. We had to remind them to share a couple of times, but they are both good-natured kids who are pretty easy-going, so we didn't have any tears or drama. The rest of the workday was relaxed and pleasant. There was a good balance of work and play for my student, and the highlight of the day was when we made another peacock out of Legos together.

At lunch time I messaged Dad to see if either of my hometown local papers had written an article about my running yet. He replied that the *Sentinel Times* had done a story, and I excitedly trawled the website and was excited not only to read the article, but also to see my friend Aya's photo, with their name credited underneath. I excitedly rang them and congratulated them on their first official published photo. I asked Dad to buy six copies of the paper for me. The other local rag in my old stomping ground, *The Advertiser*, was doing a story on me next week.

When I got home it was straight down to business. I wasn't feeling super-pumped or energetic (we're well past that stage in my training), but I didn't allow myself the time to think any negative thoughts, like, *I can't do this* or *I don't want to do this*. I was able to force myself into a relatively positive mindset.

We've established that I don't like fast running, and we've also established that sustaining it for more than 5 km is pretty challenging for me. I decided to just do my best and push myself with the most effort I could muster. I was relieved to find I had plenty of energy. Don't get me wrong—it wasn't easy, but I didn't feel like giving up or slowing to a jog at any point.

There was a point where the sunlight was behind me and I was jogging towards my own shadow. Whenever this happens, I have this funny little inner monologue—*Who is that slow, unfit person running in front of me? Surely I can run faster than her!* And you know what? I never can. I still make a fun game of trying though, and it always makes me laugh inwardly.

Wednesday, 26 July 2023
Week 8, Day 3
8 km Training Run

Something happened this morning that hasn't happened in a long time. I cried non-stop during my drive to work. I was crying a little bit while I was eating my breakfast, but I held back the tears because I didn't want my mum to see me cry. I was feeling anxious. I just had this overwhelming feeling that I wasn't ready to handle the day.

Thoughts like, *I'm not good at my job*, or *No one cares about all this marathon training, what's the point?* and *No one understands what I'm going through*. I just felt brain-fried and like the day was going to be a real struggle.

When I pulled into the car park, I was still crying. I had these conflicted feelings of whether I should pull myself together and hide my feelings or reach out to someone. There is at least one lady at work who knows how bad my mental health can be and with whom I feel I can be honest. I decided if someone asked me the question, 'How are you?' I'd reply that I was struggling and having a rough morning, but no-one asked.

I was kind of relieved, but there was a part of me that wanted to sit down with someone in a flood of tears, listen to a kind word, and drink a calming cup of tea in a cathartic little moment of honesty before the official start to the day.

As I walked into the classroom, before the bell went, and before the kids came in, I wiped away my tears and put on my 'game face.' As I started our morning routine with my student, the morning's thoughts started to wash away.

The funny thing is, there was no trigger. I didn't have a bad night's sleep; I didn't have a particularly stressful day coming up. Sometimes I just cry for no reason. It's a mystery. I just cope in the best way I can and use strategies to deal with the feelings when they arise. This morning it was partially drinking water and taking deep breaths, but the best strategy I find is just to *do*. Don't think, don't feel—just *do*. On autopilot if you must.

The trouble with that is that the thoughts and feelings don't get addressed, and they can bubble up later. I'm a master of the 'cope and crash' method of bipolar survival. Cope, cope, cope, cope, crash. Lots of coping and contained little crashes that hopefully get outweighed by all the coping I'm doing. It seems to be working out okay for me.

Please don't listen to my life advice. This is not a self-help book. I am not a guru. I'm just winging it.

Speaking of self-help books, today I downloaded a bit of an anti-self-help audiobook, *The Subtle Art of Not Giving a Fuck*, by Mark Manson. Just to mix things up a bit on my training runs. I'm getting sick of listening to music, so I thought I'd try an audiobook and see if I could keep up a decent pace without a beat driving me. So far, I'd saved my audiobooks for long runs, where pace doesn't matter.

It turns out I managed just fine, and it made the run enjoyable. There was a lot of talk of inevitable pain and suffering and choosing your pain and choosing your suffering, or something of that nature. Basically, being selective about what you 'give a fuck' about.

My thoughts were: *This. This is the pain and the suffering I'm choosing. The time sacrificed. The boredom and loneliness of the long runs. The muscle pain and the exhaustion. These are the fucks I'm choosing to give.*

Thursday, 27 July 2023
Week 8, Day 4
Rest Day

Last night, Daisy woke up at 2 a.m. and wouldn't go back to sleep until 4 a.m. When my alarm went off to get ready for swimming, I was so tired and knew Daisy would be too, so I decided we'd sleep in for an extra hour and go to the 10 a.m. swimming class.

It was kind of the swimming teacher to let us do our class later. The 10 a.m. class is technically full, but a lot of the kids don't show up, so I knew there would be room for us. I was proud we were able to turn up at all after the night we had.

When we got home, I set about doing a bunch of chores and making sure all our clothes and swimming gear were washed and on the line; the dishes were done, and Daisy and I were showered and dressed—with me in my bright pink outfit, ready to see *Barbie* for the second time with Jess and Margaret. I was even left with plenty of time to do my makeup—with pink eyeshadow and lipstick, in true Barbie-style.

Chris got home early, which allowed me to call Margaret and organise to meet at the cinema bar an hour before our session started for a proper adult mummy get-together, complete with prosecco.

The idea of having a little group of girlfriends is new to the three of us. We felt like a little sisterhood or sorority, getting together and seeing a silly, funny, but ultimately feminist and empowering movie.

I also had some exciting news to share. I received an email from Tristan at Beyond Blue wanting to do an interview in the very near future, and he'd sent some questions or key talking points to consider and prepare for the interview.

After getting home, cooking dinner and saying goodnight to Chris and Daisy, I was left to consider and ponder the questions thoroughly, and in truth, it made me a bit nervous. I didn't know where to start or begin to answer difficult questions like, 'Why are you doing this? Why Beyond Blue? What are your experiences with anxiety and depression?'

How could I encapsulate a whole life of living with these conditions into one conversation?

I wanted to be honest, vulnerable, and eloquent. I wanted to share a story that others who were struggling could relate to and offer some hope, advice and inspiration.

But I'm not an expert! I haven't got it all figured out! I'm not a role model. Am I?

Friday, 28 July 2023
Week 8, Day 5
8 km Training Run

Finally, a day where I haven't had to do virtually anything besides my training run. No alarm, nothing to do in the morning, just a visit from my Dad. He was coming all the way from San Remo, so I knew he wouldn't arrive until at least 10:30 a.m.

This morning, it was hard to get any housework done. Daisy was clingy. She was crying and wanting my attention while I was doing the dishes, and in the end, I didn't even finish doing them! I got halfway through putting the washing away too. It wasn't just Daisy—I was in a bit of a fog. I'm still recovering from a couple of weeks of doing too much and slowly re-adjusting and regaining my strength and energy.

Daisy was happy to see her Grandpa arrive. She doesn't get to see him as often as her other grandparents, so it's always extra special—for us and for him.

She was being cute, giving him lots of cuddles and attention, babbling non-stop in her own little baby-talk language. This old-style Aussie bloke, who's all about fishing, boats, football and beer, just melts in her presence. He's a big softie, my dad.

Daisy does this thing where if she wants to go outside, she goes and gets her shoes and brings them to me because she associates wearing shoes with going outside. She did this while Dad and I were having a cup of tea. I told Daisy, 'We'll go outside in a minute; Mummy's just finishing her cup of tea.' So she climbed up next to me on the couch, looked right at me, and dipped her shoe in my tea! We thought it was the funniest thing we'd ever seen! We still waited for Grandpa to finish his tea, then we got her a different, non-tea-soaked pair of shoes and took her outside. We pushed her along on her little bike around the unit complex until Dad got a bit tired, and we decided to go back inside.

Once Dad had said his goodbyes, I realised just how tired I was (what's new) and decided to lie down for a little while. I feel like this happens every day, and I feel like a broken record, but I fell asleep, woke up groggy, and realised I had to wake myself up and attempt to run 8 km at a reasonable speed, feeling like I was still half asleep!

My run was hard. I could feel in every fibre of my body that I was going significantly slower than Wednesday's run, but I was already pushing myself to my limit.

The hard part of completing a marathon is not the six or so hours of running on the day but rather the endless training, the time commitment, and the exhaustion all the time.

Sometimes I wonder what I've gotten myself into.

Saturday, 29 July 2023
Week 8, Day 6
45-60 Minutes of Strength Training

I stayed up *way* too late last night. Sometimes I just get stuck on the couch. I'm too lazy to turn the TV off, get up and get ready for bed; it's almost easier to be half asleep than to walk the few meters from one room to the next and lie down properly and attempt to sleep.

I forgot to set the alarm, and when I was awoken by a knock at the door around 7:25 a.m., my first thought was, *This seems a little early for a package to be delivered.* I'd completely forgotten about Parkrun! I answered the door to my mother-in-law, still in my pyjamas, then rushed around, getting ready as quickly as I could. I was so embarrassed! I'd even been considering foregoing Parkrun this week, as a part of my plan to dial back my social calendar and take it easy on myself, but I knew if I missed it, I'd be in a bad mood, like I'd missed out on something important—something that undoubtedly gives me pleasure.

I was volunteering today as a marshal, standing at one of the bridges, directing runners to turn left and 'loop the bridges' before coming past me one more time for the home stretch. It was a bit boring and lonely, and it was hard to keep track of who had already done the loop and who hadn't. I also felt a little awkward about being overly enthusiastic in cheering people on—after all, they hadn't reached the finish line yet. Was it too much? I much prefer tail-walking or handing out finish tokens—jobs where you're around other people and can chat and socialise. Today was my fifth time volunteering, so I'm halfway to my ten-week milestone.

As cold as it was when we arrived at the park before 8 a.m., by the end of the run the sun was out, and it was turning out to be a nice day. After breakfast, when I got home, I wanted nothing more than to sit on the couch and read. I was sort of steeling myself to turn down any social offers to get out and do anything. *Take it easy, Jacqui. You don't want to get burned out again.* Also, I had to prioritise strength training. I didn't want to repeat the last couple of weeks and wait until the end of the day when I had no energy.

Then Margaret called and suggested we take the kids to the park. She had a point. It was a beautiful day. When I was a kid, I never would have been inside on a day like this. I didn't want to coop Daisy up, so I made the effort for her sake. I stuffed her bike into the car and high-tailed it to Margaret's house, and from there both kids rode alongside us to the nearby park, swapping bikes on the way, as kids will do, always wanting what the other kid has.

It was a short outing, which was good, as Margaret and I tend to get sucked into a bit of a time void when we hang out together, and I end up rushing or struggling to do whatever is left to do in the day! Today she had to go on a bit of a drive to pick up a new bike for George on Marketplace, so when we got back to her house, we said a quick goodbye, and I arrived home with plenty of time and energy left to go to the gym.

Some of the intensity and sheer number of reps I was doing were making my muscles literally feel like they were on fire—that old cliché of 'feeling the burn.' It's amazing how quickly that pain fades between sets though. The science explaining all this in terms of lactic acid build up, etc. is too technical for me to fully understand, but I get the gist. Working out is putting the body through stress and causing it subtle, minor damage, which is why recovery and not overdoing it is so important.

In the evening, I could feel a few aches in my legs as I pottered around the house, and it felt *good* in a way. I wasn't wrecked, but I'd worked hard, and my body was registering it. My desire to be lazy and just read returned and I had a bath and got out one of my running books, which I hadn't touched in over a week, then hit the couch and decided that cooking was not going to be a thing later, and that I was craving pizza. On Parkrun days I have a big breakfast so late that I skip lunch and get ravenously hungry for an early dinner. Luckily for me it doesn't take much to talk Chris into getting take-away, so pizza it was.

I feel like I'm not painting a very good picture of myself here—always having baths and lying down and getting take-away! I must be coming across as lazy. I guess it depends on what lens you choose to look through. You could just as easily say I'm learning to look after myself and practicing self-care. I oscillate between these two views of myself constantly, and I have to admit the negative view usually wins.

I feel embarrassed to be so *tired* all the time. I feel embarrassed for just checking out so often and running out of spoons. Guilt. So much guilt. Not so much self-loathing anymore, and that little voice in my head is getting much less nasty and cruel, but self-stigma is a hard thing to shake. Why do I have to be so *bipolar* all the time? Why can't I just be normal?

Sunday, 30 July 2023
Week 8, Day 7
24 km Long Run

Last night Daisy had me up half the night AGAIN. From about 3:30 a.m. until 6:30 a.m. My alarm went off at 8:45 a.m., as my cousin was coming at 9:30 a.m., and I was hoping to be all ready to head out on my run by then, but I just turned off my alarm and stayed in bed. As 9:30 a.m. drew nearer and nearer, I thought over and over in my head, *Please don't arrive on time, Michelle.* Lucky for me she was half an hour late.

I dragged myself out of bed to open the door, and around this time Daisy woke up, so I loped around the house changing and feeding her, having breakfast and getting dressed. I felt like lying in bed for another couple of hours, but the dreaded 24 km run had to be done.

I was already exhausted and dragged my feet in the first two kilometres. My plan was to just get lost in my audiobook and let my feet move automatically, and it worked for the first eight or so kilometres, but then I had to concentrate on where I was going so I wouldn't get lost on the way back. Jells Park was busy and bustling, as was to be expected on a sunny Sunday afternoon (yes, it was afternoon by the time I made it there). There were people everywhere and paths leading off in every direction. I tried to bring up my map, but I couldn't make sense of it.

I decided to wing it and just follow my intuition. I managed to find enough pathways to take me to the 12 km mark, which would be my turnaround point, and I even managed to take the same route back to the beginning of Jells Park. That's where things started to look a bit murky and wayward.

I didn't recognise any of the paths to find out how to get back to Mulgrave and the Eastlink trail. I headed off in the direction that seemed to make the most sense, but I instantly felt that it wasn't right.

I doubled back on myself and headed in the opposite direction. It still didn't look familiar, but I was too tired, confused and brain-fried to turn back the other way again and figure out where I was. I eventually came out onto a main road, and I was totally lost. I brought up my Google Maps, but it was hard to orient myself and figure out which direction I had to head in. I eventually worked it out, and of course, the way back involved running up a huge, steep hill.

I was way off course. The huge detour meant that I'd reach the 24 km mark well before I was anywhere near home, and a five-minute cool-down walk would turn into at least 15 or 20 minutes. I didn't feel like I had it in me. Then, after about 20km, my Garmin died. I'd forgotten to charge it! I quickly brought up another tracking app on my phone and decided to let it guide me for the final four kilometres.

Everything hurt. I had no energy whatsoever.

It was hard to even take in the audiobook as I was so brain-fried. Had my training not been enough? Was I not ready for this run? Or was I exhausted because of my lack of sleep? I'd been taking in my gels and plenty of water, but they hadn't given me any sort of boost. By this stage, I'd slowed to a shuffle that was even *slower* than a walk. But I was determined to keep running.

Those last four kilometres felt like 12. I was an absolute wreck. Fresh, perky, energetic joggers ran towards me in the opposite direction, and I was embarrassed to be seen in my weakened sorry state. I wanted to shout, 'I don't normally run like this! I've been going for longer than a half-marathon, and that's why I'm so tired!' I felt like such a loser.

At last, my app announced that I'd hit 4 km, but I decided to jog a little bit further, as I wasn't completely sure whether my Garmin had registered 20 km or a bit less before it had unceremoniously carked it. Before long, I could go no further. I had to walk. Normally, after a run, I cool down with a brisk power walk, but this was a hobble, nearly a limp. I felt like I was on the brink of collapse. I was going to struggle to walk for even five minutes. I kept checking the time on my phone. Each minute dragged on. The five-minute hobble took me to a main road around the corner from my house, and I found a fence to sit down on and called Chris.

'Honey, this is going to sound lame, but I'm on the corner of x and y roads, and I need you to come and pick me up.' He found the situation pretty amusing.

Monday, 31 July 2023
Week 9, Day 1
Rest Day

This morning, as predicted, I woke up feeling so sore. Once again, I'd had night sweats and had soaked through my pyjamas, so that had left me feeling depleted as well. That being the case, I should have gotten up early to have a shower to avoid being utterly gross, but instead, I rolled out of bed at the last minute, peeled off the sweaty pyjamas, and pulled some clean clothes onto my sticky, sweaty body. I decided I'd just have a shower after work.

Today, my student came into school crying and cried for an hour and a half. He has no verbal communication, so he couldn't tell us what was wrong. Every time we offered him a drink, a tissue, or a sensory toy, he'd bang his fists on the table and cry even more loudly, so we left him alone until he indicated he was ready to engage with us by sitting up and wiping his tears away.

Then we had a meeting with his occupational therapist, who agreed it was best to give him space in those situations. She was a bit concerned about some of the behavioural and emotional issues he'd been having lately but was impressed with his improvements with fine motor activities like writing, colouring and Legos.

After work I had my phone interview with Tristan from Beyond Blue. During the day I'd put more thought into his potential questions and decided to be more vulnerable and to try to talk a bit more about my lowest periods, like when I couldn't even shower myself. I want to normalise those kinds of symptoms for people who think they're the only one, who feel embarrassed or ashamed, like I did (and still do). We talked for about an hour, and I'm still not sure that I got everything across that I wanted to.

Over the next couple of weeks, Tristan will type up my story and send me the draft so I can suggest any additions or omissions. I also sent him the intro to this book for a bit of background information. I was relieved to hear that my story is going to be in print and will not involve any sort of video!

My friends and family have been concerned that I'm pushing myself too hard or doing too much. 'You can't be out there running for four hours, it's not good for you.' I explained that I have a solid training plan that I'm sticking to, with rest days factored in, and that the marathon will probably take me six hours, so four-hour runs at this stage in my training are necessary. I think they're genuinely worried that I'm going to die out there. I'm worried too (after all, Pheidippides, the world's first marathoner, dropped dead at the end of his run), but I'm more determined and stubborn than I am worried.

My main concern and priority is that I don't end up with a DNF (did not finish). The cut-off time for the Melbourne Marathon is seven hours, and I'm confident I can finish in that amount of time, provided nothing goes terribly wrong. They have a special route for those of us whose run is going to take more than five hours, so they can open some of the closed roads a little sooner. Seven loops of Olympic Park. Seven! I'm going to be bored out of my mind! At least for that last leg of the journey my friends and family can cheer and spur me on each time I come running past. I'm going to need it!

Tuesday, 1 August 2023
Week 9, Day 2
7 km—'Race Pace'

This morning, when I woke up, I was still incredibly sore, especially my calf muscles. I seriously wondered whether I should run. I posed the question to one of my running groups on Facebook and got mixed answers, but the answer that seemed to make the most sense was, 'Take a break if you think you are injured, and running will further that injury; otherwise, it's fine to run.' I'm not injured; I think it's just normal soreness, although walking up or down steps is painful. But was running going to be dangerous? No.

The work day was lovely, as for the first two hours I got to run my playgroup, which meant seeing Mum and Daisy and watching her play with another little girl who showed up. There were only two kids today; George couldn't come because Margaret had been called into work at the last minute. The other little girl is a bit older than Daisy and is incredibly intelligent. She knows all her colours, numbers and her alphabet, and all the dances and actions to a bunch of kids' songs. Her mum is lovely too. It's important to remember that playgroup is not just about the kids, it's also about building a relationship and dialogue between parents. This mum has three other kids, so she has plenty of advice to give and a lot to teach me.

The rest of the day involved an excursion where the kids got to visit a progressive high school, where they had a farm and a nature reserve. The kids got to see goats, a miniature horse, a donkey, some sugar gliders and bandicoots, kangaroos, wallabies, and stick insects. They got to pet and feed the animals, and all the activities were run by the high school students, who are learning to do work in the wider community. They were an impressive group of mature and pleasant kids, who worked well with our little ones.

On the bus trip home, I heard someone say they felt like having a sleep, and I felt the same way. If not for my training, I'd probably have had a little lie down once I got home from work.

I put on my workout gear as soon as I walked in the door so I wouldn't have time to change my mind or give in to my soreness and tiredness. I did not want to run. I especially did not want to run fast. I thought about a compromise: some sprinting and jogging intervals, a fast 5 km run, and running the 7 km except slow. Surely some running was better than no running at all? I decided to just shoot for my fast 7 km and do my best. If I couldn't hack it and had to slow down at some point, at least I'd tried.

Once I started running, I was surprised to find that my calves weren't hurting. I felt a little tenderness in my hip joints and at the back of my thighs, but no real pain.

The other day, a friend said they had seen me running down one of the local main roads during one of my 8 km training runs and that I was "just shuffling." I hadn't been running my fastest, but it wasn't a slow run either. I'd been putting in effort. I found that comment hurtful! It spurred me on, though.

I kept checking my Garmin to make sure my speed was on target. I'd chosen a flat route and had my 170 BPM playlist blaring, but it was still a huge challenge. Seven km felt so far! I felt ready to stop after five! I resisted the temptation to slow down.

I was puffing and panting, pumping my little legs. Each time my feet hit the ground, I quickly picked them up and tried to bounce, spring and propel myself forward. Working on my cadence (or steps per minute) while also trying to open my stride. I just kept telling myself I could do it, and in the end, I could! I was so proud of myself. I remembered to stretch, and during my cool-down walk, I noticed that the pain in my calves had gone completely!

Afterwards, I checked my Garmin. The run had taken me 51:14 minutes, with an average pace of 7:19 minutes per kilometre. My fastest 7 km by nearly three minutes! And with such little energy and confidence in myself before I set out! The hardest part of my week (bar my long run) was over.

Wednesday, 2 August 2023
Week 9, Day 3
8 km Training Run

Today was an interesting and unusual day for me. It started out normal, then when I finished work, I checked Facebook and saw some disgusting news about Lizzo. Three backup dancers, three of Lizzo's famous 'Big Grrrls,' had come forward with a lawsuit, describing a toxic work environment with the famous singer at the helm, complete with body-shaming and sexual harassment.

I pored through articles and felt physically sick in the pit of my stomach and so disappointed. I'd had musical acts I enjoyed get 'cancelled' before, and it hadn't affected me, but this was different. I'd never seen a singer as a role model, as someone to look up to and to emulate, as a source of inspiration.

Who would be my Lizzo now? Who could possibly take her place in my heart and soul? Who would be the hero to fill the Lizzo-shaped hole in my life?

As I ran my 8 km, I tried to listen to my audiobook, but my attention faded in and out. I couldn't stop thinking about Lizzo, and I pictured her doing the things and saying the things that had been alleged. They played in my mind on a loop. In her reality show, she'd come across as a mother figure, a mentor, and a guide, taking those dancers under her wing. And with not one but three of those girls making such serious allegations, it seemed it was all a lie.

I felt so stupid for buying into that whole Lizzo mythology. I felt angry at myself as well as at her. For falling under her spell. For believing all her bullshit. For being taken in with the rest of the world, with the rest of the sisterhood.

I felt embarrassed about how excited I'd been to see her live in concert only a couple of weeks ago. At the way I'd swooned, whooped and cheered, and the selfies we'd taken and posted on Facebook about our 'incredible night.' It was all tainted now.

With all this spinning through my head, I didn't even notice I was bleeding. I have an anxious habit, a tick, where I pick at and chew the cuticles and dead skin around my fingers and thumbs. I can't stop doing it, even when I'm well. It seemed I'd been a bit over-zealous with it today, and my left thumb ended up trickling blood and spreading it all over my leggings as my hands brushed against my thighs with every swing of my arms.

It looked like a crime scene; the hot pink fabric was totally soaked in a reddish-brown mess. It had spread to all my fingernails and onto the cuff of my sleeve. I was very aware and self-conscious about what passers-by were thinking as I ran towards them. Who was this bizarre creature covered in blood, running as if everything was completely normal and fine? What the hell was wrong with her?

I couldn't wait to get home, get out of my blood-stained clothes and get into the shower to scrub the hell out of my hands. *Out! Damned spot!* I managed to stem the flow of blood and wrap my thumb in a Band-Aid. It was going to be hard to sleep with my thumb throbbing and smarting under the tight wrap of the Band-Aid. It was an annoying, niggling sort of pain.

Blood and Lizzo-gate. What a day!

Thursday, 3 August 2023
Week 9, Day 4
Rest Day

I was proud of myself for waking up and getting organised in time for Daisy's 9:00 a.m. swimming class. We even arrived a little early. After the lesson Margaret and I let the kids play in the shallow end while we relaxed and chatted, unloading and venting and filling each other in on everything that had happened in the few days since we'd seen each other. It was nice to decompress with another mum, who also happened to be my best friend.

Once home, I went about my day getting little things done: taking out the recycling, putting on and then hanging a load of washing, putting the dishes away. Then we had a snack before I packed a bag and headed off to Parkmore Shopping Centre.

I was meeting Margaret again so that the kids could play in the play area while we talked some more. We tried to put our heads together about my fundraising. The newspaper articles had only led to a couple of donations. Margaret suggested we canvas some local shops to try to get my poster with the QR code out into the community.

That evening, I checked my inbox and found another email from Tristan at Beyond Blue. This email discussed the plan for my story moving forward and introduced me to a colleague who would be involved with the campaign. I wanted to get a better understanding of her role, so I googled her, found her LinkedIn page, and skimmed through her resume.

Then I noticed something weird. It said she had a Bachelor of Arts in Musical Theatre from the University of Ballarat, 2000–2002. We'd been at the same university, studying the same course at the same time! I'd been in first year, while she'd been in third year!

This was 21 years ago, and I was in an extremely compromised state of mind at the time, so I couldn't quite figure out if I recognised her or not. However, it was a small school of about 60 students, so we must have interacted at some point, been in the same dance classes, frequented the same campus coffee shop, and been to the same parties.

I panicked! I'd been such a train wreck back then! So insane, so loud, so promiscuous! I'd slept with, dated, or at least kissed half the guys (and some girls) on campus! I'd spent my days and nights kitted out in provocative clothing—short shorts and midriff tops and gone out partying in the town's only nightclub every Wednesday night on Student Night, getting blind, blackout drunk, and dancing like a desperate, down-and-out stripper! Then one day, I just mysteriously disappeared, and the word on the street was that I'd had some kind of nervous breakdown . . . or something.

And this woman, who possibly knew and remembered me, had read some of the most intimate words I'd ever written about my state of mind and crazy, delusional thoughts during the exact time period that we'd crossed paths! The thought of it was mortifying.

My mind was spinning as I imagined a few scenarios. Either she remembered me and had hated me with a passion and would have to pretend otherwise in an awkward, uncomfortable correspondence. Or she remembered me fondly and we would excitedly bond over mutual friends and experiences, and she'd support and promote me with gusto. Or, in the most likely scenario, her memories of me would be as vague as mine were of her, and our interactions would be completely neutral, polite, pleasant and professional. But surely it would be a head trip for her! It was a head trip for me. She'd be bound to Facebook stalk me—hell, I Facebook-stalked her. We had three mutual friends.

I thought about the last 21 years—our parallel lives. Obviously, neither of us had turned out to be famous Broadway stars, but we'd forged our own, very different paths and collided in a mission to raise awareness of mental health.

It would be fine, right? This little 'six degrees of separation' coincidence wouldn't derail my entire relationship with Beyond Blue . . . right?

Friday, 4 August 2023
Week 9, Day 5
8 km Training Run

Today I did the bare minimum. I was tired. I was unmotivated. I was depressed. I pretty much glued myself to the couch. It was a day of bad parenting, where instead of taking Daisy somewhere to play and be social, I just put on her favourite show and let her be a little baby couch potato. Doing the dishes and putting the clothes away were both just too hard tasks.

I was embarrassed. I was ashamed. I felt guilty.

I felt like I should be doing something with my day. I felt bad that I hadn't asked Dad to come for a visit. I decided I should try to get in touch with my friend Minty, as last time I'd made a date for us to meet up, I'd completely forgotten and double-booked myself. I called him, and we decided I'd take Daisy up to Mornington to visit him and we'd go to a local pub for dinner.

When Chris came home, I apologised profusely for not doing the dishes or putting away the clothes. He was concerned about how upset I was about it. 'Why do you always think you have to do the dishes?' he asked. 'Because it's my job!' I replied. He responded by saying, 'Nobody says it's your job; it's only you who says that.' And I replied, 'But you work so hard, you shouldn't have to do them.' He was very gentle with me. 'Look, how about I do the dishes while you go and put away the clothes?' I was so grateful to him. He is so patient and kind.

Soon after I got ready and went for my run. I chose a flat route and went easy on myself, listening to my audiobook. I was pleased to see that I'd given myself plenty of time to do my run before leaving to see Minty, with a bit of a break in between. I wasn't rushed or stressed, and I was feeling a bit better about things. I may have felt like I wasted the day, but going for a run and seeing a friend were pretty good outcomes.

I got ready, bundled Daisy into the car and we drove to Mornington. We had made a booking at one pub (I always make bookings; I have huge anxiety about not getting a table), but Minty wanted to go to a different pub, so I agreed that if we could get a table we'd go there, and if not, we'd stick to the original plan.

We got a table for two with a high chair and perused the menu. Everything looked pretty good. In the end, I settled for a seafood linguini, nuggets and chips for Daisy, which I knew she'd barely touch. No sooner had the food arrived than Daisy managed to dip her hands in the tomato sauce and start sploshing it everywhere.

In my haste to take it away and clean up after her, I knocked over my full-to-the-brim Coke Zero and got it all over myself and the table! I swore loudly, and Daisy started crying, and I must have seemed stressed because a stranger got up from their table and offered to help us. In the end, we sorted it all out, and we were able to resume eating, but Daisy was too upset to go back into the high chair, and I had to try to eat with her on my lap!

Minty is quite a successful and famous YouTuber, with a channel discussing pop culture and movies that is beloved by fans worldwide. Because of this success, he's been able to buy himself a big house with a pool, a pool table and an air hockey table, as well as multiple arcade games, including my favourite, Big Buck Hunter. His house is also a virtual museum, with a replica of a Blockbuster Video store in his garage and movie and pop culture memorabilia meticulously displayed everywhere you look.

After dinner, Minty was keen to show me all the latest additions to his house, so he invited us in, and I made sure to hold onto Daisy on our little tour so she wouldn't get into anything. Among the new additions to his collection were a life-sized Batman sculpture and a Terminator arcade game. Minty also gave us a paddle pop ice cream, and Daisy was suddenly interested in eating! I left early to hopefully catch Chris before he went to bed, but when we got home, he was already peacefully snoring.

I checked my inbox, and I saw an email from Natalie, my ex-university colleague at Beyond Blue. She thanked me for what I was doing to support Beyond Blue, explained that they were working with the organisers of the Melbourne Marathon, and asked if she could include my story in a piece about the Marathon in a newsletter.

> *Hi Jacqui!*
>
> *So great to hear from you and yes, I remember you too! Such a small world isn't it? Those days just seem like a lifetime ago!*
>
> *Thanks so much for everything you are doing for Beyond Blue. It was really inspiring to read your story recently – thank you for being so generous and open in sharing it.*
>
> *We are working with the organisers of the Melbourne Marathon to create some content for their emails, and I was wondering if you would be happy for me to include your story in a piece about the marathon, fundraising and Beyond Blue, to share in their newsletter?*
>
> *We already have some great content from your fundraising page, so I am happy to use some of that, but only if that's ok with you – can you please let me know if that's ok, or whether you would like to add or include anything else?*

If you are happy to send me a couple of photos to go with the piece that would be amazing as well, but only if you're comfortable to do so.

Let me know if you have any questions! Thank you so much once again

Thanks

Natalie

Saturday, 5 August 2023
Week 9, Day 6
45–60 Minutes of Strength Training

This morning, I did not want to get up for Parkrun. This is not like me—usually, I look forward to it and to seeing everyone. Maybe it was because I knew I'd be skipping breakfast and coffee afterwards—Chris's mum had to head into work, so I'd have to come straight home after volunteering. My job was handing out finish tokens, so I got to relax and chat with some of my friends while we waited for all the runners and walkers to cross the finish line.

Stuart was also at the finish line, and I asked him how his new job was going. He'd been working as a security guard in a psych ward. He said that one of the patients had become aggressive with him and the nurses and had to be put in isolation. His story triggered some unpleasant memories of when I'd been put in isolation, many years ago.

Isolation is exactly how it sounds. An empty room with no stimuli, nothing except a heavy, weighted, waterproof, hard mattress in the corner. Not even a pillow or a blanket. Nothing to do, nothing and no-one to interact with. Not even a clock, so you have no sense or awareness of the passing of time.

It only happened to me twice, in the earlier days of my illness, on two separate occasions when I'd been admitted to Frankston Hospital.

The first time was so long ago that I can't remember what I'd done to get put in, but I think it had something to do with interfering with other patients, annoying them and getting up in their business.

For some reason, whenever I'm in isolation, I tend to tap dance and sing at the top of my lungs, which sounds weird, but it seems like the only way to entertain myself (and also a desperate grasp for attention!)—maybe a sort of bizarre, convoluted sort of protest.

That first time in Frankston Hospital in 2002, I was convinced I could somehow escape, and I became obsessed with the idea of proving that I could—to outsmart everyone and prove my superiority. In a failed MacGyver-like display, I'd snapped my glasses into pieces, thinking I could use them to pick the lock. Afterwards, I was so regretful and ashamed, feeling incredibly guilty towards my parents, who'd have to fork out all that money for a new pair of glasses.

The second time I was in isolation was in 2016, during a hospital stay that followed a manic episode triggered by the breakdown of my first marriage and the paranoia that my ex-husband was 'out to get me.'

This time I could remember exactly what I'd done to get put into 'iso.' I'd been followed around and badgered by a younger, intellectually disabled patient who had taken a shine to me. She was in my face all the time, and I just wanted some space from her.

She asked, no—insisted—that I come and watch *Home and Away* with her, and I'd flat out refused. But she was having none of it. She just wouldn't give up. So I barricaded myself in one of the visiting rooms. I pushed all the furniture up against the door and refused to come out, screaming, 'I just want to be left alone!' Be careful what you wish for.

I was seething and indignant over being punished when I felt like I'd done nothing wrong. I was consumed with intense hatred towards the nurse who had locked me up.

I was batshit crazy. I was out of my mind. I was determined to make the nurse suffer, and I did something utterly shameful and disgusting that makes me feel physically sick to remember. I had pulled down my pants, squatted in the centre of the isolation room, making direct eye contact with the camera, and I had urinated on the floor, knowing the nurse would have to come and clean it up. Looking back, I can't believe I did that. I profusely apologised to the nurse once I came to my senses, but it doesn't change how I feel about the incident.

It was incredibly hard making the decision to even write about it in this book, because of the intense shame, self-hatred and regret that memory brings up. I had behaved like an animal; inhuman. I had repressed the memory until today.

As I drove home from Parkrun, I had these moments replaying in my head: being on the opposite side of Stuart's security guard position, being the aggressive patient, the crazy patient, the unmanageable patient, the patient who made the staff's life hell.

At least my last two admissions to Dandenong Hospital had been without incident, and the memory of my isolation periods is mostly distant, apart from the trigger of today's conversation. I didn't even know where the isolation room in the Dandenong psych ward was. Isolation had never even crossed my mind during my last two admissions. I'd been there to heal, to recover. I had nothing but respect for the staff. I'd become compliant. A model patient. That thought was at least a little comforting as I pulled into the carport at home and brought my attention back to the present.

When I got home, Daisy had just woken up, and Tonia was changing her nappy. 'Mum! Mum!' she called out to me. I love hearing her say 'Mum.' It took her a long time to say it, she'd been calling me 'Ba' for a long time, and I'd been worried she might not be able to form an M sound. But recently, she'd not only been saying 'Mum' but specifically calling me Mum and Chris Dad, distinguishing between the two of us. Now, one of her favourite things to do is to run into the bedroom, where I've stuck my newspaper articles on the wall next to my bed. She points to the pictures of me and shouts, 'Mum! Mum!' She does the same with our family pictures on the fridge, pointing to us and exclaiming, 'Mum! Dad!'

I gave Daisy breakfast and decided I'd do some strength training at home, so I'd only have to make a quick trip to the gym. I used some free weights and did a few different types of reps, and did some squats. Daisy copied me and did some squats as well. Then Daisy got a bit sooky, so I stopped working out and picked her up and gave her cuddles until Chris came home.

I was happy to go to the gym—feeling positive about it. Maybe because I knew it would be a quick and painless visit, with the bulk of my training already completed. I worked my core and used two machines, the leg press and the chest press; then I was ready to head home and have a shower.

Sunday, 6 August 2023
Week 9, Day 7
26 km Long Run

Last night I had terrible night sweats. I literally soaked the bed sheets and doona cover. My whole body was wet. In the morning, I felt exhausted and totally depleted. All day yesterday, I'd made a conscious effort to hydrate through the day and night so that I'd be ready for my long run today, and now here I was, totally dehydrated and in desperate need of electrolytes. Chris brought me some coconut water as I lay in bed, barely able to move. I'd shifted over to his side of the bed once he got up, as the bedding there was dry.

I drifted in and out of sleep until late morning, when I was surprised to see my mum had come to visit. We'd told her she didn't need to watch Daisy, as Chris had the day off, but she came anyway in case we needed help with anything. I was walking around in a fog, chugging down more water and coconut water to rehydrate myself enough for my long run, while Mum flitted around the house, doing dishes, washing and roasting vegetables. She had brought food to do some meal prep for me in case I didn't have a chance to do it myself, in a repeat of last week. She was pleasantly surprised to see I was already on top of it but decided to cook anyway—we could always use the extra food.

Chris would be leaving at midday to take Daisy to visit his grandparents. Chris had a shower, and while he was getting ready, Mum dressed Daisy up in her nicest clothes and put her hair up in two little pigtails. By then, I'd returned to the land of the living and was ready to set out for my run.

I had my gels, headphones, phone, keys, and camelback. I wasn't exactly in peak condition, but I was adamant that I needed to stick to my training plan and do my best to complete this 26 km run.

As I set out, my feet were heavy, and I felt like I was dragging myself through concrete. It was hard enough just to get through the first two kilometres—24 more seemed impossible. Every time I ran down a hill or even the slightest incline, I was all too aware that it would be an uphill climb on the way back. The whole run was difficult—I was just letting my legs move automatically while I tried not to think about running and just listened to my audiobook—but around the 13 or 14 km mark, I just hit the wall. How could my body be ready to quit already? Even in my half-marathon I hadn't felt like this until 18 km in.

I was not enjoying myself. I just kept plodding on. I was dreading those hills. I had no energy—the energy gels weren't helping. I started to concede defeat. I thought about cutting my route short of stopping at 24, or even 21 km.

As I ran a little closer to home I came to a park with an easy loop of track, which I decided to just run around on repeat until I could no longer go on. By then I'd managed to make it to 21 km, so at least I'd done a half marathon.

My audiobook had run out, and I had started to listen to another audiobook about running. It was not a good choice. The opening chapter was all about how bad running is for your body and how inevitable injury is for most runners. It was psyching me out, big time.

After about 25 km I slowed to a walk. I paused my Garmin. Would I save the run or press resume and continue? I had hoped to run the whole distance, but my body wasn't allowing it. I decided to resume my Garmin and keep moving in any way I could. I wasn't walking for long when I decided to pick up the pace again and try a light jog. I ran/walked in little intervals until I reached the 26 km mark and pressed stop on my Garmin.

I looked at my stats and was pleased to see that even with walking breaks, my pace was still better than it had been for last week's long run. I decided to shift my stubborn attitude that I was going to run the whole marathon without stopping to walk on race day. Just like every friend and every running book had been telling me, there's nothing wrong with walking breaks. It's just about getting across that finish line in less than seven hours—walk, run or crawl.

**Monday, 7 August 2023
Week 10, Day 1
Rest Day**

It was hard to get out of bed. I wanted to call in sick. I wanted to stay at home. I wanted maybe a week where I could lie in bed and not have to do anything or talk to anyone. I realised that with the advent of motherhood those days were over. No more self-indulgence. No more checking out. No more giving up.

As I was eating my breakfast, I was crying a little. I just didn't feel like I had it in me to face the working day; the working week. On the drive to work I oscillated between being okay and tuning into the breakfast radio coming through my speakers and fretting and stressing about the day ahead and holding back tears.

Once again, I obsessed over answering the question, 'How are you?' I decided to reply with an honest, 'Struggling a little bit.' But of course, when I got to work, I defaulted to a chirpy, 'Fine, thanks, how are you?' when greeting my co-workers. In the staff room, as I put my lunch in the fridge, I debated whether to use my spare time before the working day getting ready and photocopying work or allowing myself to sit down with a cup of tea and gather my strength. I went with the photocopying.

My student was in a bit of a state. He didn't seem to want to do any work and was very touchy all day, bursting into a wailing mess at the smallest trigger. *I know how you feel, buddy,* I thought.

After work, I had an appointment at the gym for another Evolt scan and a consultation with my personal trainer. I was certain I'd put on weight since the last one, as I'd pretty much thrown away the scales and started eating more carbs for fuel, plus my jeans had become a bit snug.

I was pleasantly surprised to find that there had been very little change and that my overall score was still 8/10, in the 'optimal range.' I'd managed to maintain a healthy weight and body composition over the last nine weeks. Then we quickly went over the use of a couple of exercise machines I was less familiar with, and I took off to spend time with my family.

**Tuesday, 8 August 2023
Week 10, Day 2
7 km—'Race Pace'**

Last night, Daisy woke up crying and just wouldn't go back to sleep. Every time I tried to put her in her cot, she'd just start crying and reach up to be picked up. In the end, I took her in my arms and lay down next to her in the spare bed, hoping we could both fall asleep together, but she was wide awake. She was babbling away nonstop, in a little baby-talk diatribe about God knows what!

Eventually, things got a bit quieter, but then she just started whispering in my ear as if she was telling me a secret. She'd do this whispering thing, then lie down and go quiet, and just when I thought she was asleep, she'd lean over and start whispering again. I would have found it funny if I wasn't so exhausted and it wasn't the middle of the night!

In the end, after what seemed like hours, I was satisfied that she was asleep, so I went to transfer her to her cot. She immediately woke up and started screaming bloody murder. At that point I was having none of it. I was just too tired, and I'd had enough, so I decided to close the door, go back to my own bed and let her cry it out. It took a long time, but she eventually settled.

I expected to wake up this morning feeling drained, but I was fine. My mood was better than yesterday too. No overwhelming feelings, no tears. Maybe yesterday was just a touch of Monday-itis, or maybe I was feeling better this morning because Mum arrived early to come and watch Daisy, and I wasn't eating breakfast alone with my thoughts.

Playgroup went well, with three little girls including Daisy. There was a new girl who hadn't been before, and I had a good talk with her mum, who would be sending her daughter to our school. I assured her the staff were good and welcoming and would be able to cater to her needs, even if she was a bit behind and not quite feeling ready for school.

Unfortunately, the rest of the work day wasn't so pleasant. I was on yard duty when there was a huge blow-up between two kids. They'd been swearing at each other and one of them had threatened to punch the other one. As each of them was fighting and arguing to tell their own side of the story, they were shouting and dropping F-bombs and C-bombs all over the place in front of the preps. One of them (the one who started it all) was crying and getting emotional.

I ended up having to talk to his classroom teacher, write three separate incident reports (all while trying to work with my student) and contact leadership and the school's counsellor via email. I also had to organise for another little girl, who was feeling very upset, targeted and victimised, to speak to the school counsellor as well. All this took up most of the day's last session.

Once I got home, I had to face the fact that I had to do a fast 7 km. Always my least favourite run of the week. I procrastinated. I sat on the couch. I told myself I needed to 'unwind after work' and that I needed a moment to just have a little break before I got changed and did my run. I did this for 47 minutes. So much for a 'little break.'

I considered *not* running. Surely one missed run wouldn't hurt. I hadn't missed any so far. Then I considered just running fast and slow intervals for a little while. I settled on that idea and got ready, and it was only when I was walking out the door and setting up my music and my Garmin that I decided to stick to the plan and go all out for 7 km.

I had figured out that I was much more motivated by my own music than pre-set BPM playlists. I'd put together my own playlist, entitled *Fast Running*, with Spiderbait, AC/DC, Beyoncé and Britney Spears, among others. My favourite songs to run to are *Thunderstruck* by AC/DC and *Black Betty* by Spiderbait. It's a short playlist, so I put it on shuffle, and some songs get repeated, but I'd rather listen to a good song two or three times than several bad songs, which seemed to be the norm when I just searched '170 BPM' on Apple Music.

I was committed to going hard for the whole duration, but once again, I was chasing my shadow, and my shadow did not look like it was running fast. It looked like it was chugging along and struggling. I couldn't decide if that was more disheartening or motivating. I kept looking at my watch. One moment, my pace would be seven minutes, the next, it would be 750. I was all over the place.

In the end, the run took me 50 minutes and 57 seconds—my fastest 7 km time, with an average pace of 7:16 min/km. I was proud. I was making progress, getting faster, and getting stronger. My training was working. I screenshotted my stats and posted them to my running groups on Facebook. It always feels good to share and brag.

Wednesday, 9 August 2023
Week 10, Day 3
8 km Training Run

This morning, when I got up, Daisy was awake and lying in the single bed having cuddles with her grand-mère, as she refers to my mum.

I tell Daisy the same things over and over every day. 'I love you so much. I'll love you forever. You make me so happy. You're my favourite person. Let's be best friends forever.' Then I go through the long list of everybody who loves her. Parents, grandparents, great-grandparents, aunts, uncles, cousins.

I already had plenty of work prepared at school, so I didn't need to be at work as early as usual. Mum made me toast with eggs and bacon, which felt very indulgent for a Wednesday morning.

Work was good, as usual. I'm enjoying working with the student I'm paired with, so much so that in my preferences for next year, I've requested to be with him again. I remember having him in prep when he couldn't even write his own name. He's come *so* far.

After work I changed and headed out. The run felt hard, not exhausting, but like a real effort, and so boring. I was beginning to feel like training had taken over my life and I was regretting making such a big commitment. Just because it's physically possible to achieve something doesn't mean you should. I was thinking about how my runs would soon be increasing in distance, taking up even more of my time, and for the first time, I felt like giving up.

Not just that run, mind you, but giving up on all of it. The training. The marathon. What was the point? I'd barely raised more than $2,500, a quarter of what I was hoping to, and I was embarrassed. It was enough to pay a Beyond Blue telephone operator's salary for a couple of weeks, maybe?

Then I thought about the newspaper articles, the exposure. I'd been hoping they'd lead to donations, but that hadn't happened. But maybe it wasn't about that. Maybe it wasn't about the money. Maybe it was about raising awareness, being a spokesperson for bipolar, for mental illness in general, for suicide prevention. Maybe that was the role I had to play in all this.

Or had I just embarrassed myself and my family by 'coming out' in my small town's local paper? Was I just fuelling rumours and judgements against my family for 'allowing' my suicide attempt to happen? Had I made a mistake? And was it all too much? The training? Writing it down? Would it all just defeat the purpose by leading to a decline in my mental health?

I didn't entertain those thoughts for too long. Instead—*You can do it. Just keep pushing. You may have only raised $2,500, but that's still a lot more than most people raise, and you've still got until one month after the marathon to raise more.*

I was more than halfway through my training. It will all be over soon, and instead of being something elusive that I might do one day, a marathon will instead become my crowning achievement. I had a look at my stats after my run, and saw that it had been my fastest 8 km! Two records this week—for my race pace run and for my training run! The training plan is working, and my trust in it and adherence to it is paying off.

I'm not ready to give up. Not yet.

Thursday, 10 August 2023
Week 10, Day 4
Rest Day

I woke up just before my alarm, feeling like I'd been hit by a bus. I turned the damn alarm off before it had a chance to ring. There was no way I was getting out of bed. It just wasn't going to happen. There was no way Daisy and I would be making it to that 9 a.m. swimming class. Just an hour's sleep in, that's all we needed. I messaged Margaret to tell her we wouldn't make it. Jess had also had a rough night with the kids and had messaged the same thing. I drifted back to sleep, bargaining with myself that I'd try to make it to the 10 a.m. class.

Just before 9 a.m. I was awoken by the piercing sound of my phone ringing loudly, followed by Daisy crying. The phone had woken her up too. It was Margaret, checking in to see if I was alright. I think I replied 'No,' then tried to lie back down in the hopes that Daisy would stop crying and I could get an extra 15 minutes of rest. I wasn't so lucky.

As I started going through the motions of getting ready, I was crying. Not only would we not make it to the 9 a.m. class, but we were going to be late for the 10 a.m. class as well. I was a failure as a parent. I was so embarrassed. What a terrible start to the day.

When we got home, the thought of washing and hanging out our swimming gear and showering away all the chlorine was too much. I just felt like lounging around with Daisy, smelling like the pool all day. I wouldn't be going out for any play dates. It was going to be a 'bad mum' day. TV and not much else.

I was so relieved when Chris got home early. Daisy was upset. Was she tired? Was she hungry? Both? I had no idea, and I didn't have the mental energy to sort it out. I passed the responsibility over to Chris. 'You handle this. I just need to lie down.'

I closed the door to the bedroom and curled up into the foetal position. I lay there for hours, listening to my phone beep and ring. I didn't so much as roll over. At one point, I managed to sleep, and I think that helped.

When I emerged, I was ready to be a proper mum again, and I walked with Daisy to the nearby playground, where we played peekaboo and went on the swing and on the slide. She'd brought her Bluey doll to the park, and we pushed Bluey down the slide a few times too. It made Daisy break out into gorgeous little peals of laughter.

Friday, 11 August 2023
Week 10, Day 5
8 km Training Run

There were tears again this morning. Lots of tears. I just woke up with this overwhelming sense that I couldn't cope. I looked around the house and it was like a bomb had gone off, and I just didn't know where to start. My Dad was coming at some point in the morning, so I had to make a dent in the mess before he arrived because I didn't want him to be critical or concerned. Over and over in my head, the words 'I can't do this. I'm a bad person.' Feeling so lost and pathetic and panicky. I was hyperventilating.

I just wandered around crying, doing what I could, as I could. Taking the recycling out. Putting away some of Daisy's clothes and a few things that were cluttering the table. I felt like I was alone, with no-one to talk to, and I felt worried that things were getting out of control, as I hadn't found time to see my psychiatrist or psychologist since this whole marathon training thing started. And yet in the beginning of this book, I bragged about how good I am at staying on top of all that.

Not long before I started writing, I had a sort of miniature breakdown in which I felt tearful, stressed, upset and wound up. I'd gone to see the GP about finding a new psychiatrist, as the one I see is quite expensive, and she's very in demand, with very limited availability. I also must travel if I want to see her in person.

The 'mini-breakdown' led to me almost writing off my car. I'd been so wound up and stressed driving home that I'd crashed into one of the pillars in our car park at home. That, of course, led to more stress—huge stress and a bad week in which I also broke my phone and realised it wasn't insured, and locked myself out of the house and had to wait with a neighbour for Chris to come home. Bad things always come in threes. I had a day off work that week, which helped but was only a temporary, Band-Aid solution.

This morning and yesterday were not quite that bad, but I still had the sense that things were building-up, and that I was like a pressure cooker, just pushing everything down and feeling like it was only a matter of time before the steam had nowhere to go and everything boiled over. I thought about calling Parentline just to be able to tell someone what a hard time I was having, but I didn't know if talking would make it better or worse. I also thought about making an appointment with my psychologist, who was usually fairly easy to see at short notice, but I'm so conscious of what little free time I have that just the idea of making an appointment is almost more stressful than it's worth.

I did the dishes, and as always, for some reason, getting that done was soothing. It was one very tangible, house-worky thing that had been accomplished—something concrete that took a load off Chris. It was some evidence that my dad could glance at and think, 'Okay, the dishes are done; things can't be that bad.'

By the time Dad came, it was less like a bomb had gone off and more like we'd just been peppered with a few grenades, which was good enough for me, and apparently, good enough for Dad. He asked how I was doing, and I said I was a little flat. He asked if the marathon training was getting to be too much for me, and I said I didn't think so. It's just motherhood and life in general that's too much. It's just being me. Having bipolar.

Chris came home early, and Dad left after Daisy went down to sleep. I went to lie down as well. I'd have to keep it to an hour or two; then I had my 8 km run, and then it would be time to shower, get dressed and go to the city to see a movie with my friend Christoph.

When the time came, I didn't want to run. I considered skipping it—in the scheme of things, one missed run wouldn't make a difference, but it's a slippery slope from that to going right off track with my training or giving up altogether. Plus, I wanted to reserve missed runs for times when I might genuinely be ill or injured.

It was my first run in my new shoes, which had arrived earlier in the day. They felt amazing, like running on clouds. I'd asked for some advice for breaking in running shoes on one of my Facebook running groups, and the consensus seemed to be that if they were appropriate shoes, they wouldn't need breaking in.

It didn't feel like long before I got to the halfway point, and I was surprised at how quickly I reached the place where the Eastlink trail ended and I was back on the road home.

I managed to get ready and make it to the city with plenty of time to spare, and we were lucky enough to get a table at Tiamo, my favourite Italian restaurant in Melbourne.

Then we perused Readings—an iconic bookshop that's always open late—before checking out the new Wes Anderson film, *Asteroid City*. I'm not a die-hard Wes Anderson fan, but I do like his aesthetic and absurdity. This film delivered on both counts and I was glad I'd taken the time to see it.

Christoph and I drove back to our house, where Chris had set up a blow-up mattress in the lounge. The night was still young, so I forced Christoph to watch one of my favourite films that had just been put on Netflix—*Eagle Vs Shark*, a New Zealand film directed by Taika Waititi. We were halfway through that film when I was outraged to hear Christoph had never seen *Boy* (also directed by Taika Waititi)—my favourite film of all time, a coming-of-age story about a young Māori boy set in the 1980s. So of course, we had to watch that as well! We went to bed much too late, but it was worth it for a night educating one of my best friends in fine cinema.

Saturday, 12 August 2023
Week 10, Day 6
45-60 Minutes Strength Training

Even though it was such a late night, I did have comfortable, good quality sleep, with pleasant dreams. Unfortunately, I was awoken by Daisy at 7:15 a.m. I lay there listening to her cry for a moment, praying she'd go back to sleep, but she was well and truly up and in need of attention. She'd also awoken Christoph, who had never met Daisy before and was feeling pretty groggy, waking up to a toddler running, crawling and rolling around all over his makeshift bed.

After feeding Daisy we tried in vain to watch another movie, but Daisy just kept crying and wanting to go outside or watch Cocomelon. Fair enough, we'd had plenty of grown-up movie time the night before—this was her time. We gave up on the movie, and it was soon time to drop Christoph off at the station anyway.

When we came back, Daisy was ready for a nap, and I decided I'd set aside some time to write. I hadn't written since Wednesday, and I needed to catch up. I spent a couple of hours in front of my laptop at the kitchen table, (despite writer's block and a bit of a foggy brain), with disorganised thoughts swirling around in my head. I was able to put together something cohesive that I was relatively happy with, and Daisy woke up right on cue as I was finishing. I can't write when she's awake—she just wants to watch YouTube on the laptop or press all the keys! She doesn't like anything that takes Mummy's attention away from her.

As I was writing I'd gotten a bit teary—not feeling sad about the present moment, but rather getting swept up in the content and feeling all the emotions of the words on the page. Chris had kept asking if I was okay, and I assured him it was all part of the process. The catharsis left me rather drained.

I got dressed and drove to the gym. While I was working out my arms, I couldn't help but focus on my wrists as they were laid out in front of me. They're completely criss-crossed with layers of scarring from self-harm and suicide attempts.

One thing I've been reluctant to write about is self-harm. Just like suicide, it's too easy to romanticise and also such a big trigger for some people.

When I was in my worst period of self-harming, reading about it would just make me want to do it more.

People don't realise it's an addiction, like substance abuse or gambling. We continue to do it because it serves us in some way; it relieves us. But it's never enough. The cuts have to be deeper, more numerous, more painful. The relief is only temporary, and it's like a high you're forever chasing.

I first started self-harming to punish myself. I'd just gone through a difficult break-up with my first love, and neither of us was taking it well. He was already an alcoholic before we broke up, but afterwards, he started getting drunk, cutting himself and ringing me.

Every time I got one of those phone calls I wanted to run to him so badly. I wanted to be there for him, to soothe him. But I told myself that if I did that, I'd set a precedent and 'reward' the behaviour, and he'd be more likely to do it more often, so instead, I'd ring his best friend, explain what was happening, and get him to promise to go over there.

Every single time it killed me, and I felt so guilty that, before long, I started doing it to myself as well.

At first it was just about getting out the anger that I felt towards myself, about inflicting pain, about doing damage. I'd get a safety pin or a steak knife and swipe it violently across my thighs, repeatedly, creating what is referred to as 'superficial' wounds. Just red, angry welts and scratches.

I hate that term. 'Superficial.' It implies that the self-inflicted wounds aren't serious, that it's a small problem. Anyone who is hurting themselves in any way should be taken seriously. You might not need stitches or to have your wounds glued shut, but you do need help.

This sort of behaviour is not normal. A happy, healthy person doesn't do these kinds of things to themselves. People throw around terms like 'cry for help' and 'attention-seeking behaviour,' but I've come to have the attitude that if they're crying, help them. If they're seeking attention, give it to them.

Even now, all these years later, I wonder if things would have been different if I'd gone to the aid of my ex-boyfriend instead of making it someone else's problem. I still don't know if I made the right decision, if I helped him or hindered him.

Things got worse for me in terms of self-harm; they always do. I started dating a guy who was covered in scars and had a serious history of self-inflicted damage. I would ply him with questions. It was an obsession.

When did you start doing it? Why? How often? What would you use? Did you have to go to the hospital each time? What did they say? Did you have to be admitted? I had to know everything.

I even remember reading books and watching movies where the characters would self-harm and how this would feed my obsession.

I decided if I was going to be serious about this new 'hobby,' I had to graduate from knives and safety pins to razor blades. I remember the first time I bought a packet from the supermarket. It was before the days of self-checkouts, so I had to physically interact with a cashier to purchase them.

I was crying. I was buying razor blades. I expected some alarm, concern, or worry. I was embarrassed and nervous. The cashier didn't even notice. She just scanned them like any other item and didn't even look at me. I've bought razor blades countless times and never had anyone ask why I was buying them or if I was okay.

With razor blades, there's a lot less pain and a lot more blood. It's a lot more dangerous. There's that knowledge in the back of your mind that if at any moment you change your mind about just wanting to punish yourself and suddenly want to end things, you have the means to make a serious attempt.

The cutting became a ritual. Literally a fucking ritual, to the point where

I would light candles and put on my favourite music, like I was meditating or something.

It was beyond sick.

It became a knee-jerk response to any negative feeling in my life, feeling fat in ballet class, jealousy over a female friend of my boyfriend's, or any sort of disagreement or confrontation. It became a coping mechanism of the unhealthiest kind.

I was manipulative. I was horrible. I would blame my self-harm on other people, on things they'd said or done. 'Look what you made me do!'

When I look back at those times, I'm disgusted with myself. How could I have put so many people through that?

I self-harmed consistently for three years from 2004 while I was studying dance at university, while I was on exchange in London, and the year after uni.

There would be times when I'd stop, then 'relapse' like a recovering alcoholic.

When I look back on those times, I realise I didn't have any real friends, not friendships that I'd nurture anyway. Not friendships that were based on any sort of emotional maturity. I would get obsessed with people, throw myself at them and demand so much from them, not giving anything in return.

Many of my 'friendships' would last a day, a night, a week, a month. I thought that was just me being wacky, wild and impulsive. That was my personality. It was normal for me.

The worst I ever cut myself was in November 2005, when I was living in London, just after Halloween. I'd had a fight with my boyfriend, where I'd said something awful about him and his family, and I thought the only way to express how sorry I was was to kill myself.

I decided to get as drunk as possible to work up the nerve, so I went to the supermarket and bought a bottle of brandy, a magazine and a packet of razor blades. The magazine was just to make it less obvious what I was about to do.

I went back to my dorm and gulped down mouthful after mouthful of neat brandy, then realised I'd never cut myself particularly deeply before; never even enough to need stitches. I figured I'd need to take a 'practice swing' just to figure out how much force and pressure I'd need to use to make a decent slash.

I turned my left arm over and with a big swipe, cut as deep as I could bear to cut into my forearm.

There was a moment when there was no blood at all. My arm opened, and everything was white. I'd cut into the layer of fat, and that's what I was seeing. Then the blood came. So much blood! It got on the carpet; it dripped all over the magazine. Suddenly, I didn't want to die anymore; I just wanted to stop the bleeding.

I ran to the kitchen, wrapped my arm in a tea towel and called one of my university friends, and we went to the hospital together. I was terrified to take off the tea towel, but the nurses finally convinced me, and they wiped away as much blood as they could, pressed the sides of my wound together, and glued it shut. It stung like crazy!

My brother was called, as he was also living in London at the time, and he rushed to the hospital to be with me. He was beside himself, so was my mother back home. The episode had been extremely triggering for one of my dorm mates, who I'd also been fighting with at the time, and I was kicked out of my dorm and sent to live in another one on the other side of the campus.

The sobering shock of all that was enough to put me off for a long time after, but late in the following year, when I was back home living in Australia, I relapsed after another breakup. I've had lots of long periods of feeling like it was all behind me, but in 2016, after yet another breakup, I slashed my wrists to shreds and needed stitches on both arms.

A couple of years later, I was experiencing stress at work, and a few times I'd skip work and lock myself in the bathroom and start cutting, threatening to kill myself. There would be days when I was on the way to work, and I'd come to a certain intersection and think: *I can keep driving straight and go to work, or I can turn left, drive to the supermarket, buy razor blades, and never have to go to work again.*

Even as late as 2021, I had an episode at work where I spent a couple of days obsessing over a utility blade that I'd seen in one of the teacher's offices and started concealing it in my pocket and ducking to the toilets as often as I could cry and cut. That was before I had Daisy.

Thinking about any sort of self-harm makes me cringe now. Anything about it on movies or TV is extremely triggering. I get flashbacks. I physically feel what I'm seeing play out on the screen. I have to look away, my breath catches in my chest.

I haven't hurt myself since my daughter was born, and I'd like to think that I never will again, for her sake. One day, I'll have to explain my scars to her, and I still don't know what I'll say or how I'll say it.

Those days are long gone, and I can look at my scars without feeling triggered, but I often think about covering them up with tattoos. I already have a tattoo of *The Little Prince*, from the French novel, on my back, which is sort of a homage to my mother, but I'd often thought about getting something nautical as a tribute to my father, who was a fisherman.

I'd thought about pelicans and cray pots but had decided that crayfish would be better suited to the elongated shape of my wrists and forearms. I'd seen good cover-ups and bad cover-ups, and I thought if I did eventually get it done, I'd seek out a tattooist who specialised in scar coverage. The one thing holding me back is the fact that I work in a conservative school, where visible tattoos wouldn't necessarily be frowned upon but would be enough of an oddity that I'd constantly have to be fielding questions about them to the students.

It did feel like a nice idea to get a tattoo as a treat to myself after the completion of the marathon, though—a sort of badge of honour. I thought about another idea I'd floated around—a semi-colon. The semi-colon is a symbol for survivors of suicide attempts, indicating a pause as opposed to an ending. They were often tattooed along with the words, 'This is not the end of my story,' but were more commonly stand-alone symbols, making a small but powerful statement. Understated. Subtle. Mostly recognisable and decipherable to other survivors—a kind of code.

It made sense.

After telling my story so many times as a part of this journey it seemed fitting not to cover up my scars, but to acknowledge them, with a small semi-colon on my right wrist, on top of the scars, but not concealing them.

Sunday, 13 August 2023
Week 10, Day 7
Long Run 21.1 km (Half-Marathon)

Thank God Daisy slept in this morning, until just before 9:30 a.m. I needed the extra sleep. I was just changing her nappy when Chris's dad arrived to pick her up. I'd asked him to come any time between 10 a.m. and 11 a.m., but he was early. I was a bit embarrassed that I was still in my pyjamas, and I hadn't even packed Daisy's bag yet, or fed her breakfast. I was so dishevelled when I answered the door, but Daisy was happy to see him and of course, the feeling was mutual.

I helped carry her out to the car, then went back inside to have breakfast. As I was sitting at the table I started crying. I felt helpless, lonely, panicky, overwhelmed. I didn't want to spend half the day running. I wanted to watch TV. I wanted to relax. I thought about the hills. I thought about the boredom. It was five whole kilometres shorter than my last long run, but I still didn't feel like I could do it.

My inner monologue was whining like a little baby, then reprimanding itself. *I don't want to do my long run* the voice would say, then I'd try to summon a stronger voice to counter, *You can do this! You'll be fine once you start listening to your audiobook!*

There was a mental back-and-forth for what felt like an age until finally the whiny voice got softer and the encouraging voice got stronger, and I managed to get dressed. Then I was in 'go' mode. Fill the camelback, click on the bum bag, pack my phone and two gels, put on my headphones.

The first two kilometres were hard—I think they always are. After 3 km, part of me was thinking, *Only six more of those,* and part of me was thinking, *Oh no! Not six more of those!* After I conquered my first and biggest hill, I finally found my stride. I wasn't tired, I wasn't sore. I could do this. I was listening to an audiobook about ultra-running, and hearing about feats of endurance involving 100 mile runs up and down cliffs and rocky terrain. I found it inspiring.

For me, this marathon was my ultra. I wasn't fit, I wasn't strong, I wasn't athletic. I would never run 100 miles. I would never run up a mountain. But

I would do this! I would conquer this marathon the way the world's toughest runners conquered the world's most gruelling races. And it would be equally impressive because I was an ordinary person doing an extraordinary thing.

The Melbourne Marathon and Beyond Blue wanted to promote me as an example and an inspiration, and I was finally beginning to understand why. If I could do it, anybody could.

Monday, 14 August 2023
Week 11, Day One
Rest Day

This morning, when I woke up, I felt like I'd been hit by a bus. I felt like I needed at least two extra hours of sleep and a whole day of decompressing and winding down. I thought about calling in sick, but I knew if I could just get as far as pulling back the covers and sitting up—that would be half the battle.

I was right. I still wasn't feeling 100%, but I no longer felt like work was completely impossible. As I was getting ready, Daisy woke up, and I quickly got her ready while I also juggled having breakfast and preparing my lunch. As I was doing all this, I felt anxious, tense, and frazzled. I felt so sorry for myself that I had to do hard things—hard, normal person, adult things, like getting out of bed and going to work.

Halfway through breakfast, Daisy came up to me wanting to be picked up, and I lifted her onto my lap and promptly buried my face in her hair and cried. I thought about how I'd been crying nearly every morning and how it was not a good sign in terms of my mental health. I'd tried on the weekend to book a session with my psychologist, but the website wasn't allowing me to select the person I usually see. I considered asking to step away for a moment today at work after the practice opened at 10 a.m. so I could make a phone call and book in.

Once I got to work, I realised that I'd completely forgotten the kids had an all-day excursion to the Cranbourne Botanical Gardens. This meant a reduction in the normal work-related stress, but the added stress of organising the First- Aid kit and the realisation that I hadn't packed a suitable lunch to eat on the go. I managed to run to the staff room and scrounge together a few snacks from my pigeon hole, and before long, we were off.

Not long after arriving at the Gardens, the kids had a short break to eat, and I had a chance to call my psychologist's practice. I was hoping and crossing my fingers to get an appointment as soon as possible, but the soonest I could get was Thursday next week. If I desperately needed to talk to someone before then, I could call Beyond Blue, Parentline, or one of my friends. I'd just have to hold out.

Tuesday, 15 August 2023
Week 11, Day 2
7 km—'Race Pace'

I woke up feeling rested this morning and went about my morning routine without any tears. Margaret had sent me an early message saying she was bringing George to playgroup this time, and that put me in a good mood. I'd been looking forward to having her around on a Tuesday morning, but for the first few weeks of term, life had gotten in the way.

The kids all had a great time with each other and with all the toys. We put on some music, and they danced to 'Baby Shark,' 'The Wheels on the Bus,' and 'Heads, Shoulders, Knees and Toes.' There was time to draw, time to eat snacks, and time for Play-Doh.

The woman in charge of playgroups in the area came and introduced herself and also had a volunteer with her. She asked me to make a flyer to advertise the playgroup, and I panicked. I was terrible at that stuff! When would I find the time? Luckily, Margaret came to the rescue and whipped up a flyer using an app on her phone in minutes. I was also asked to attend a two-hour Zoom meeting on Thursday (my day off), and I had the balls to email the principal and ask for that time in lieu.

She said that was fine and to nominate whatever two-hour block I liked.

I was a bit on edge for the rest of the day. Not bad, but just this sense of slight emotional discomfort. I was catching up on classwork that my colleague had done with our additional needs student, and I always have this imposter-syndrome sense that she's better at her job than me and that she gets more work out of him.

When feelings like that come up, I try to fight them in my head and come up with reasons why I'm good at my job. I buy a lot of useful and helpful resources. I come up with new ideas, particularly regarding his speech therapy and occupational therapy. I am a good team member and a good communicator in terms of sharing information and keeping everyone posted. I document everything. I'm too hard on myself.

I got home just in time to see Margaret and George walking up my drive. She had some new headphones for me that she'd originally bought for herself but couldn't use. They'd given her an allergic reaction around her ears. They were the same as my favourite pair that died on me a while ago, so I was excited to buy them from her at a discount.

As we were all coming in the door, I got a phone call from a frazzled, depressed friend who had had a hard day and needed to decompress. There had been an issue at work, and she'd ended up crying, then was reprimanded for crying and being 'unprofessional.' I tried hard to be there for her and sympathise and offer my advice, but I was also aware that Margaret had gone into the other room to take a phone call of her own, and George was crying out for her. I multi-tasked as best I could, soothing my friend over the phone and soothing George at the same time, then I offered some parting words of encouragement and said I had to go so not to be rude to my visitors. Then, I felt like a bad friend.

Margaret, George, Daisy and I went outside so the kids could play, and we tried to get the headphones to connect to my phone via Bluetooth. They were fancy portable bone-conduction headphones that allow you to hear what's going on around you (traffic, etc.) as well as your music, podcast or audiobook. Unfortunately, they needed charging, so we couldn't set it up. I'd already told Margaret earlier in the day that I couldn't hang around long and had to do my 7 km run, so we wrapped things up and I got changed and headed out with my old (crappy) headphones.

I reverted to the Apple Music 170 BPM playlist, just for a bit of variety, and found it quite annoying, with a lot of cheesy music and bad re-mixes. I can't even begin to tell you how bad it is to listen to an obscure country music track sped up and accompanied by a *doof-doof* beat. But I was running too fast to stop and change my playlist, so I just put up with it.

I'd decided to do my short, fast run of the week along my usual 8 km route in the hope that it would comparatively feel like a piece of cake. The psychological ploy worked! The mistake I'd been making was to run my usual 5 km route and add on the extra 2 kilometres, which must have made me gauge the run as 'difficult' in comparison. Today, I could turn back for the second half of my run a little bit earlier than my usual turnaround point, so I ended up with this confident feeling in the last 3.5 km. Keeping up a steady pace for 7 whole km was starting to feel like a walk in the park, and I was finally starting to feel less scared of the looming 8 km pace runs coming up in my training plan.

When I checked my stats, it wasn't quite a PB, but still a lot faster than my average for a 7 km run. I was happy with that.

When I got home, I found that Chris had already made dinner, and it just needed to be heated up in the oven. It was like Christmas Day, seeing that neat little casserole dish waiting for me on the bench.

Wednesday, 16 August 2023
Week 11, Day 3
8 km Training Run

I woke up feeling completely brain-fried. My mind was absolute mush. I thought about the work day ahead. I couldn't even begin to imagine how I was going to arrange my thoughts cohesively enough to facilitate learning for another human being! I was also having a bit of a panic attack at the thought of the rest of the week and the fact that I had no room to breathe in my schedule. Work, run, cook, sleep, swimming lessons, meeting, cook, sleep, and many hours in between of being climbed all over and nagged by a toddler.

It was too much. I called in sick. When Chris woke up, I told him a little white lie that I hadn't slept all night and needed a day to catch up on sleep. I don't know why I felt the need to lie. Maybe just the thought that I was being lazy and self-indulgent and that I had no right to call in sick. Chris never calls in sick. How could he possibly understand?

When Daisy woke, Chris looked after her and closed the bedroom door so that she wouldn't know I was home. I stayed in bed for hours and even managed to go back to sleep for a while and had bizarre dreams. I was hot. I was sweaty. I'd had night sweats again and was feeling completely depleted. When I awoke, I could hear Daisy in the next room, and I was dreading going in and interacting with her. I just didn't have the energy. What sort of mum did that make me? I tried to work out how much time in bed I could justify. I was crying and feeling so guilty. I knew I had to get up and eat something to be able to take my antidepressant.

Then Chris opened the door and said he had to pop out and help a neighbour with something, so I had no choice but to get up. Chris had made pancakes, and they were sitting on the table ready for me to eat. Between mouthfuls I was wiping tears away and barely holding it together.

I thought about how long it had been since I'd seen a psychiatrist. During my last 'mini-breakdown' I'd gone to my GP to get a referral for a new psychiatrist. I'd contacted them with my referral, and they'd said they'd get back to me. That was 11 weeks ago. Eleven weeks! That's three whole months. I'd basically sought help because I'd reached a crisis point, but I'd been told by the world in no uncertain terms to put my crisis on hold. I was in desperate need of some support, but going through the normal channels had failed.

When Chris came back inside, I was still crying. He asked how I was and a fresh wave of desperation hit me as I answered, 'Not good.' He was concerned and gave me a hug but wasn't sure what else to do. He suggested we go shopping to get out of the house; besides, Daisy needed a haircut, and we were in need of a few grocery items. I needed a haircut too.

Once we were out in public and had a few errands to run I wasn't crying anymore, but I still wasn't myself. If I had all the time and money in the world, I would have loved to have a massage, a wax, a manicure, eyelash extensions—a proper day of pampering. I just needed *something*. Some sort of release, but I had to make do with a ten-minute fringe trim. After all, I'd just blown $200 on a pair of headphones! We had some lunch, got the shopping, and headed home.

I intended to lie down for an hour, or an hour and a half, and then go for a run. I lay there and cried and cried. I didn't go for my run. My first missed training session in over ten weeks. I felt like a total and utter failure.

My whole life was unravelling. Work, home, the marathon. I was no longer keeping those balls up in the air.

They'd all crashed to the ground.

Thursday, 17 August 2023
Week 11, Day 4
Rest Day

Another day of failures. I failed to take Daisy to swimming in the morning; I failed to go for a run to make up for yesterday.

I got a message early from Margaret saying that she wouldn't be able to make it to swimming as she'd been called in to work. I decided that if George wasn't going to be there, it wasn't worth making the effort in my current state. Daisy had been up late last night, much later than I'd wanted to stay up myself.

At 7:50 a.m., when we were supposed to get up and get ready for the 9:00 a.m. class, Daisy was still sleeping, and I just let her. I needed the sleep in too. We could have gotten up just before nine to make it to the ten o'clock class, but I was too ashamed and embarrassed to show up late again, revealing my incompetence as a mother to Daisy's swimming teacher!

My phone was beeping constantly as I tried to lie there and relax. Margaret was concerned and checking in, but just replying to her messages was too much for me to handle. When I feel this way the sound of a text message coming in is just a trigger for anxiety. The sound just pierces my brain, and my heart rate goes up. I'm trying my best to shut the world out, and it keeps forcing its way in. I know she means well, but sometimes I just shut down and don't have the capacity to communicate. She left a voice message, 'Tell me what I can do to help you get through this. . . . ' I didn't know the answer.

I called my psychiatrist and asked to be put on the waiting list for the next available appointment. They said they could fit me in next Wednesday at 8:15 a.m, so I contacted my boss and asked to have Wednesday morning off for my time in lieu.

There were dishes and clothes to put away. The house was a pigsty. I still had the chicken and vegetables I'd bought on Sunday that needed to be cooked. It was overwhelming. I started crying and hyperventilating. I called Parentline. They were very supportive and understanding and tried to reassure me that I was doing a good job. They also said to not be afraid of asking for extra support from Chris and the rest of the family.

When I hung up, I was still crying—maybe crying even more, and I decided to call my mother-in-law, Tonia. It was a last resort. I hated asking her for help. I wanted to be able to handle things on my own. She could hear how bad I was over the phone and said she would come over. Then, I took a deep breath and put the dishes away.

Just then, Chris came in the door and gave me the biggest hug. I texted Tonia not to worry.

Friday, 18 August 2023
Week 11, Day 5
8 km Training Run

I'm back, baby! After a slip, a dip, a drop, a dry spell, whatever you want to call it, I'm back on track with my training.

Daisy and I had nothing to do today, so we both slept in until nearly 10:00 a.m.! I know it's terrible to let your kids get into these sorts of habits, and I knew it would mean a late night tonight, but hey, I love a good sleep-in.

This morning, I wasn't crying—but I was feeling low. There was a huge, chaotic pile of dishes, and just looking at the kitchen with dirty oven trays and bowls and cutlery strewn on every surface of bench space gave me a panic attack.

The cycle goes like this. I see a number of things that need to be done—for example, the dishes, the laundry, taking out the rubbish. Then the panic sets in. I don't know where to begin, my breathing gets shallow. I hyperventilate. Then the shame spiral starts. I find normal stuff like this overwhelming; ergo—I must be a bad person. I literally bully myself, internally of course.

You suck, you're such a bad person, you're the worst person in the world, rinse and repeat. It's like a mantra. A negative mantra of low self-esteem.

Last year I was doing this a lot, and I decided to do something about my self-esteem. I bought these self-esteem workbooks, with exercises in self-love and self-acceptance, and I put my heart into filling them out and teaching myself the doctrines of some positive self-help books.

A lot of the work in self-esteem building centres around finding your strengths and celebrating them. My strengths are mostly creative. Singing, dancing, acting, visual art.

I hadn't done anything creative (bar the odd karaoke session) since January. Being back at work makes it hard—the marathon training makes it even harder. My self-esteem books are getting kind of dusty on the shelf. It might be time to pull them out again.

This morning, I just sort of pulled myself together, and went about things. It was so weird—I was standing there doing the dishes, while at the same time silently berating myself for not even being able to do the dishes. Even after I'd completed the task, I was ashamed of myself for not having *wanted* to do them. Who ever *wants* to do the dishes though? It's ridiculous! I took out the rubbish, put away the washing, and all the while I was still telling myself, 'I'm a bad person.'

Don't get me wrong, I have another, more rational voice in my head that is telling that first voice to shut up, but the 'bad person' refrain is like a metronome or a heartbeat. On those mornings at home alone with Daisy, it never fully goes away. It's like a nagging whisper.

Luckily Chris got home from work nice and early, and as soon as he'd showered and eaten, I was out the door for my run. As always, I didn't feel like it, but as always, as soon as my headphones were on and I was into my warm-up walk, I was on a mission.

During my training runs, I don't worry about cadence. It's not about how fast my feet are moving; it's about stride length. Being light, bouncy, springy. Propelling forward. Steady, determined and energetic, but it's not a fight. I wouldn't say it's completely effortless, but *almost*.

Middle-distance runs are my favourite runs. Not too fast, not too far.

Mildly challenging but not difficult. I never get the feeling of 'I can't do this' that I get with most fast-paced or long-distance runs.

Coming back, I was walking on air. It was like those last two days of doing nothing and feeling sorry for myself were completely erased—struck from the record. It was Chris's turn to cook, and after my shower I relaxed on the couch with the memoirs of a female mountain runner.

Saturday, 19 August 2023
Week 11, Day 6
45-60 Minutes Strength Training

Last night was a late one. After waking at 10 a.m. and napping late in the day, Daisy had stayed up 'til almost midnight. So, this morning, when I heard her crying at 6 a.m., I gave her a bottle and lay her down in bed next to me so we could both get some more sleep.

I'd decided to skip Parkrun for the second week in a row, as I'd be going to a friend's house to babysit their little boy from the afternoon until around midnight, so I needed to use the morning to get my strength training in.

Tonia (Chris's mum) arrived around 9 a.m., as both Daisy and I were just getting up. I made Daisy her porridge, which her abuelita fed to her, while I downed two pieces of toast with peanut butter and a cup of tea.

Once I got to the gym I tried to get my new headphones to work, to no avail. I'd have to get my tech-savvy other half to have a look at them and sort them out. The music from the gym's TV screens would have to do.

I started with the chest press, on 7.5 kg (2.5 kg heavier than the 5 kgs I couldn't budge at the start of last year) and managed five lots of 20 reps. Then I steeled myself up for the dreaded Russian Twists.

I *hate* core work. I hate *all* core work. I have a weak core, and I probably always will. At the start of last year, I'd been so weak that a ten-second plank would cause my whole body to shake and tremble.

But I pushed through, five lots of 40, then moved on to some easier machines. I went from one to the other, working on my legs, then my upper body, before reluctantly returning to the mat to do some bug crawls for my weakling abdominals.

For once I stayed at the gym for longer than 45 minutes, although I couldn't be bothered to push it to a whole hour. I wiped down the mat I'd been working on, grabbed my bag and headed out the door for the short drive home.

After I showered, I forced myself to eat a tin of tuna. Margaret is always telling me 'Protein after exercise!' so I was choosing to take her advice. I also remembered that I needed to consume plenty of carbs to load up for tomorrow's long run. Chris called me on the way home asking if I wanted KFC and I responded with a resounding— 'Yes, please!'

Then Daisy and I headed to my friends' place where I would be watching their little boy, Noah. He's only a few months older than Daisy, but he's already in size 2 clothing, while pint-sized Daisy is still getting around in a size 0.

It was so cute watching them play together. Noah had a little teepee that they were running and crawling in and out of; then Noah hid in the wardrobe and slid the door open and closed, playing peek-a-boo, much to Daisy's delight!

Around dinner time, Mum stopped in to pick up Daisy and take her back to our place so that Noah could go to bed. Unlike Daisy, he's a good little boy, who goes down at 6 or 6:30 p.m. Tonight he stayed up a little later, but once he was down, I turned off the TV and the house was *so* quiet you could have heard a pin drop. All I could hear was the blowing of the heater and the buzzing of the fridge. Even when everyone else is asleep at our house you can still hear Chris snoring!

This gave me a nice chance to just enjoy the calm, peacefulness of my surroundings. Their house is much bigger than ours, and much less cluttered. I was able to stretch out with my laptop on an otherwise empty kitchen table and write, then take indulgent little breaks to lie back on their big comfy couch and read my mountaineering memoir.

Such freedom!

Sunday, 20 August 2023
Week 11, Day 7
27 km Long Run

Mum and Daisy woke up together, so I got to have a little sleep-in after being out babysitting late last night. I got up at nine, had breakfast and got ready to go out running. For once I wasn't dreading my long run. I was feeling pretty enthusiastic about it.

It was a beautiful day, and the sun was out and shining. I was listening to my audiobook as I set out on a route upon which I was sure not to get lost.

Unfortunately, my legs felt heavy and tired. Less than 5 km in, I already felt like I'd run more than 8 km. *How am I going to get through this?* I thought.

I've heard a lot of runners say the first 5 km are the hardest before you get into a rhythm, and I was hoping that was the case for me today. Luckily for me, sometime after the 5 km mark I started to feel comfortable and energetic again—I'd found my stride.

I had my gels with me, and I'd decided to have them at 7 km or 8 km, at 14 km and at 21 km. I also had my camelback for sips of water on the go. I sucked little squeezes of the thick, sweet gel between the 7 to 8 km mark, hoping it would help sustain my energy well past the halfway mark.

After I hit about the 12 km mark, things got hard again. I still had 1.5 km to go until my turnaround point, and that distance seemed to stretch out and go on forever. My left Achilles was starting to hurt, as well as the ball of my right foot. I thought about all the various injuries that could befall a runner: runner's knee, plantar fasciitis, shin splints, cuboid syndrome.... I think I vaguely remembered reading somewhere that something like nine out of ten runners get injured every year. I almost hoped I would get injured to put an end to all this madness!

Once I turned back and reached about 14 km, I was exhausted. I decided to try 'Jeffing'.

'Jeffing' is short for the Jeff Galloway method, in which you intentionally break up your run into intervals of running with short walking segments in between.

I'd seen a lot of people using this technique in races, and I'd always be surprised when I'd run past a walker, only to have them overtake me once they started running again. The idea is to start with your intervals early before you feel so tired that you have to walk nonstop.

I settled on a two-minute jogging, 30-seconds walking ratio. I was curious to see how much it would slow me down—or if it would indeed slow me down at all.

Each two-minute run felt difficult to get through, and the walking breaks felt so quick, but going through the cycle and keeping my eye on my watch made the time in general pass more quickly, and soon I was ready for my second gel.

It didn't give me any sort of boost in energy—in fact, I was petering out. I felt there was no way on Earth I'd be able to get through the whole 27 km, and I seriously considered stopping to take a shortcut home when I still had over 6 km to go. I was so tired. My legs felt like lead.

Somehow I pushed through. I just concentrated on each two-minute running segment, and tried to walk as fast as I could in between. The running seemed to numb the pain in my legs, and each time I stopped to walk I'd feel it again, but I needed to conserve that energy. As I trudged on, I felt certain that my overall time would be abysmal and that Jeffing on race day would lead to a DNF, with a time *way* longer than seven hours.

I wanted to give up, abandon the run and just walk—or better still, sit down. I was dreading each hill. Somehow, I dug deep and pushed hard, and made it up all the overpass inclines, and that one big hill I'd been dreading the whole way.

When I got to the last few blocks, I decided to stop timing intervals and try running the rest of the way. I pretended it was just the end of a regular 5 km run and I was going for a big finish. I surprised myself by running steadily for more than three blocks!

As my run came to an end, so did my audiobook. I'd timed it perfectly! My legs were on *fire*. I wanted to collapse during my cool down, but instead I steadied myself, held onto the brick fence in front of our units and did some slow, deep stretches. Emotionally, I felt amazing! I couldn't believe I'd done it! I'd run 27 km. I checked my pace, worried about the jeffing, and it was faster than some of the long runs I've done without walking at all! I was a convert. I was now an avid Jeff Galloway disciple!

Monday, 21 August 2023
Week 12, Day 1
Rest Day

This morning Daisy woke me up much earlier than I'd usually get up on a Monday, (or any day for that matter). On the one hand, I was annoyed and tried to get her to go back to sleep, but on the other hand, it turned out to be a blessing. It gave me time to have a shower and freshen up and prepare for the day.

Since I started this journal, I can count on one hand the number of days I've woken up early enough to shower in the morning. It makes a difference. But getting out of bed is one of the hardest things for me to do every day. It means facing the world. It means facing reality and responsibility. It means being an adult—something that, at the ripe old age of 39, I still haven't quite gotten the hang of!

There were no disasters or meltdowns today. No tricky situations that I had to deal with. My student was cool, calm and collected, working co-operatively. My biggest issues at work were that (a) I was sore (understandable) and (b) I was hungry, for some reason. I'd had two pieces of toast with peanut butter for breakfast, but by 10:00 a.m. I was starving and had to have an apple while all the kids had their fruit.

At lunch time, I had my roast vegetables that Mum had prepared, with some chicken and couscous, but it just wasn't hitting the spot. It was a big enough serve, it should have been plenty to keep me going, but I was just ravenous and felt like eating something more substantial. I knew my yogurt afternoon snack was not going to be enough. As soon as the bell went at 3:30 p.m. I made a bee line for McDonalds to enjoy a quarter-pounder with cheese. In the days when work stress had been a big issue, this had been a regular occurrence, but it was only the second time this year that I'd caved in and had fast food after work.

Knowing that today was my rest day, and my only afternoon with free time after work, I went to Rebel Sport to stock up on more carbohydrate gels and then to the library to see if I had any books waiting on hold for me. There was nothing there. Going up and down the steps to the library was hell. My calf muscles and my thighs were killing me. I felt like an invalid, practically limping. My mind cast forward to tomorrow—a 7 km pace run. Would my muscle pain ease up in time for me to be able to run? Sometimes I feel like the effort of a long run warrants two rest days.

Tuesday, 22 August 2023
Week 12, Day 2
7 km—'Race Pace'

This morning I slept in. I didn't set my alarm. I woke up at 6:30 a.m., checked the time, then rolled over and thought, *I'll lie down a little bit longer. I won't fall asleep.* And of course, I did.

I have these weird recurring dreams that I'm back at university, high school, or my old job in special education, often all at once and juggling all three. Sometimes in my dreams I'm living in a share house again or living both in my current house and a share house, constantly going back and forth, leaving things at one place or the other.

My conscious mind kind of creeps in, and I try to remember whether I have a job or a conflicting schedule in my real waking life that interferes with my dream studies. I sort of wrestle with that sleeping, dreaming state and end up waking up and reminding myself that, no, those studying / old job / share house days are over—and I'm kind of disappointed, but I try not to dwell on it. My life is what it is. Maybe I'm resenting the idea of getting older and being past my prime or my 'heyday.'

It was lucky I woke up when I did and that it was only a five-minute sleep in. But I think we've established I hate not being on schedule, so I was worried about running late. Again.

I was feeling groggy this morning. I'd had night sweats again, and I felt disgusting, but I didn't have time for a shower. That would have to wait 'til after my run this afternoon. I thought about the day ahead. Playgroup, then three sessions in the classroom. I wish I had a spare hour or two somewhere to just read and write. I didn't feel like working. I was feeling lazy. As is often the case, I was just resenting the fact that I'm so busy.

Margaret was a little early to playgroup, so we had a chance to talk, just between the two of us, about some things that had been troubling her. She'd had a lot on her mind, and we'd been hoping to catch up on Sunday, but time got away from both of us.

Sundays are a bit of a write off because I spend most of the day running and the rest of the day recovering. There's not much time for anything else.

As soon as the kids all started trickling-in, I felt so positive and uplifted. Watching them grow and become more confident each week, learning to relate to each other and play together, rather than just individually side by side—parallel play, as they call it.

The rest of the day was normal and uneventful. As the work day was ending, I was starting to become more and more aware of my impending pace run and dreading it as usual. I was still so sore from Sunday.

At home, I greeted Daisy, Chris and Mum and started getting geared up right away before I could change my mind. Then Daisy came into the bedroom and wanted to play, and that was the perfect excuse to procrastinate—anything to delay the inevitable pain and discomfort I was about to put my body through.

When Daisy had had enough of our little peekaboo game with the blankets, I got my head back in the game. The weather was extremely crappy, and it had been raining on and off all day, so I was torn between running outside in the rain and going to the gym to run on the dreaded treadmill (or 'dreadmill' as we runners like to call it).

In the end I decided to brave the elements, and I popped in some contact lenses and grabbed a jacket. I hate cold-weather running because a singlet never feels like enough, but long sleeves make me hot once I get going. I usually settle on being too hot as the lesser of two evils, as freezing during my warm-up affects my mood and my ability to get in the right mindset. It's just one more thing to whinge about before I even start.

Today I was blasted by the frigid chill as soon as I stepped out the door. I felt it penetrating my bones. My hands in particular felt positively icy. *Remind me why I'm doing this again?* I thought to myself.

The run was hard yakka. Just two days after that epic 27 km, my body wasn't exactly in peak condition. It still hadn't recovered from the shock. I was pumping my little legs like the Roadrunner from Looney Tunes, but it wasn't having the desired effect. I was thinking the whole time, *Cadence, cadence, cadence,* but I was painfully aware of how slowly I was going.

I didn't even have it in me to look at my watch as I ran. I didn't need any data. My body was all the data I needed. I thought, *Hey, let's just get through this. All you can do is your best.* It ended up being one of my slowest 7 km by far, embarrassingly slow, but at the end of the day I got it done, and that's the main thing.

I've been thinking a lot about RPE, which stands for 'Rate of Perceived Effort.' I initially didn't realise this when I first looked at my training plan, but it has a little guideline of RPE for the different types of runs.

For a pace run, it says RPE 4-5, in which you should still be able to hold a conversation but with some difficulty, according to the RPE charts I've looked at online. I've been working way harder than that on my fast, short runs. If I even tried to spit out a few words, I'd quite possibly die.

For training runs, the RPE is 3-4, 'a comfortable pace' in which you should be able to hold a conversation without getting out of breath. Ha! I could probably get out a couple of sentences, but it would be an effort.

For my long run, the recommended RPE is 2-3—'light and easy, could continue for hours.' My long runs are comparatively easier than the rest of my training, but 'light and easy' is probably an exaggeration. 'Bearable' would be a more appropriate adjective. But to be fair, I do continue them for hours—my last one was almost four hours in duration.

Analysing all this and reassessing my training strategy is partially to avoid overtraining and burnout, but if I'm honest, I'm just looking for an excuse not to punish myself so damn hard every Tuesday. Running, above all else, is supposed to be fun. Is there any point in training so hard if it's just going to make me miserable?

I'm tempted to consult with a running coach just to get my head around it all. I could discuss my heart rate data and consider being a bit easier on myself. I could also pose the question in my Facebook running groups. I'll sleep on it.

Wednesday, 23 August 2023
Week 12, Day 3
8 km Training Run

This morning, I didn't have to be at work until 11:40 a.m. as I had a couple of hours of time in lieu of having a meeting on my day off last week. I did, however, must be up and ready for a telehealth appointment with my psychiatrist at 8:15 a.m.

After waking, I had just enough time to have a bit of a morning cuddle with Daisy, then have a quick banana and a cup of tea before settling once again in the privacy of our bedroom with my laptop in front of me. It had been a long time since my last appointment in February, so there was a lot to catch up on.

I said I'd been stable and functioning well for the most part, besides my two little episodes of burnout, or 'mini-breakdowns,' which had happened 13 weeks ago and two weeks ago, respectively. I also talked about how overwhelmed I was feeling with everyday household tasks, and how that was affecting my self-esteem.

My psychiatrist felt that these were not 'bipolar' problems, related to manic or depressive episodes, but more to do with psychological or personality issues—a recurring thing that I would need to work on, rather than something that needed to be managed with medication.

I also surprised myself by getting emotional about my inability to say no to people and set boundaries and how just maintaining a normal social life was leaving me mentally and emotionally drained.

I tend to prioritise other people's needs over my own, and I gravitate towards people who can relate to my problems. This means that my closest friends all have their own issues. One of the things I like most about myself is how supportive I am as a friend and how emotionally available I am in terms of being there for people—but it's a double-edged sword.

I've lost track of the number of times I've had to set a good half hour aside to help a friend debrief after a hard day at work, when I was just getting in the door, feeling frazzled and in need of my own debriefing. Likewise, I'll agree to meet up with someone, and tell myself I only have a couple hours to spare, resolving to leave at a certain time. Inevitably, I'll then lose track of the time and end up stressing and rushing around to keep up with my other commitments afterwards.

It's definitely not just an issue of having demanding or needy friends; it's a 'me' issue. I'm co-dependent. I have an intensity when it comes to friendship, where I feel the need to be intimately close to the people around me. I don't do acquaintances. All my relationships are just deep. It's also a trope, but very true, that it's easier to get wrapped up in other people's problems than to confront your own. I use social responsibilities as an excuse to shirk out of my other responsibilities and then feel guilty for doing it.

I didn't expect to end up talking about all that; in fact, I hadn't even realised how much it was affecting me until I tentatively started mentioning it and burst into tears.

Maintaining friendships can often be complicated for people with bipolar disorder. For one, we often do 'crazy,' unforgivable things when we're manic, and sometimes that's hard for people to get past. Sometimes we're so embarrassed and ashamed by our actions that we can't bring ourselves to face these people afterwards.

Depressive episodes can affect our friendships in a different way. We withdraw socially and don't want to leave the house or see anyone, sometimes for months. We just don't have the social energy. People get offended by the lack of contact; we drift apart, or again, we're so embarrassed by ourselves that we can't face people once we come out of our funk.

For most of my adult life, I haven't had any enduring friendships. I haven't kept in touch with anyone from primary school, high school or university, bar the odd exchange on Facebook here and there. I'd be involved in amateur musicals and never make friends or keep in touch with those guys either, even though they all seemed to bond with each other and form lasting friendships.

For a long time, this has made me feel fundamentally unlikeable, like there was something wrong with me. Most of my birthday parties have just been dinners with my mum, my grandmother, and whatever boyfriend I had at the time. I literally had no-one to invite who would turn up. Even my 30th was just a few family members and a bunch of my ex-husband's friends.

Another barrier for bipolar with regards to friendships is that our life seems to be separated into phases, as our moods dominate and come and go, and along with them different obsessions and connections to people and places.

For example, there was a period in my 20s when I was quite obsessed with making visual art, involving myself heavily with a particular gallery and the community around it. I'd go to all their openings, exhibit in group shows, and network and socialise with all the other artists. They became my friends; they became my whole world.

Inevitably, when a depressive phase hit and all my creative energy was spent, I withdrew from that world and all those friendships petered out. I told myself it was because those people were shallow, and once I stopped making art, I held no value or currency to them, but the truth is—I also had a big part to play in it.

Many of my friendships have also revolved around whatever relationship I happened to be in. Right into my late 20s, I struggled to maintain a relationship beyond the one-year mark, so losing all my friends became a practically annual thing. My obsessive nature meant that I'd pour all of myself into these relationships and, like an immature teenager, drop off the face of the Earth in terms of maintaining any of my already flimsy existing friendships. I was so inconsistent and unreliable.

A couple of times I've said and done things to people I care about that were horrible. Those moments haunt me and make me feel like the worst kind of terrible person.

My breath catches in my chest just thinking about those things.

At one point, a friend posted online about a tattoo she'd gotten. The words, 'No man's woman' emblazoned on her arm. I was manic at the time and couldn't keep my big mouth shut. 'Literally, all I've ever heard you talk about is men,' I posted. There was a ring of truth to what I was saying, but the truth can hurt, and it was a horrible thing to say to any person. Totally inappropriate. I got a lot of understandable and justified backlash from that post, and I was unfriended, blocked and never heard from that person again. And she meant something to me. I don't know why I said that.

Looking back, I think I was deeply jealous. I've never had the courage to be 'no man's woman.' I've never been single. I've always jumped from relationship to relationship, afraid to be alone. Until just now, I've never admitted that to myself or thought about the motives behind the incident in that way.

Another time, when I was in a mixed episode, I insulted one of the people who was supporting me the most. She was letting me stay with her and her family while I went through a break-up. She's a social person, who's always the life of the party, and she usually has a lot to say. Nothing wrong with that.

We were relaxing outside when she commented on the peace and quiet. I remarked that I was surprised she liked peace and quiet, as she 'never shuts up.' She was so insulted and offended, and so was her husband. I can't blame them. Another friendship that was important to me just suddenly cut off. I miss those guys all the time.

After the appointment I ended up with more than an hour to spare. I dropped into the McDonald's near work and treated myself to a muffin and a coffee, spending some time on my laptop, typing away. I was enjoying myself so much that the time flew by and I didn't want to tear myself away, but I reluctantly closed my laptop and drove around the corner to start my working day.

Throughout the day, I was in a bit of a fog—distracted, lost in thought. I was preoccupied with everything Lucinda, the therapist, and I had discussed and also with the notion that perhaps it was time to reevaluate my training process. Sometimes, after a psychiatry session, I just get this feeling of being depleted. I'm sure it's not uncommon. Therapy is hard work.

I have an appointment with my psychologist tomorrow as well. After my last crash I'd sort of gone into survival mode and reached out for all the professional support I could get. It's often the way that by the time you can get in to see someone, you've managed to naturally avert the crisis on your own, and this time was no exception.

I usually try to space my appointments out, as there's no point going over something with one person and just repeating it with another, but it's too late to cancel tomorrow's appointment, and Stuart (my psychologist) often offers a fresh perspective and some helpful strategies.

During my break today, I got a chance to think about the idea of consulting a running coach. I'd seen a coach offering his services and expertise on one of my Facebook groups, so I decided to contact him. He got back to me right away, and I was pleasantly surprised to see that he did indeed do one-off sessions, and that they're within my budget. We've organised for a 30-minute Zoom consultation tomorrow, right after my appointment with my psychologist.

After work, I decided to sit down and analyse all my running data that I'd gathered from my Garmin. I made three lists: one of all my 7 km runs, one of all my 8 km runs, and one of all my long runs. I had three columns with the date, my average pace, and my heart rate zone percentages. I also looked at my average stride length.

Doing all this helped me identify a few trends. Firstly, my pace had improved in all three types of runs; secondly, almost all my running was in zone 4 (145–162 beats per minute or 'threshold'); and thirdly, my stride length was significantly longer during my training runs than in my pace runs, which would explain why the former felt so easy and the latter felt so hard. I had been conservative about my stride length, as almost all the literature warns against the risk of injury with overstriding, but I think in my case, I'm an understrider if that's even a thing. Lots of little, tiny steps add up to an inefficient way of moving.

It was a beautiful day, and despite being so tired, I was looking forward to my 8 km run. Maybe it was the time to myself, the space to decompress?

I'd selected a new audiobook to listen to but was disappointed to find that, even at maximum volume, I couldn't hear it over the sounds of the traffic. I had no choice but to switch to music mid-run, which meant a lot of slowing down and fumbling with my phone. I expected this setback to affect my overall pace and time, but that wasn't the case at all.

It'll be interesting to see how I cope with the 10 km training runs coming up in the next few weeks of the program. Historically for me, a 10 km run has been categorised as a 'long run,' in which I'd allow myself to trudge along, basically at a crawl. Such runs had been reserved for the weekend, when I had all the time in the world. I wonder how it will be fitting a 10 km run in at the end of a work day. Would I end up running in the dark? Would I get home in time to eat dinner at a decent hour? How was I going to make it all work?

Hopefully, this new run coach will help me tweak my program to make it less demanding and intense, allowing me to spend a bit more time with my family and a little less time pounding the pavement. I'll see how it all goes tomorrow.

Thursday, 24 August 2023
Week 12, Day 4
Rest Day

This morning I got up early enough to get Daisy ready on time for swimming! I did it! Me! On time for the 9:00 a.m. class on a Thursday!

I felt so proud of myself. It turns out Daisy was the only one who showed up, but that was fine, as she got extra attention from the teacher.

When we got home, I did all the things I was supposed to do: I hung up the towels, we had a shower, and I washed and hung our swimming gear. I was ready, bright-eyed and bushy-tailed, for my 12:00 p.m. appointment with my psychologist.

I took the laptop outside into the sunshine, and it felt good to be getting on top of everything and touching base with my professionals again. My psychologist was pleased with how I'm doing and had some tips about being assertive with my friends without being mean. Framing it all in an 'It's not you, it's me' sort of way.

Straight after that I was ready for my Zoom meeting with Stuart Marshall, the run coach I'd found through the Slow Runner's Society. Stuart was amazing. It was only $40 for a half-hour session, and it was so worth it. I feel like every runner who is training for a race should consult a run coach. It's cheaper than a massage, which is something we don't hesitate to treat ourselves to, and it's a total game-changer.

He'd done his homework, looked at my existing training plan and the Melbourne Marathon course, and calculated what my average pace would have to be to finish on time—ten minutes per kilometre—WAY slower than I was currently going on my long runs.

He had so much advice for me there's barely room for me to type it all here! Firstly, he revamped my whole training plan. He swapped my strength training from a Saturday to a Tuesday and made Saturday a rest day, as he didn't want me with tired, sore muscles for Sunday's long run. He also suggested some recovery exercise on a Monday, just 20–30 minutes of moving my body. A slow run, a walk, the bike, the elliptical, even a swim or some Pilates. He made Wednesday another rest day and scheduled a couple of runs on Thursday and Friday, both 45–60 minutes, favouring 'time on my feet' over kilometres, as any more than that was just 'junk miles and overtraining.

He even said Thursday could be another rest day if I felt like it, and that Friday would be my fastest run, but that it wasn't necessary to go as fast as I had been on my Tuesdays—as my goal was only to finish the race—and there was no point torturing myself for a fast time that wasn't even part of my goals.

For my strength training, he suggested doing my leg exercises on one leg, as the actions in running all involve just one leg at a time. He also suggested doing my calf raises on a bent leg as well as a straight leg, as it would use different muscles and strengthen muscles that are crucial to running. He also suggested some step-ups.

He said one day of hydrating for a long run wasn't enough and that I should pump myself full of water for three days before a long run. He suggested pizza the night before a long run and banana bread for breakfast. He asked me about my fuelling during my long runs and said I was under-fueling. He recommended half a gel every 4 km.

In terms of the walk-run method, he said to play around with it and see what worked best without expelling too much energy. He said the 10 km mark was a good point to start 'Jeffing'. One of his clients does four minutes of running alternating with three minutes of walking, and he said something like that could work for me.

He was a big advocate of listening to my body, which was reassuring. It made me feel like skipping workouts, as needed, was intelligent and necessary when I'd just been seeing it as weak and felt like a failure whenever I did it.

After I spoke to Stuart, it was as though a huge weight had been lifted off my shoulders. I felt inspired, enthusiastic, and like I was now going into this thing with a solid game plan that would suit me—that wasn't just a one-size-fits-all.

Friday, 25 August 2023
Week 12, Day 5
Rest Day

Today wasn't a scheduled rest day, but I just didn't feel up to running and gave myself permission to skip a day. It was empowering. I don't think I've ever done that before without feeling guilty.

Daisy and I both woke up late after another ridiculously late night, and it wasn't long before Dad was at the door, coming over for another visit. Daisy was watching Cocomelon, and I was trying without much success to give her breakfast, but in the end, she ate a banana and some mandarin, and I was happy with that.

It was a sunny day—beautiful—so we went outside, and Daisy played with her outdoor kitchen and wrote on the ground with sidewalk chalk. It was nice to be just chilling in the sunshine with Dad and Daisy, watching her play and having cuddles with Grandpa. I remembered to hydrate, and I discussed my running coach session and my training plan with Dad. He seemed impressed.

He did a quick calculation in his head and said, 'Hang on a minute; if you run at 10 minutes per kilometre, for 42 kilometres, that's seven hours of running! That sounds like a long time to be running.'

I explained that a lot of it would be walking and that it'd probably be closer to six than seven hours. He was curious about my fuelling, and I showed him my gels, and it was nice to have someone to talk to who was interested in all that stuff.

Saturday, 26 August 2023
Week 12, Day 6
Rest Day

This morning I woke up feeling like I'd been run over by a bus. AGAIN. I could hardly move, and my head felt like someone had filled all my sinus cavities with concrete. It was partly due to the late night, partly due to last night's night sweats, and largely to do with three days of early spring weather and the accompanying hay fever. My eyes were itchy and watery, and I was rubbing them constantly. Even after drinking water nonstop yesterday, I was completely dehydrated. I had no energy. Berocca didn't help, hydralite didn't help, and anti-histamines didn't help.

I had a shower to feel more human, and I guess it sort of worked. Being upright was probably good for my sinuses too. Sleeping in had just made things worse. I decided to do the dishes, as that always gave me a little sense of accomplishment, and it did the trick of lifting my mood somewhat.

Chris came home, and we all decided to go to Waverley Gardens Shopping Centre for lunch, to go to the supermarket, and to hit the chemist up for some strong cold and flu tablets and some psych meds I was low on. While we waited on my prescriptions, we went to TK Maxx, and I found a calendar for writing up my new training plan. I was excited to get organised and ready for a fresh start with my training! I geek out and get excited about things like that. I'm a big planner.

When we got home, I put Daisy down for a nap and did a steam inhalation. It's one of my favourite tricks for clearing out the sinuses. I was able to breathe a bit better, but my eyes still felt terrible, and I was still exhausted.

I wanted to go to sleep, but I got out my laptop instead and decided to get some work done. Meanwhile, Chris fell asleep on the couch. The cold and flu tablets and the steam inhalation were making me feel a bit less like an invalid, but I was still sceptical about my ability to pull myself together for a long run day. I hadn't missed a long run yet, and I wasn't happy about the idea of possibly being benched on a Sunday.

I worried that it would be a big setback. Would it affect the rest of my training? Would it affect race day? All the literature I'd read suggested it was okay to miss a day of training here or there, but the long runs were the most important. Apparently, you should never miss a long run if you can help it.

But what would running while sick do? Maybe I'd have to cut my run short, or I wouldn't be able to keep up the pace, and then that would affect my confidence. People keep telling me it's 90% mental, so having a demoralising run can't be that good. I'd have to see how I felt in the morning and decide. I was just praying that I'd wake up and suddenly be magically fine.

Sunday, 27 August 2023
Week 12, Day 7
29 km Long Run

Guess what??? I woke up suddenly feeling fine! Well, fine is a strong word, but I felt well enough to run. I'd woken up early, taken a cold and flu tablet and started hydrating for the day ahead. I'd said to Mum to come over at nine or ten o'clock and I was out of bed before eight. I had time to eat breakfast (banana bread, as suggested by my new running coach) and to get dressed, do my hair and fill my hydration vest.

I felt prepared.
I felt ready.
I felt positive.

When Mum arrived, we quickly greeted each other. Like she always does, she asked what needed doing around the house and explained what food she'd brought over to cook to help us out for the week. Then I said goodbye to Daisy, and I was ready to set off.

My headphones were charged, I'd downloaded an audiobook, and I had all my gels.

Feeling hydrated made a huge difference. Last week, I started drinking before I even hit 4 km, and I was out of water before I finished my run. With three days of copious water consumption under my belt, hopefully, this wouldn't be an issue today.

I felt confident about my new plan. Run for 10 km, then alternate walking for three minutes and running for four minutes. Ten km was going to be nice and easy. I'd managed dozens and dozens of 10 km runs without getting tired.

It was refreshing to have a new attitude of confidence that I was on track to finish my race before the cut-off time, that as my coach Stuart had put it—I had an hour of 'wiggle room' to play around with. The walk-run intervals were something I had plenty of time to experiment with. If I was too slow with today's plan, maybe I could cut down my recovery walks to two minutes instead of three on my next run. There was no pressure.

The run was going well apart from the fact that I had the sniffles. It was annoying to say the least. I just wanted my nose to stop running; was that too much to ask? At one point I nearly dislocated my shoulder trying to get a handkerchief out of the back of my hydration vest. I blew my nose, then tucked the hanky into the strap of my bum bag, and at some point, without my realising it fell out, and I was back to sniffling again.

The next issue was gels. Stuart had suggested I consume half a gel at a time, starting at 4 km, but unfortunately, the opened sachet in my bum bag leaked everywhere and made everything sticky! My phone, my hands—it was a mess. I kept trying to lick my phone clean, but then it would just get sticky again! I must have looked like a crazy person, running around, licking my phone. *Never again.* As of my next run, I'd be switching to gummies. Much less messy!

My next issue was that my headphones stopped working. They just ran out of battery after about an hour and a half, even though I'd been sure they were completely charged!

Oh no! I thought. 'The next couple of hours are going to be TORTURE!' I hate running without something to listen to. It also meant I had to listen to my huffing and puffing and be reminded of how unfit I was. Margaret had given me the box and the receipt for the headphones, so I'd just have to exchange them for a new pair.

The new plan of run-walk intervals was going pretty well. Three minutes was a great amount of recovery time, and whereas last week I'd resorted to intervals once I'd become exhausted, I hadn't let it get to that point today. I was just a bit worried about the hills on the way back. It was just my luck that every hill seemed to coincide with a running interval, and with about 8 km to go, I started to get a bit tired. Not exhausted, but tired. My battery was wearing down.

When I got to the biggest hill on my route, I steeled myself for a tough time. It was a running interval, and I was determined to last the whole four minutes. Half-way up, I noticed I was out of breath. I probably wouldn't have been as in tune with myself if I'd had my headphones on. At the end of four minutes, I was beyond the out-of-breath stage, and I was gasping. Shallow, quick breathing.

I was having an asthma attack.

I couldn't remember the last time it had happened. I didn't even have an inhaler on me—I'd just never needed it before. It must have been the hay fever that had weakened my respiratory system.

I decided to put the intervals aside and walk the rest of the way. I had to look after my body and my lungs. I was able to maintain a fairly fast walking pace while still getting my breath back. I only had four kilometres to go, so I was optimistic that I'd maintain an average of less than 10 min/km. After a big walking break, I tried to run again, but the attempted burst of energy was short-lived. I had to walk.

I was proud of myself for seeing the run through and not giving up. Walking part of a 29 km run was better than not making the distance at all!

I needed to learn how to cope in the face of adversity. I wouldn't be able to give up on race day. As I rounded the last corner and only had a few blocks to go, I started jogging again. I was excited to finish up my longest run yet, save it on my Garmin, and check my pace.

I was relieved and happy to see that my average pace, despite all the walking, was nine minutes per km; 42 minutes ahead of the cut-off of seven hours if I kept up that pace for the actual marathon. I did notice that a few of those last kilometres were over the ten-minute average, though, so once I was in better health, I'd try to push myself through those intervals for a bit longer, as the further I walked, the more I'd slow my average pace down.

At this point, it's all looking do-able and realistic. I'll have to talk to my doctor about some preventative asthma medication and get a new small puffer to put in my bum bag or hydration vest. I'm so pumped for my first full week of the new plan, without those dreaded pace run Tuesdays—and with a lot more resting.

Time to put some Xs on that brand-new calendar!

Monday, 28 August 2023
Week 13, Day 1
20–30 Minutes of Recovery Exercise

Chris had the day off work today, so I didn't have to wake up alone in our bed. It can be hard being the partner of a baker, as almost every day he's up and out of the house hours before me, and I sometimes wish we could spend the morning waking up and having breakfast together.

It can also be a bit sad having to say goodnight to him at 8:15 p.m. every night.

Sometimes as he leans over and gives me a goodnight kiss, I say, 'I'll miss you,' and I mean it. There are times when it's nice to sit in the quiet after everyone has gone to bed and times when it's quite lonely. And times when Daisy's still up and won't go to sleep, and I wish that I could just crash.

Today Daisy was sleeping in, which gave Chris a chance to stay in bed while I got ready for work. It was nice just having him there. Being able to kiss him goodbye when it was time to go.

I felt positive about the day ahead and proud of myself for getting up and making it into work again without being depressed, anxious or burnt out. Just feeling normal and like I could function like a regular human being.

My student was in a good mood too. Mondays are often hard for autistic kids, as they must make that big transition from the weekend to the school week, and more often than not they come in at the start of the day feeling quite unsettled. Who am I kidding? Mondays can be hard for all of us! Unfortunately, his good moods can be as disruptive to the rest of the class as his meltdowns, as he gets excited and makes loud "happy sounds," which I barely notice anymore, but the teacher and other students find it distracting.

I completely forgot that tomorrow is a curriculum day, which means the kids will all be staying home while we do professional development. I thought

I'd still be doing playgroup, but Mum and Margaret both got text messages saying it would be cancelled. On the one hand, it's a little bit sad because I enjoy those sessions so much, but I'm not going to lie when I say that all staff members in every school look forward to curriculum days.

During my yard duty, and again as I drove home, I noticed what a nice sunny day it was, so I decided to spend my recovery exercise going for a walk with Chris and with Daisy in the pram—some nice family time. We walked and talked about the shows we'd been watching, and I brought up a little training conundrum I was having. Should I continue to run on the same long run route, with its hills (which seemed like unnecessary training for a flat course on race day), or should I do laps of the local neighbourhood, which would be flat and, therefore easier, but less pleasant and scenic and incredibly boring?

Both options had their pros and cons, and we both remarked that overtraining did have its benefits, as it meant I would find the marathon easier in comparison and I'd be more prepared. I also thought that days when my asthma and hay fever were bad, were probably good days to avoid those hills. I'd have to play it by ear.

Tuesday, 29 August 2023
Week 13, Day 2
45-60 Minutes of Strength Training

I was able to have a big sleep-in on purpose! I didn't have to be at work until 9:00 a.m., with no work to prepare and no playgroup room to set up. I didn't even have to pack lunch. On curriculum days our school provides lunch, usually fancy sandwiches and wraps, fried chicken, spring rolls and other delightful treats. One of the many reasons I love curriculum days. There's also no yard duty (so no going outside in the cold) and usually an early finish time.

Today, the school went all out. Not only did they provide lunch (chicken, chips, and salad), but they also provided morning tea. I'm not talking cheap plain biscuits; I'm talking Tim Tams, mint slices, and the good kind of chocolate chip cookies and Anzac biscuits.

The professional learning was mostly focused on student well-being and creating a sense of community in the classroom. There was also a segment on staff well-being and self-care, which often gets overlooked. I think the staff were embarrassed to talk about it, and we kind of pushed through it and glossed over it, in favour of moving on to the 'real stuff.' To me, it seemed tokenistic, but then I'm biased, as self-care has basically had to be the centre of my life—for me to stay sane and remain functional.

I made a point of wearing my workout clothes to school so that I could go straight to the gym after work. The gym on the way home wasn't my usual gym, where I feel completely comfortable and at home; it was the new, 'fancy' gym that my membership also covers, where I always feel a bit intimidated and out of place.

On the way there I started feeling tearful and overwhelmed, and I couldn't pinpoint any reason why I was feeling that way. I'd had an easy, pleasant day, which required hardly any strenuous thought or decision-making, and yet I felt spent, and in need of a breather, or some down-time.

I decided to park the car and sit down reading or scrolling through Facebook before going in. Instead, I just burst into a full-on torrent of tears—as if something earth-shattering or traumatic had happened. I just sat there blubbering for a while, still clueless as to what had caused such a breakdown, then pulled myself together and dragged myself inside.

I decided to put my bag in a locker, which I never do, but it seemed like the proper thing to do in this pristine, sterile monument of a building. I have an irrational fear of lockers. I get this anxiety that I won't be able to open or close them, or that I'll forget which locker I used. I also feel like my gym bag is sort of a security blanket that I like to keep in sight. I went through the process of locking and unlocking my locker several times, which involved scanning my membership fob, just to make sure I had a handle on the whole thing; then I reluctantly backed away out of the change rooms and into the glaringly bright fluorescent lights of the gym itself.

As I wandered into the workout area, I was immediately accosted by a severe-looking, uniformed woman who asked me if I had a towel with me. I confessed that I didn't, and she scolded me, 'No towel, no workout. We're enforcing it.' I said I'd be happy to buy one ('happy' was a strong and largely inaccurate word!), and she quickly dismissed me, saying they had some to give away but that this would be the 'last time.' She handed me one sternly.

Then I made my way over to where the yoga mats were and did some core work. I'm sure I've mentioned before that I hate it, so I thought I'd get it out of the way first up. When I went to use the machines, I felt awkward. Where do I even put my towel? Under my butt, on the machine? Or is it for wiping the sweat off my forehead? I don't sweat, and I always wipe the machines down afterwards with the wipes provided, so the towel just seemed superfluous. I went with placing it underneath me and set about trying my new workout tips from Stuart, my running coach.

The two main pointers he'd given me were to do my leg work one leg at a time, and to do my calf-raises on bent legs as well as straight. The one-legged thing was extremely difficult, and I felt so uncoordinated and awkward. And weak! I had to put the machine on its lowest weight setting, and my legs were trembling under the strain. I was incredibly self-conscious that people must be looking at me and judging me (which of course they weren't).

A couple of guys walked past, and the towel lady intercepted them. They assured her they had towels in their bags, which she looked at disapprovingly. 'Are you members?' she asked. They said no, and then she snapped, 'Just make sure you don't put your bags in the way of people,', and they promised not to. It was a weird request, as if they intended to put their bags right out in the gangway where anyone could trip over them. I was glad I'd used the lockers.

Just being in this somewhat unfamiliar space made me feel uneasy. It seemed like the sort of place where hard-core, young, Instagram-able gym junkies flocked. So pristine. So unlike the daggy old gym around the corner from my house where almost everyone seemed either old or overweight, just doing their best. The machines were so new that I felt scared I'd get them dirty or break them. I just wanted to get *out* of there.

But I forced myself to linger, using the upper body machines—the shoulder press (which I surprisingly handled like a boss), the chest press and the lat pull-down. They have some of the machines bizarrely close and facing each other, which felt oddly intimate. I tried not to make eye contact with anyone. I had no idea how long I'd been there—I hadn't looked at the time when I'd started, but surely it had been at least 45 minutes? It felt like an age.

I got out of there and went home to my family, where I showered with Chris while Mum looked after Daisy.

We'd agreed to go out to dinner with friends and I didn't feel completely keen on going, but I wasn't sure I wanted to stay home either. I just had this feeling—like I didn't know what I wanted. I usually try to look nice when I go out, but I just threw on any old thing, kissed Daisy goodbye, and headed out with Chris.

We were the first ones there, then gradually everyone else trickled in. The group we go out with are not close friends, just a meet-up type group with similar interests, and it's usually a table of about 20 people or more.

I'd decided to eat something healthy, after the sugar-fest at work, so I went for a salad with chickpeas and lamb cutlets.

I was seated next to a girl I'd met the previous week, and we had a nice chat about mental health. Bipolar disorder, borderline personality disorder and co-morbidities (the two often go hand in hand), and the minefield of applying for support from the National Disability Insurance Scheme (NDIS). We also talked about different types of therapies and how hard it is to find an appropriate psychologist who doesn't cost an arm and a leg. I recommended my clinic, as they bulk-bill, but admitted I wasn't sure if they practice the type of therapy she needs.

Then it got to a point where conversations were happening on either side of us that we weren't involved in and we were sat awkwardly in the middle. I felt super uncomfortable and wanted to leave, but it took a while for Chris to agree with me, even though he just had his head in his phone. Eventually, we left with the good (and true) excuse that Chris had to be up early.

Wednesday, 30 August 2023
Week 13, Day 3
Rest Day

This morning, I woke up feeling completely brain-dead. It was like I'd forgotten to plug in my mental battery charger or something. I just couldn't think. There was no way I was going to be able to function and make simple judgements and decisions at work.

My mum tried to get me to get out of bed in the hopes that I'd snap out of it, but I stood firm. I was staying in bed, and not even an earthquake would move me. I spewed forth some feeble excuses about hay fever, stomach troubles, night sweats and lack of sleep, all of which were true except the latter, but I avoided elaborating on the brain fog. She could never seem to fathom that it couldn't be easily reversed with a little attitude change and some magically summoned positivity.

She brought Daisy into the room, thinking she would cheer me up, but Daisy just fell asleep next to me and didn't wake up until 10 a.m. Up until that point I hadn't even gone to the toilet, had a sip of water or even looked at my phone messages that I'd heard beeping. I picked Daisy up and wordlessly and mindlessly carried her into the kitchen, where I dumped her in front of my mother, not even making eye contact. Then I turned around and promptly went back to bed.

I felt guilty. Of course, I felt guilty. I was worrying my poor mother. I was being childish. I was shirking all *normal* adult responsibility. As the next couple of hours dragged on, I knew I should get up and eat something so I could take my antidepressant, but the thought of dealing with the intense joyful energy of my daughter held me back. I couldn't face her. I couldn't handle her. I couldn't smile and laugh and talk and kiss and hug and play.

I just couldn't.

After a while I heard the door open as Chris came home from work. I emerged from bed, only to find that Mum and Daisy had left the house and gone somewhere. I'd thought things had become quiet.

I'd been overheating and sweating profusely under the stifling covers, so I had a shower to freshen up. I was crying. I tried to eat some lunch, but the thought of food disgusted me. I shovelled it in my mouth anyway as huge droplets of tears landed in my bowl of chicken and vegetables—I couldn't take my antidepressant on an empty stomach.

When Mum and Daisy got home, Mum looked at me and said, 'You look like you've been crying.'

'Of course I've been crying,' I responded.

Mum was still surprised and a bit confused. 'Did you forget to call work this morning?'

'No.'

She prepared to leave as she had an appointment, while I called my GP and two other clinics before finding a doctor who could see me for a medical certificate and some help with my hay fever and asthma. I could tell Mum felt guilty leaving me but she had to go. She was already running late. She reminded me that she'd be going away for another week on Friday and pleaded with me to 'stay well.' I recognised the mum guilt. I was an aficionado by now.

I told Chris I was feeling stressed about not having written in days and my overdue books, and he joked, 'Fuck off! Go to the library.' I was in no mood for jokes and scolded him for telling me to fuck off. He apologised and said he just thought it would be a better place for me to concentrate without 'this one,' indicating Daisy.

I felt terrible for leaving my child and even worse for being relieved about it as I drove to the library to get some work done. I returned a pile of unread books that had been sitting on my nightstand and found a little corner bench where I perched on a stool and opened my laptop. I managed about a third of the work I had to get done before I noticed the time and had to rush off to the doctor.

He gave me a medical certificate and some scripts for an inhaler and a nasal spray, and I found a chair in the chemist, pulled out my laptop once more and tried to get in some more writing as I waited for my scripts. It wasn't enough. It was too late in the day to find a café to sit in and finish as I so longed to, so I just made my way back to the car and drove home.

I was still in a useless state. My nose was dripping like a tap, and I couldn't tell if it was hay fever, a cold or the fact that I'd been crying. I tried to assess the dinner situation and just threw my hands up in the air over it. I couldn't cook, and I could tell Chris didn't want to either. I ordered a sickly, greasy burger and some disgusting loaded fries and couldn't finish it all.

Daisy went to sleep far too early. She hadn't had a day nap after sleeping 'til 10 a.m., and I knew it meant she'd wake up at an ungodly hour in the night.

There wasn't much we could do about it. We tried keeping her up, but she was floppy in Chris's arms and couldn't keep her eyes open.

We found some shows to watch for once, and I tuned in and out, reading a short story draft that Christoph had sent me on my phone. It was only a first draft, so it was full of typos, but it was good.

Just after 8 p.m. Chris had no choice but to say goodnight, and I admitted that I didn't want him to go to bed and leave me alone. I could tell he felt bad, but he did what he had to do, and I pulled out my laptop one last time to finish what I'd started at the library.

Thursday, 31 August 2023
Week 13, Day 4
Rest Day

Today is International Overdose Awareness Day. I wouldn't have known had someone not posted about it in my bipolar Facebook group. It's hard to think about, but it bears contemplating. I grimly remember each overdose that punctuated my past with shame over the misery and pain inflicted on my loved ones.

All those pills. The resignation. Convincing myself that there was *no* other option. Being found. Waking up. The life support. The tubes down my throat. The fear of having done irreversible physical damage to my body that I'd have to live with for the rest of my life.

I've been *so* lucky so many times. And so many times I've looked back and thought the luck was undeserved—that it would have been better for everyone had I died. I think of the years I lived in limbo, wanting nothing more than to end it all. The wasted years when I felt like a burden and a leaden weight on the world and the people around me. The shame of having had no coping mechanisms and no sense of survival, to the point where downing whole bottles of pills were my knee-jerk reaction to any kind of adversity.

It's a part of me and my personal history that I have to accept and can't deny, but in order to live the full, rich life that I've finally carved out for myself, I have to detach myself from it, just like the cutting of the umbilical cord. I've had to emerge, like a phoenix from the ashes, anew, changed, altered, improved. An entirely new person. My life has been re-booted and it's unrecognisable. A total overhaul and facelift. A new cast of characters.

This house that I live in, this family, this darling baby. All gifts. Proof that things can change for anyone. That pain is not forever. Anyone can rewrite their story. I try to instil this notion for other suicidal people who reach out to my online communities. You never know what could be waiting around the corner. But I know it's almost impossible to believe. I wouldn't have believed it. I wish I could do more.

Today I googled a list of celebrities who have died from overdoses: River Phoenix, Mac Miller, Heath Ledger, Prince, Michael Jackson, Phillip Seymour-Hoffman, Dolores O'Riordan, Judy Garland, Marilyn Monroe. The list goes on. Is public awareness making a difference? Will talking about it change things?

I'm so afraid of romanticising suicide. When you're in that moment of despair, it's hard to see it as anything other than appealing, but it's not. It's ugly. It's damaging. I think of Chris coming home to a bedroom covered in vomit after my last attempt. How with everything he was going through, he had to clean that up. He had to mop up that floor. He had to soak and wash those sheets. He had to face that stark reality that I had carelessly tried to check out of. After hearing what had happened, I'm sure all he wanted to do was just collapse into a comfy bed, but I'd even ruined *that* for him.

This day has meaning. It has gravity. I'm trying to honour it. I'm trying to step forward and take my place in the narrative and the complicated, problematic landscape. I am fine now. I am happy. People say 'Hi' to me every day and see a person who belongs and deserves to be here—someone worthy, needed, and loved.

And it's true. I am.

But I've taken pills and tried to kill myself. Many times. Countless times. It's not just nameless, faceless, homeless junkies. It's that person who you like or even love, who smiles and laughs like a normal human being. They go through this. Sometimes they fail, but too many times they succeed. They leave giant holes in the fabric of the universe, the unknowable potential of what and who they could have been.

If I did it, anyone can.

The only thing I can think of is the power of saying it out loud, and therefore making it real. 'I'm suicidal.'

It's a fact, a problem, an illness. If we start to think of it like cancer, which affects so many normal, seemingly healthy people and which we immediately treat with measures like chemo and surgery with compassion, maybe we can act.

I have my action plan. My immediate go-to list for times of crisis. A plan other than the finality of that fatal full-stop. The semi-colon is my new reality. And I'll never do it again. Never.

I believe there's nothing a person can't come back from. Bring it right back to survival. What do I need to do in this moment to survive? And there's always something. The first step is just to put those pills back in the drawer, close it and walk away.

People have begged me to make them a solemn promise never to do it again, and I've broken that promise.

You need to make that promise to yourself. If you're reading this, and you've ever been tempted by the idea that an overdose is the simple, easy way out, make that promise to yourself. Imagine letting go of that powerlessness and replacing it with strength and fortitude.

The choice to live is the most powerful choice you can make.

Friday, 1 September 2023
Week 13, Day 5
45–60 Minute Training Run

This morning I woke up with a resounding mantra pounding in my head 'I can't cope.' As I woke up, 'I can't cope' were the words I said to myself. As Daisy woke up, and I changed her nappy, 'I can't cope.' I went about these bare minimum actions, like breakfast for both of us and taking my medication, just crying and hyperventilating. I just wanted to curl up in a ball in the corner of the couch and cry all morning. I thought about calling a friend or a hotline for support. Maybe I needed someone to talk to. I thought about reaching out to my bipolar group. I thought about calling my mother-in-law and saying, 'Please come over, I can't do this.'

In the end, I felt that all of those things would only make me feel worse, more desperate, and isolated, so I decided to flip the narrative on its head.

So, little voice, you think I can't cope? Just watch me cope! Watch me cope like a boss!

I was still hyperventilating and crying a little, but I was determined to get some things done around our bombsite of a house. I cleared the kitchen table a little, bit by bit. I put the dishes away, also in dribs and drabs between doing other things. I put the washing away. I picked up Daisy's toys and books off the loungeroom floor. I did the dishes, took out the nappy bin, the recycling bin, and washed and hung out more clothes, plus the sheets and pyjamas I'd soaked through from another bout of night sweats. I put fresh sheets on the bed. In other words, I coped.

My asthma was still bad, so I decided to do a steam inhalation. I boiled the kettle, poured the boiling water into a bowl, and hovered my face over it, with a towel covering my head to trap the steam. It didn't feel like it was working or helping. I tried to put my face closer, then accidentally dipped my chin into the scalding water and burned the heck out of it. I touched my chin and felt a huge blister. When I went to dry my face, I broke the skin and looked into the mirror to see a huge red welt on my face. I felt like such an idiot.

I was so frustrated about my asthma. When I went to the doctor on Wednesday (who was not my usual doctor, by the way) he prescribed a reliever inhaler and told me to take it four times a day, as well as before and after exercise, and also gave me a nasal spray for the hay fever. It seemed like strange advice. My understanding of asthma treatment plans is that you're supposed to take a preventative every day and just use the reliever for attacks.

All day yesterday I had trouble breathing, so I went to see another doctor last night. I said that my asthma had been triggered by hay fever and that I'd like a preventative puffer to take over the spring period, and I mentioned that I was training for a marathon. He just looked me up and down and said, 'The problem is running. You need to try some gentler exercise.' I said I'd been running for three years without asthma bothering me, but by that point he seemed impatient for the appointment to be over. He had already made up his mind not to give me a preventer. I was so mad!

Today I reluctantly decided to give running another go for the first time since my asthma attack on Sunday. I still wasn't feeling 100%, but I was determined to try. I took my puffer about 15 minutes before I went out and I felt OK. I ran at a moderate pace—just what I was aiming for, and didn't struggle or have an asthma attack. When I finished my run I took my puffer again, just in case, but I don't think I needed it. I decided I'd do my 21.1 km on Sunday but stay close to home and just go around the block, avoiding hills. That way, if I have an attack, I won't be in the middle of nowhere.

Saturday, 2 September 2023
Week 13, Day 6
Rest Day

I was trying to sleep in this morning when I got a flood of texts from Margaret. I decided I'd have to have a talk to her about how I'm not very good at handling early morning text messages. She wakes up at 6:30 a.m. every morning, and after a late-night Daisy and I are often not up until 9:30 a.m. or even ten on a particularly bad day.

She wanted to get together and have the kids play, taking advantage of the sunshine, but when I summoned the energy to respond, I said something like, 'I'm still a zombie right now; I'll call you when I enter the land of the living.' It took a while to get my act together. I had to sort out breakfast and housework, and by the time Daisy and I were ready, George was already having his morning nap.

Daisy was keen to go outside, so I took her out the front and pushed her around on her bike. I noticed the neighbours were home, so I invited the kids to come and play with Daisy. They drew with chalk, explored the gardens of the unit complex and got the bubble machine going, which Daisy always loves. When Chris finished work and came up the garden path, Daisy's face lit up, and she ran to him as fast as her little legs would carry her, and he enveloped her in a big hug.

Chris was keen to go to the shops as he was craving burritos (typical Chris). I invited Margaret and George to come, but she encouraged us to just have some family time. She wanted to catch up when we got back, but surprise, surprise, Daisy was asleep! She said her husband and George had gone out and she was just out the front of her house, chilling in the sun. I decided to join her, and it was nice to just relax and have some girl time. While the Spring weather has wreaked havoc with my hayfever, I do love some sunshine. I'm like a lizard; I just bask in it.

When the boys got back, George just looked at us with wide eyes and said, 'Daisy?' We told him Daisy wasn't here, and he just looked so confused and betrayed. The poor thing! He didn't know what was going on! I messaged Chris so he could ring us when Daisy woke up, and she was awake, so we all went to the park.

Surprisingly, for such a nice day, we had the playground all to ourselves. We pushed the kids on the swings, watched them run around, and Daisy was brave enough to go down the slide a couple of times by herself. At one point Daisy was on the swing and George ran up and shouted, 'Daisy! Come!' and it was the cutest thing I'd ever seen. There was a nice picnic table to sit at, and the kids sat down and had a snack. It was so nice I didn't want to leave, but we had to go and get ready for a birthday party.

I went home, quickly wrapped a present and drove with Daisy to see the birthday girl, my friend Cherisse, who I hadn't seen in far too long. She hadn't seen Daisy since before she was walking, so she was super excited to see how much she'd grown.

The party was fun; we watched karaoke videos on YouTube and sang along. One of Cherisse's friends is a seven-time marathoner, so we had lots to talk about. His advice to me was, 'Never run when you're tired. Only run when you're fresh as a daisy.' I thought if I followed that rule, I would never run at all, but it was a nice sentiment!

Sunday, 3 September
Week 13, Day 7
Long Run, 21.1 km (Half-Marathon)

I woke up feeling so exhausted. *Not long run day! Please tell me it's not long run day!* Daisy woke up crying, and I brought her into bed with me and gave her a bottle. She was still thirsty, so I gave her a second bottle, then we both lay there, her sucking her little thumb and me resting my eyes, neither of us wanting to get up.

Eventually we plied ourselves out of bed and started getting ready for the day. My inner monologue was particularly dramatic today. 'I hate everything,' over and over, then, out of nowhere, 'I wish I was dead.' Where did that thought come from? I've talked to my psychiatrist about having these thoughts and feelings in the morning, and she's basically told me it's not a bipolar or depression thing, it's just part of having a negative personality.

A normal person would have a reasonable thought like, *I don't feel like running 21 km today.* That's perfectly valid. Every runner feels that way sometimes. But for me that somehow spirals quickly to wishing death upon myself. Luckily, I know how ludicrous that all is, and I'm able to sort of laugh about it—but it's still concerning.

Despite having to navigate the doomsday self-talk, the reasonable part of me knew that I'd feel great once I was out there running, and of course, I was right. Running locally meant there was no deafening traffic, so I could listen to my eBook, which made it all rather enjoyable.

The author of my running book talked about his school days and how terrible he'd been at P.E., and I realised how interesting it was that I'd been the same.

I've talked about being an ordinary person doing an extraordinary thing with this marathon, but I don't think I've even come close to getting across just how un-sporty I've always been. In both primary and secondary school, I'd been completely useless in all team sports. I couldn't catch a ball. I couldn't throw a ball. I couldn't even kick a ball. I virtually failed all my fitness tests. In the end, my physical education teacher gave up on me and let me sit out just about every lesson.

My only saving grace had been my ability to be a good sport and 'give it a go' on School Sports Day. We had a system where everyone who entered an event got one house point just for trying, and I had a tremendous amount of team spirit. Knowing full well I'd lose every single time, I entered every event, coming last and getting my house point, with my fellow yellow house supporters cheering me on like I was Cathy Freeman! At the end of the day, I always ended up with more points for my house than the people who were coming first in their favourite events! I remembered all this fondly as I made my way around and around the block.

Every now and then, I'd notice something like a nature strip of freshly cut grass or a wattle tree, and my heart would pound as I thought of my hay fever, but my airways decided to co-operate. We'd been blessed with another day of springtime sunshine, and my mood was great. I was a little bored with the whole 'running in circles' thing, but not enough for it to feel unpleasant. I was aware that the Melbourne Marathon would finish with six laps of the same streets, so it seemed like a good idea to prepare for a little boredom.

I felt great after my run. I still had plenty of energy. Nothing was sore. No blisters. I marvelled at how far I had come. How epic and strenuous my half-marathon race had been back in July. Now, a half-marathon felt like nothing. Just a little jog. Maybe it was the three-minute walking breaks that my coach had suggested. They made a big difference to my energy levels.

I checked my average pace, and it was still nine minutes per kilometre, giving me that extra 42 minutes of 'wiggle room' if I had to slow down on race day.

Monday, 4 September 2023
Week 14, Day 1
Recovery Exercise—Yoga

I woke up full of dread and anxiety. This happens every day now. I'm so sick of being like this. I was crying, and it was hard to breathe. I felt like I needed to stay in bed. But I'd already had one sick day last week, so I had no choice but to try to pull myself together.

They talk about waking up on the wrong side of bed, and I feel like that happens to me every day. I wish there was something I could do to change that, but I'm probably doing all that I can already. Putting on a brave face. Pushing through. Pretending I'm okay. I don't know what the solution is.

Maybe I need to come up with some strong positive affirmations and force myself to say them when I wake up. In the past, positive affirmations haven't worked. I'm just not good at them. It's hard for me to believe in what I'm saying. I sort of say little things to myself in a quiet voice once or twice. Things like, 'You can do this. You're capable. You've done this a hundred times before.' But it doesn't remove the lump in my throat. I'm barely able to hold in the tears.

This morning, I was so bad I had to take a Valium. Chris was still in bed, so I got out the key and opened the portable safe where the medications are kept. I took one pill and worried that it might not be enough. I grabbed an extra pill and searched everywhere for my little pillbox so that I could take it with me to work, but I couldn't find it anywhere. In the end, I just put it back in the Valium bottle and thought for a second, *Should I just take the bottle with me?* Then, the thought crossed my mind that I couldn't trust myself not to take the whole bottle in a moment of weakness. That's a scary thought. I hadn't had that feeling since before Daisy was born. I've seen so many posts in bipolar forums of mums saying that they'd just end it all if it wasn't for their kids, and been so glad I've never felt that way. It worries me that I'm having these kinds of thoughts. I don't know how long I can cope with feeling like this every single morning. It seems like there's no end to it.

I was hoping the breakfast radio on the drive to work would distract me and put me in a better mood. I was just oscillating between crying and trying to take deep breaths and noticing the blurriness from the tear stains on my glasses. As I got closer and closer to work, I panicked more and more. Was the drive nearly over? Why wasn't I feeling better? Literally, right around the corner from school, I was still crying. Would I have to sit in the car park and sob until I could pull myself together?

In the end, I didn't, but I tried to think of a contingency plan if I was struggling. How would I respond to people asking how I was? In Norway they say, 'Up and not crying.' That was a good one, but I felt like I had to elaborate by saying, 'But barely.'

Luckily no-one asked me how I was. I had decided I would say to my classroom teacher that I needed to step out for a few minutes to take some deep breaths if things got bad (he knows I have bipolar and is supportive), but we had a relief teacher. There goes that option, I thought.

By the end of the first lesson, I was in a good enough mental state not only to get through the day but also to do a good job. My student had been jumping up and down in his chair, so I'd taken him out of the classroom for some physical activity. It occurred to me that one of my strengths as an Education Support worker was being attuned to my students' needs and having an arsenal of solutions to cater to them and get them back on track.

All my panic from the morning was gone. The sky was not falling. I was coping, functioning, and succeeding! My brain was working perfectly fine, and I was able to plan, teach, multitask, provide occupational therapy, and do all the things that were required of me.

At the start of the day, I'd been worried that there were two whole weeks left of school, or for me, six days, and that felt like forever. Now, I was feeling like it would be a good couple of weeks if every day was like today.

The weather today was very 'Melbourne.' We're known for having four seasons in one day—*Crowded House* even wrote a song about it! On my way to work, I'd had to turn the air conditioning on in the car because it was so sunny, and by the time I left work, the sky was oppressively dark, and it was windy, rainy and muggy.

For my recovery exercise I'd been thinking of going for a run, but I didn't feel like going outside in all of that. Instead, I decided to check the schedule at my gym for a yoga class. There was one at 6 p.m., so I booked myself in and asked Chris to make dinner early so that we could eat at around five and I could get there nice and early.

I was the first one into the yoga studio, and I noticed that the heater wasn't working, so I went to reception and asked them to turn it on. When I got back, two other ladies were setting up their mats and other equipment, and I asked if the Monday class was hard. They said there was a bit of a mix of standing and sitting poses but that it was fairly easy.

When the instructor came in, I recognised her as someone I knew and liked, and she started us with some easy resting poses, lying on the bolster releasing all the muscles and opening the back. Then we did some of my favourite back-twisting stretches, and I felt relaxed and present, focusing on lifting my posture and deepening the stretch. We spent quite a bit of time on the legs, which was perfect for me the day after a run.

Then she mentioned the word 'balancing' and I audibly let out an 'Oh no.' I think the instructor was a bit shocked, and she asked, 'Are you okay?' and I replied with embarrassment, 'I have terrible balance,' and she assured me that it was fine and that I could move over to the wall and use the wall for support. I did okay and didn't wobble around like a Jenga tower at the end of a game! I felt serene and composed—like a bit of a pro, to be honest!

When the class was nearing the end, she said, 'Now we're going to do a bit of core work.' I restrained myself from repeating another 'Oh no,' but I'm pretty sure I groaned. But the other ladies did too, so I'm not the only one who hates core work!

All three of us struggled and fumbled through the pose with total inelegance, wobbling and collapsing, then trying to compose ourselves and resume the position. None of us were able to extend our legs out to where the teacher had hers, and when the torture was over, the teacher was kind but a little patronising—'You all did well!'

Tuesday, 5 September 2023
Week 14, Day 2
45–60 Minutes of Strength Training

A miracle!! I woke up this morning feeling fine. Nothing negative coming from my pesky brain. Just something like, *Oh, it's 7:30. I suppose I should get up in a minute*, like a normal person. Could I be cured? Have I matured overnight? Have I tapped into some rational part of my grey matter that was lying there dormant all along? Whatever it is, it doesn't matter; I'm just glad to be back!

It was an easy day at work today. In the morning, there was a playgroup, and then there was a special morning tea.

The class I work with, the grade 3/4s, had gone on an excursion until midday, so that gave me an extra 20 minutes after recess to photocopy resources for the day and get everything ready. I decided to be brave and try a maths activity that my student had previously grown frustrated with and given up on, this time using concrete materials to assist with his learning. I'd just take a deep breath and go through it all slowly and patiently. If he screamed or banged the table, I would just abort and calm him down with one of his favourite activities.

Speaking of his favourite activities, we seem to have lost one of his Lego sets; one that I had paid for with my own money! I've been searching high and low for it, going through his cupboard and going through it again, and I've asked everyone he's been working with, and no one has any idea where it is. This set was his favourite—with instructions to make a robot, a dinosaur and a fighter jet. They were more advanced than his other Lego kits, which meant they kept him occupied for longer and challenged him more. I'm so annoyed.

After my fruitless Lego search, the kids returned from the excursion and ate their lunch. They had a fill-in specialist teacher, which happens once a term during planning week, so as a treat, she had them watch a movie. That took up most of the day, so I put aside the work I'd prepared, ready for tomorrow.

After today, there are only four more school days until the holidays. I'm powering through these working days and kicking goals. The sessions aren't feeling like they're dragging on, and I'm not feeling at a loss in terms of what work to prepare or second-guessing myself about how good or bad I am at my job. I feel secure in myself, and it's a nice, comfortable place to be.

After work, I went straight to the gym. I was back at my regular gym, the gym where I feel most comfortable and I don't get confronted over whether I have a towel or where to put my bag.

I got in a good balance of upper body and leg work today and got that awful core stuff over with right off the bat. The one-legged leg-presses and calf-raises were challenging, but I enjoyed working so hard. I felt less uncoordinated than I did last week.

I noticed some teenagers hanging out together and working out. The girls had their long hair out and flowing down their backs, and it made me inwardly chuckle. No one wears their hair loose to the gym unless you're a pubescent girl trying to impress the boys.

I never went to the gym as a teenager. Come to think of it, I never lived anywhere near a gym, so it wasn't an option. But I have no memory of ever hearing my classmates talk about going to the gym or working out. Maybe it was because all my friends were performing arts students, or maybe the '90s was just a different time when social media was non-existent, and body-consciousness was less rampant. I think I'd be okay with Daisy having a gym membership in her teens if we emphasised that it's about being strong and healthy—and not an obsessive focus on looking a certain way.

Wednesday, 6 September 2023
Week 14, Day 3
Rest Day

You wouldn't believe it, but I had another morning where I woke up with not a single anxious or depressed thought in my brain! I woke up 20 minutes before my alarm, and stayed in bed for those 20 minutes, just slowly waking up and getting ready to get up. I had a drink, went to the toilet, and let the kettle boil while I got dressed to save a bit of time.

As I drove the familiar route to work, I marvelled at and appreciated feeling so *good* two days in a row. There had to be a formula or some optimal conditions. What was different about today and yesterday?

For starters, I haven't had night sweats for two days in a row. When I wake up soaking wet, it's hard to get out of bed, as it's one thing to be wet, but being wet and cold is even worse.

Another issue in the mornings is waking up after having nightmares or disturbing dreams.

Last week, there was one morning when a dream had brought up all sorts of buried trauma that I hadn't thought about in years.

I dreamed of an ex-boyfriend from my teen years who had been a compulsive liar, who suddenly disappeared and wasn't there for me after my parents split up. Then I'd been raped by an older man, all in a short space of time. He'd just vanished off the face of the earth, and I couldn't get in touch with him for months. When I finally tracked him down and got a chance to speak with him, he explained that he'd felt angry and betrayed by me for having slept with somebody else, even though I'd been raped.

Dreaming about all this had left me panicking, and I couldn't bring myself out of the past, feeling as though it was all suddenly happening again. I was bawling my eyes out in my PTSD (Post-Traumatic Stress Disorder) moment; I didn't even think of doing a safe place meditation, a technique that my psychologist had taught me.

In the past, my psychologist has led me through some guided meditations aimed at addressing trauma, but it involves a commitment to daily meditation to make it work.

Each day, you meditate for roughly ten minutes, picturing yourself in a place where you feel calm, comfortable, safe and protected. You go through each detail of your 'safe place' in your mind's eye: the sights, smells, sounds, temperature, etc. For me, it's a secluded beach in San Remo called Shelley Beach, where every inch of the sand is covered in white shells. Wavy and windy, with cool air thick with salt spray. When things were bad for me, back in 2020 and 2021, I was arriving to work ten minutes early every day and doing a safe place meditation, sitting in the car park and 'visiting' Shelley Beach before going inside.

In terms of trauma, the purpose of building a strong sense of this 'safe place' serves as a basis for revisiting and reframing traumatic situations and moments from the past.

You form a clear picture in your mind of yourself in that place and time of trauma, feeling all the feelings and thinking all the thoughts you had. This can be difficult and painful. Then you picture your current self, visiting that former self and taking her by the hand and guiding her to your 'safe place,' which is already so familiar in your head. Ideally, the process provides a sense of resolution, but it does take work.

Maybe it's time to start working on my mind again the way I've been working on my body. I've got to find a healthy way to deal with those sorts of dreams so that they don't end up affecting me for the whole day.

But I digress, back to today. Two days in a row of waking up in a healthy state of mind is significant. It means that these terrible feelings aren't endless. They aren't inevitable. It means that on those bad mornings, I can take courage in the knowledge that there are, in fact, better days ahead. A couple of weeks of feeling terrible almost seems worth it, or at least more bearable, when I can go for two whole days like this where I feel positive, capable and grateful.

Thursday, 7 September 2023
Week 14, Day 4
45-Minute Easy Run

I'm on a healthy streak! *Mentally* healthy, I mean! No anxiety, no depression and no dread when I woke up this morning. Unfortunately, I got a phone call from my stepmother, Val, with some troubling news. Dad had fallen off a ladder yesterday and broken nine ribs and one vertebra. She said he'd gone to the Wonthaggi Hospital, but they'd transferred him to The Alfred and that he was in intensive care, but she said, 'Don't worry. He's fine. He can walk and everything.'

I guess I didn't have time to process her words and what they meant, because I'd only just woken up, but the last bit—the 'he's fine' bit was the main bit I took in, so I wasn't overly worried. Anyway, I had to go to swimming, so I had no time to stress about Dad, as I had to get ready and get us to the pool. I sent Dad a quick jokey text, saying, 'No more ladders!' before I left the house.

Daisy was the only one at swimming today. It felt a bit weird, to be honest. It's the second time she's been the only one there. It was still nice though, and Daisy had fun, but just when we were about to finish up, disaster struck.

Imelda, the instructor, got out a Bluey doll, and it was exactly the same as the treasured Bluey doll Daisy has at home. *Oh no!* I thought. *Daisy's never going to want to give that back! She'll think it's hers!* I was right. When it was time to finish up the lesson and give back the doll, she was having none of it. She cried and screamed at the injustice of it all. I kept telling her that her Bluey was at home, but of course, she didn't understand. Luckily Daisy always calms down pretty quickly, and once I got her dressed in the change room, she was right as rain.

Just as we were heading to the car, I got a call from Margaret saying she was at Waverley Gardens shopping centre having breakfast and did we want to come and meet up with her? I said that we were still covered in chlorine from the pool and Daisy had no shoes and socks, but I thought *fuck it*, and instead of going home we went straight to the shopping centre.

While we sat in the café, I told Margaret I was worried about my Dad. If he was 'fine,' why was he in intensive care, and why had he been taken all the way to the city from Wonthaggi? Dad has a history of being, let's say, not exactly forthcoming about his health. He had previously had a heart attack and never told any of us about it. I wouldn't put it past him to be in a seriously critical condition and telling Val to protect me from the truth so as not to worry me.

When we went home, I rang The Alfred to ask about visiting hours. The lady on the phone said that Dad was allowed to have two visits a day, of two people at a time, and that the visiting hours were pretty much all day. Then she paused. 'I'm sorry, you're not on the visitor's list. Valda Swallow's in charge of that; you'll have to talk to her about putting you on the list.' So I texted Val to see about her putting me on the list and went about my day.

It got to the evening, and I still hadn't heard back from Val. I got a text from Dad saying, 'I'll call you later.' Something was up. My mind was ticking over, and I was spiralling. Why hadn't they just asked Dad to put me on the visitor's list? Had he been unconscious? Why hadn't Val gotten back to me? Was that text even from Dad, or was Val using his phone? Yes. I was that paranoid.

I googled 'complications from broken ribs.' I shouldn't have done that! Ruptured and collapsed lung, ruptured spleen, ruptured arteries and internal bleeding.... Now I was worried. It got to 10 p.m., and I still hadn't heard from Dad. At this point in my mind Dad was in hospital dying, and I wasn't going to get a chance to visit him before he died.

I called my brother Pierre. He didn't know anything either but told me not to panic. Too late. In the end I sent a long email to my brother Ricky in LA. He was the one Dad had told about his heart attack, so maybe he could extract some information that the rest of us couldn't.

With the time difference, it was way too early in LA to call Ricky, but I texted him to call me when he woke up and not to worry about the time difference.

Friday, 8 September 2023
Week 14, Day 5
40-Minute Pace Run

Daisy and I both had a bit of a sleep in, which was nice. Again, no thoughts of existential dread. Had a normal, uneventful morning pottering about the house and getting things done.

I was in the kitchen when my phone rang—it was my Dad, but before I could answer it, the ringing stopped. I was about to call him back when I got a text message from him. I went to open the message and saw that it was a voice recording. I pressed play and immediately realised he'd clicked record by accident and could just hear him and the nurse or doctor talking to each other.

I heard a voice saying, 'I want you to roll on your side and try to get up for me. Does that feel ok?' I then heard Dad's voice saying, 'Yeah, that's fine.' I listened for groaning or shouts of pain. Nothing. Then the nurse asked, 'Did you sleep OK? Was the pain OK?' and again, Dad saying it was fine. Then the nurse asked, 'Is it more painful to lie on one side than the other?' and Dad replied that the left side was a bit worse, and that it was more comfortable on the right side. Then the message cut out. I breathed a huge sigh of relief. Dad sounded OK.

Soon after, Dad rang me and we talked about me visiting. He apologised for the mix up yesterday, and in his humorous style he said, 'They call it intensive care, but it's more like intensive prison. They don't let anyone in or out.' I said I was busy until the afternoon, but that I'd try to get there with Daisy a bit later in the day.

It was Margaret's birthday, and she had her friend Juliet from Sydney with her. She had a simple birthday wish to be with Juliet, George, Daisy, and me at the new burger place at Waverley Gardens and then watch the kids play.

A bit before 11 a.m., she called me to say they were at the shopping centre, so I got a few things together (including her present), and we made our way over.

Both she and George were so happy to see Daisy. I carried Daisy over to George's pram so she could greet him, and she just reached in and started gently stroking his face. Those two love each other so much.

Juliet had been getting her nails done, and when she finished, she came over and joined us. I gave her a big hug and said it was nice to meet her and that I'd heard a lot about her. She said the same about me.

Margaret explained that she and Juliet had known each other for 20 years.

We made our way over to the new burger place—'Burgertory'—and took a seat in one of the booths. The whole time we were in the restaurant Daisy was on one side of us and George was on the other. Daisy was shouting 'George!' and he was shouting back 'Daisy!' and it went on all through lunch. I felt sorry for the people around us. I was a bit embarrassed to be one of 'those families,' who interrupt a perfectly nice, relaxing lunch for everyone else.

We had to get the kids out of there and off to somewhere they could play, so we up and left before poor Margaret and Juliet could even finish their chips. We ordered some dessert set off for the play area. Finally, the kids could run feral!

After a while Daisy was showing signs that she was tired—rubbing her eyes and getting a bit sooky, so we went home. Once we were home, I thought about what to do in terms of visiting Dad. Either we could go now, and I could let Daisy sleep in the car on the way, or I could put Daisy down for a nap at home, and I could go later.

I confessed to Chris that I was exhausted and wouldn't mind sleeping while Daisy had a sleep, so I went to lie down and just crashed. I lay there and slept for hours, and by the time I woke up, it was too late to visit Dad.

We had some dinner, then I decided to go to the gym to do my 45-minute run on the treadmill. I *hate* treadmills, and I can't remember the last time I ran on one. I much preferred being outside, but it was too late (and too dark) to go out.

I hopped on and started doing my five-minute warm-up. I set the treadmill to a nice, brisk, walking pace. I'd never used these treadmills before, and they had a screen showing a virtual walk/run through a hilly, rocky landscape, which looked like it was possibly filmed in Colorado. I *wasn't* hating it; it wasn't that bad!

When it was time to run, I had no idea about pace. I thought I was running at a moderate pace, but it was hard to say. Running outside was so different. There was a lady a couple of treadmills down from me who looked to be doing an identical work-out. I fell into stride with her, and it almost felt like we were companions, training together.

I finished at virtually the exact same time as the other lady I'd been pacing with, and as we were both leaving the gym, I struck up a conversation with her. 'Are you training for a race?' I asked her. 'Yes,' she said. 'The Melbourne Marathon Festival on October the 15. I'm doing the 10 km.'

'Me too!' I said. 'I'm doing the marathon.'

'I'm just getting back into running after having my baby. She's 16 months old.'

'Me too!' I exclaimed. 'My daughter's 20 months old.' We wished each other good luck and parted ways as she chimed, 'I'm sure we'll see each other again. My name is Rahini.'

'My name is Jacqui,' I replied. In the car driving home, I realised we probably wouldn't see each other again, as I wasn't usually in the gym at that time on a Friday.

Saturday, 9 September 2023
Week 14, Day 6
Rest Day

This morning, I got up nice and early, ready to volunteer for Parkrun. I waited for Chris's mum, Tonia, to arrive and look after Daisy. I waited. And waited. And waited. She never came. I had to message the volunteer chat and apologise profusely for not showing up. I texted Tonia to see if she was OK, and she'd simply forgotten. She felt bad.

Daisy had a huge sleep in and it gave me some time to write. I enjoyed a cup of tea and some peanut butter on toast. The house was quiet. I thought about how nice it was and thought, *I should wake up before Daisy more often and spend the time writing*, but I knew it was wishful thinking and wasn't likely to happen, knowing my body clock.

I spoke to Dad, and he said he'd had a bit of gastro, and I decided it was best not to visit him. He also said they were thinking of discharging him soon.

Sunday, 10 September, 2023
Week 14, Day 7
31 km Long Run

This morning, I did not want to get up. I was so tired, and I'd had night sweats again. Mum arrived at 9:30 a.m., the time I'd asked her to come, and I let her in, groaned, and said, 'I'm just going to go back to bed for a little while.' Knowing me the way she does, she knew better than to question it.

After a while, she came into the bedroom and said, 'If you don't get up and go for your run soon, you're going to still be running at five!' She had a point.

Reluctantly I got out of bed, and as I got dressed, my head pounded with the words *I don't want to run 31 km today*. As I ate my breakfast, *I don't want to run 31 km today*. Over and over in my head as I drank some coconut water to replace last night's sweat with some more electrolytes, took my asthma and hay fever medication and got together everything I needed for my run, *I don't want to run 31 km today*.

I knew it would be the case, but as soon as I started running, I felt better. As I'd rolled out of bed, I'd thought to myself, *I've got better things to do than to spend the whole day running*, but when I thought about it, that was not exactly true. In reality, what was I going to do if I stayed home? Scroll Facebook?

I put on an audiobook about a prolific amateur marathoner, and as I listened to tales of 'qualifying for the Boston Marathon' (an elite event only for the fastest runners) trying to 'break the three-hour mark' (for a marathon?! That was my goal for a half!!!) and doing all six 'majors' (London, New York, Boston, Chicago, Tokyo and Berlin), I started to feel discouraged.

My little quest was so humble, so modest, so *pathetic*. Would anyone even be proud of me? Would my mum? What if I came last? What if I just ended up being an embarrassment to the people who came to support me? Would they be disappointed? Would they feel sorry for me? Would they feel like cheering on sloth-like, shuffling old me was a waste of their day?

I felt negative. I would *never* qualify for Boston. I would never run all six majors. I would never break the three-hour mark. I'd be lucky if I broke the six-hour mark! Heck, I'd be lucky to finish! After this marathon, I wasn't even sure if I'd ever run one again. I just wanted to tick it off my bucket list—to be able to say I'd done it.

I was back to my usual route, out and back across several suburbs via the Eastlink trail, with a few hills thrown in for good measure. I was determined to get up those hills without having an asthma attack or totally exhausting myself (but of course, I had my asthma puffer on me, just in case).

I decided to follow Stuart's recommended plan of 10 km of running, then alternating three minutes of walking with four minutes of running until I finished. I felt fresh and energetic after the 10 km but decided to begin my walk-run method (or 'Jeffing,' as we runners call it) anyway. Stuart had said that I'd want to start Jeffing *before* I felt exhausted—not *after* I'd ran out of steam. The last thing I wanted to do, he'd said, was slow down significantly towards the end, as it would be terrible for my morale, and the psychological element is *so* important in a 42 km run.

I was roughly at the 23 km mark when it started to get hard. Not excruciating, not impossible, but I certainly noticed a drop in energy. I still had 6 km to go—17 km on race day! I just focused on one interval at a time— *Just four, three, two, one minutes until the next walking break,* repeatedly. I felt determined not to let this 31 km run beat me. I'd run 29 km two weeks ago— this was only two extra kilometres.

By now I'd abandoned the audiobook and was listening to my favourite playlist. I pounded my feet in time with the beat, singing along to each tune in my head. I came across quite a few walkers going in the same direction ahead of me, and I focused on catching up to them and moving on past. Each walking break was rejuvenating, and three minutes certainly felt like enough recovery time.

I just wondered how tough it would be on race day and worried about whether I'd be able to maintain less than a ten-minute pace for the duration of the whole 42 km. With a much longer distance than the previous week, and therefore a much higher percentage of Jeffing, I was bound to average a slower pace than the nine minutes per kilometre I'd been hitting. Just how much slower, I'd have to wait and see.

When I finished up, I felt like I still had a little more left in the tank, which was a good sign. I checked my pace nine minutes and 24 seconds. It was good enough, but I knew I'd be slowing down significantly for the last 11 km on the day. I thought about playing around with the initial run distance and the Jeffing ratios. Maybe next week I could try running 12 km, then walking two minutes and running four. Stuart had encouraged mixing it up a bit to see what worked for me.

It was worth a shot.

Monday, 11 September 2023
Week 15, Day 1
20-30 Minutes of Recovery Exercise

It's like I've found the right side of the bed and started waking up on it! I'm feeling pretty good. When I'm at my worst, I believe I'm not even capable of feeling good, like I've *never* felt good in my life. Your brain plays tricks on you like that.

I have no doubt in my mind that I'll experience profound depression again several times in my life. It's not negative thinking; it's realistic.

It's just a part of the illness.

There have been times when I have spent the better part of a year depressed—literally crying every day, with everything an effort. It sounds like an exaggeration, but it's not. I'm predisposed to it, and I'm starting to feel a level of acceptance that seemingly unbearable episodes will come (and eventually go), but that it's no reason to fear or dread the rest of my life. I've gone through the fire and come out the other side before.

I can do it again.

It was sunny again today. Apparently, it's going to be sunny all week! Maybe the weather is lifting my mood. Maybe I have a couple of seasons of good mental health to look forward to, buoyed by the Australian sunshine. It puts the kids at school in a good mood too, as well as the other staff. It's infectious!

Work was so-so. Not great, but not terrible. Being completely in charge of one person's curriculum is not without its challenges.

After work I went straight to the gym to do my recovery exercise. I'd decided to do 20 minutes on the exercise bike, just to mix things up a bit. God, it was boring. I tried to kill the time by watching the swimmers out the window in the pool outside, but I just ended up with my phone in my hand, scrolling social media as I pedalled. I hadn't brought my headphones, as the gym's music is so loud anyway, but I'll consider it next time so I can listen to my audiobook.

I was just going through the motions today. Stuart has said that recovery exercise is just about getting the body moving again after a long run, so I don't need to worry about calories burned or heart rate or working up a sweat. It just all felt like such a chore. I'm getting bored with all this exercise!

Can the marathon be over already?

Tuesday, 12 September 2023
Week 15, Day 2
45–60 Minutes of Strength Training

This morning during breakfast I had a little moment. I glanced across the messy table and noticed a form I had to fill out for a gallery membership, and I just burst into tears. I just have so many of these little things I need to get done, and it's all piling up.

I never have time for the little things. I have to complete my VIT (Victorian Institute of Teaching) registration, log my recent sick leave, do an online module on anaphylaxis, and then get tested by our school's first-aid monitor. I must ring up and cancel an appointment to test my lung function (it's not an issue anymore), and I also have books on hold at the library that I need to pick up. They're just little tasks, but when do I have the time? We also need a few things from the supermarket, and I feel like grabbing them should be my job today, as Chris is with Daisy.

By the time I got to school I was feeling a lot better and happy about it being playgroup day. I'm an old hand at setting up the room by now, and the kids all trickled in a bit later than usual, so I had a bit of time to organise the cupboards and throw some things out, Marie Condo-style. This does not spark joy. In the bin it goes.

Once the kids arrived, we decided to go out to the sandpit and the playground, as it was such a nice day. I put up a sign on the door in case anyone else turned up, and we wandered over.

Daisy did not want to say 'Bye-bye playground' when it was time to go. There was some crying, and anguish on my poor child's face as she was forced to depart, but she's a tough cookie. She gets over these things quickly.

Today was an interesting and productive day, as my student's speech therapist finally had a chance to come in for a consultation in person after so many Zoom sessions. We were both proud of the progress he'd made with his communication device, and we had a bit of a discussion over the relevance (or lack thereof) of the rote learning he was doing academically. He's not taking things in or understanding the underlying concepts, and things like learning sight words or memorising books or times tables aren't functional or useful for him.

I also saw first-hand the intensity of his required focus when he was engaging in meaningful and challenging learning with her. It made me realise how taxing and mentally draining learning can be for him and how important it is for him to take a break and unwind after a brief but difficult session.

After work I went straight to the gym and committed myself to working hard and getting some difficult exercises out of the way, right off the bat. Things like one-legged calf raises on a bent knee are still quite new to me. There were a few more people around than usual, and I had to wait to use a few machines and even skipped some that were being used, like the chest press and the lat pull-down. I was happy that I'd sufficiently pushed myself though, and that I left feeling energetic and motivated, instead of exhausted and brain-fried.

I even had the mental energy to stop by the grocery store on my way home and pick up a few things, including protein bars and a protein drink, which was supposedly banana-flavoured (and tasted like medicine). I also picked up some veggies and chicken to cook myself some Udon noodles for dinner, as I'd be home alone with Daisy while Chris went to his weekly social dinner.

To my surprise and delight, Daisy was interested in the noodles and ate a fair pile of them, as well as some pieces of carrot. I think she has a taste for strong flavours, as I'd used a lot of oyster sauce and ginger.

As the night wore on, I started feeling quite excited about my upcoming 40th birthday. Tomorrow I'd be having a celebration at work, as it was going to be my last day before the holidays, when my actual birthday would be happening. It was also only a few days until my birthday party—a two-parter, with high tea and a five-course dinner.

When you have bipolar it's almost like you're not allowed to be excited. Like it's not permitted. Is it excitement, or is it hypomania, with the potential to turn into full-blown mania? Will the excitement affect my sleep? How will that impact my mental health?

It's as though we aren't even able to just feel and enjoy positivity for its own sake. Health and normality are some kind of fairy tale or myth for the bipolar individual, and anything that isn't depression must be some kind of mania. We can't just be *well*. We're always on guard or high alert and second-guessing ourselves. It's exhausting.

Wednesday, 13 September 2023
Week 15, Day 3
Rest Day

This morning, I got out of bed early, which is unheard of! I even got up in time for a morning shower before work! It was warm enough for me to wear the new pants that Margaret bought me for my birthday, with my matching tan leather jacket. No jumper or sweater was required! I felt stylish.

When Mum arrived, I proclaimed, 'Today's my birthday!' She looked at me, confused. 'No, your birthday's not until next week!' she answered. 'No,' I explained. It's my work birthday. They're having a special cake for me because it's my 40th.'

Mum seemed amused that I could be excited about something so trivial, but I brushed it off. I was feeling happy, and nobody was going to take that away from me!

I arrived at work happy and greeting everyone cheerfully like a little ray of sunshine. I popped my lunch in the staff room fridge and noticed a box from the Cheesecake Factory tucked away in the bottom. As our break time approached, I was glancing at my watch every few minutes in anticipation.

Finally, the bell sounded, and I headed to the staff room. I got there in record time, and there were only two of us, the Acting Principal and me. When the others came in, the cake was unveiled, a carrot cake with cream cheese icing—my favourite!

They popped four candles on, signifying each decade of my marvellous existence, then the candles were lit, and 'Happy Birthday' was sung. As I blew out the candles, a co-worker took a couple of snaps of me with my iPhone. I cut the cake, and we started handing the pieces out. It was delicious and went down nicely with a hot cup of tea.

I felt warm inside and loved.

Thursday, 14 September 2023
Week 15, Day 4
45–60-Minute Easy Run

I'm an absolute legend in that I got up with plenty of time to get ready for swimming this morning! In fact, we were ready a bit *too* early, and I put Daisy into her swim gear and onto the couch, only to have her wet her very thin swim nappy and soak through her bathing suit until she was sopping wet. I only noticed this as we were about to head out the door. It was a quick fix, as she has plenty of bathers and swim nappies, so I re-dressed her and we ended up at our lesson on time.

This time both George and Tabby were there, so Daisy was able to see and play with her friends. There were lots of toys for the kids to play with in their lesson, lots of songs to sing, and it's so sweet how much Daisy loves her teacher.

She's so confident in the water. Too confident. She thinks she can swim (spoiler alert, she can't) and she runs into the deep end until the water is lapping around her face and she's standing on her tippy toes. Sometimes she tries to launch herself in, almost like a dive, and I'm forever having to re-direct her into the shallow end.

After swimming I just couldn't be bothered with showering and washing both our hair, etc. I did manage to wash our bathers and hang them out. Just before lunch, Margaret called and invited us to her house to sit on the back porch in the sun while the kids played on George's little cubby house and slide. I admitted that we were still covered in chlorine and hadn't even thought about lunch, and she assured me, 'Don't worry, we haven't showered either, and I've cooked lunch for us and the kids.'

I was so relieved and so thankful. We sat together on the patio, drinking in the warmth of the spring weather, and discussed Daisy's christening.

When Daisy started to get grumpy and tired, we headed home so she could have a nap, and I went out for my easy run.

I felt at peace as I trotted over the pavement, on one of my favourite routes, happy with my life, and grateful for the people in it.

Friday, 15 September 2023
Week 15, Day 5
45–60-Minute Training Run

I woke up feeling such anticipation, positively buzzing! It was still four days until my real birthday, but it might as well have been today. The forecast had predicted another perfect, sunny day; in fact, it was expected to stay that way until Wednesday.

I had a light breakfast—just a banana—I didn't want to fill up before my two big gastronomical extravaganzas. Chris skipped breakfast altogether. We both intended to pig out, big time.

I took my time relaxing before getting ready for my run, then got kitted up and donned my headphones, saying a quick goodbye to Chris and Daisy. I went through all my ritual warm ups, set my watch, and off I went.

Today I was in the zone. I felt light, I felt fit. Big, springy strides in quick succession. Other runners and walkers greeted me with genuine smiles. Everyone was feeling that joy that comes when spring has finally sprung. No asthma today, no hay fever. Just healthy, rhythmic inhales and exhales.

Once I got home, I carefully chose my outfit, showered, sprayed on my favourite perfume, dressed, and twisted my hair up into a neat high bun. Then I put in my contact lenses and carefully did my makeup. I couldn't remember the last time I'd used proper makeup brushes and applied the works—foundation, bronzer, eye shadow, etc. I looked good. I felt even better.

It was a nice, pleasant drive into the city, and we easily found parking at Federation Square. We made our way down to the quaint riverside bar, arriving early and being treated to our first glasses of prosecco. There was a gorgeous atmosphere, with joggers in the Botanical Gardens across the Yarra, and rowers gliding past in perfect synchronicity.

One by one, my beloved guests arrived, and boy, had they turned it on. Everyone looked fantastic! Some of my friends I hadn't seen in ages, and it was a joyous reunion. A few of them had taken the train in, ready to ply themselves with alcohol as we were offered three bespoke cocktails and bottomless prosecco.

Once we were all seated with drinks in hand, the immaculately arranged trays of delectables arrived, and each morsel was carefully described by our waiter.

Everything was infused with subtle hints of unique flavour and perfect balances of texture, lightness, and crunch. It was the perfect amount of food: eight tiny servings, a mixture of sweet and savoury.

I received hugs, cards and gifts, and we all talked and laughed and caught up on each other's news and gossip. A few of my friends were meeting for the first time—none of the others had met Christoph or Jess (mum Jess), and everyone got along. Non-mum Jess was violently ill and couldn't make it, but she was thoughtful enough to Facetime us all as we excitedly crowded around my phone screen and fought each other to get a word in.

In no time, phase one of my party crawl was over, and we headed to Fitzroy for dinner. My cousins and my brother had made it, as well as some friends who hadn't been able to come to the high tea.

I was given the honour of selecting all five dishes from the impressive menu, and as each dish arrived, we all enthusiastically dug in. It was an exclusive restaurant with a degustation menu and tiny courses concocted by the magnificent chefs. Lots of fresh seafood and poultry and a myriad of sauces, some subtle, others rich; all nuanced with hints of exotic and creative ingredient choices. My foodie friends and relatives were impressed.

As dinner ended, I decided to kick on at a city nightclub for a themed party night, where I knocked back a few too many beers, danced like a maniac, and hustled for Beyond Blue donations, raising over $300!

It was the perfect end to a perfect day.

Saturday, 16 September 2023
Week 15, Day 6
Rest Day

I fared pretty well this morning, all things considered. I wasn't all that hungover, more just exhausted because I was too wired and drunk to sleep last night. And obviously dehydrated. Water, water and more water. A shower. Back to feeling human again.

At first, I thought, *At last, a day where I have nothing I have to do*, then I remembered I had to go to an exhibition opening in Mornington. I'd entered a portrait prize, which I'd placed in last year, so I wanted to be there for the announcement of the prizes. I'd also promised Mum I would go.

I put on a pretty, colourful dress, with matching earrings, headband and necklace and was surprised how reasonably fresh and not hungover I looked. I was pretty sure I was going to avoid a lecture from Mum. I dressed Daisy up in her little mustard yellow pinafore with the matching hair bow, and she was as pretty as a picture.

I managed to get us organised and into the car on schedule and arrived at the gallery before Mum. The exhibition was impressive—intimidatingly so. I'd entered a couple of appropriations, a portrait of Frida Kahlo and another of Van Gogh, both created in my signature collage style of tiny ripped-ed up pieces of magazine paper, carefully arranged.

I was proud of my work, but it paled in comparison to the pieces I'd entered last year. They'd been hung in prime real estate, smack bang in the middle of the main room, but today, my pieces were tucked away in a couple of less prominent corners of the gallery. Not a good sign in terms of potential prizes. I doubted they'd award the same person two years in a row anyway.

It was a beautiful sunny day, and the gallery had stunning surrounding gardens, so we spent most of the opening outside, with Daisy running around between the rose bushes and abstract sculptures. Everyone there was besotted by her. They kept commenting on how gorgeous she was and how beautiful the name Daisy was and asking all about her. I was beaming from ear to ear, a proud mum.

Soon it was time to announce the prizes, and we gathered around the gallery director as she made her speech. She congratulated all the artists on their wonderful entries and remarked on the outstanding standard of work this year. I missed out but was pleased to see that the winning entry was one of my favourite pieces. A colossal oil painting of several people gathered around a dinner table, carefully painted in meticulous detail.

After the opening, Daisy had a quick play at Mum's house before I headed home. I'd arranged for my friends Shorna and Paige to come over with their little boy to celebrate my birthday with a few drinks, as they hadn't been able to make it yesterday.

It was nice having them over. It's hard to find time to catch up when we have little ones and we all work. The others had a few alcoholic drinks while I wisely abstained and drank water like a camel, preparing for tomorrow's long run. We ordered some pizza, and it was a nice, fuss-free, easy night.

Sunday, 17 September 2023
Week 15, Day 7
21.1 km Long Run (Half-Marathon)

I had no get up and go this morning. It was as though I was glued to the bed. I'd told Mum to arrive at 9 a.m., and when she knocked on the door, I was still in my pyjamas and hadn't eaten. Daisy was just waking up.

I'd like to say I rushed around getting ready, but it would be more accurate to say I slowly lumbered from room to room in a daze, trying to put off my run and even googling things like, *What happens if I skip a long run?* It turns out nothing happens, but the truth was, I was just being lazy, and if I was going to skip any long runs, it should be next Sunday, when I'm on holiday in Magnetic Island.

I was even holding back tears. I just wanted to lie in bed all day. Sound familiar? In terms of personality and mindset, training for a marathon doesn't suit me. I'm lazy by nature, a total sook, and the queen of whingeing. But despite all that, I always seem to get it done. I push those thoughts way, way down and I do the work.

Today was no different. I told myself it was only a half-marathon—a whole 10 km shorter than last week's 31 km, so I'd be finished in much less time and still have a few hours in the day left to do as I pleased.

I laced up and went through all my pre-long run rituals. I had everything I needed; all I had to do was decide what to listen to. I didn't want to spend money on another audiobook, so I went into my podcast app, typed in 'bipolar' and found a journal-style podcast called *The Bipolar Diaries*.

I decided to switch up my walk-run plan to make it a little more challenging and hopefully increase my overall pace, without sacrificing too much energy. I decided to run for 12 km, then alternate walking for two minutes with running for four minutes. It was manageable.

I maintained a pretty good level of energy. My mood was good. Once I started, I didn't struggle or feel like giving up. I convivially greeted the cyclists, walkers and joggers I came across and once again concluded that it was a pretty good way to spend a Sunday. The sun was out, and I knew I would have been miserable and feeling sorry for myself at home in bed.

The last few kilometres are often the hardest, but today I felt optimistic hitting the home stretch. It felt good pressing 'Stop' on my Garmin. I had nailed this run. Not so long ago a half-marathon was a huge achievement, now it was an indulgently easy Sunday. I had a spring in my step as I power-walked my cool-down. As I diligently completed my post-run stretches, I felt like a proper runner rather than an imposter.

Monday, 18 September 2023
Week 16, Day 1
20–30-Minute Recovery Exercise

I had disturbing dreams last night and night sweats. I'm starting to think I have some sort of sleep disorder because I spend so much time dreaming, and my dreams are so vivid. I often dream of intense emotional things, like apologising to people I have wronged or confronting people who have wronged me in the past, particularly in my romantic relationships.

I revisit all these gut-wrenching feelings to the point where it feels even worse than living through them the first time. I usually spend about an hour in the morning half-asleep, aware that it's the morning but still completely in a dream-like state, like I haven't let go of the warped reality of my dreams and latched onto my actual reality yet.

Daisy properly woke me up, calling out, 'Mum!' and I went to greet her and change her. My nightgown was still soaking wet with sweat, and I felt disgusting. Seeing the state of the house I immediately felt overwhelmed.

The nappy bin was overflowing. So was the kitchen bin. Last night was bin night, so the big bins had been taken way out to the front of our block of units. I felt a pang of annoyance at Chris for not checking the rubbish situation before taking out the bins. There was a pile of clean dishes to put away and a pile of dirty dishes in the sink. Clothes all over the floor in our room, all over the bed in Daisy's room, plus a laundry basket of clean clothes to put away.

I had to give Daisy breakfast, eat my own breakfast, take my antidepressant, my asthma medication and my hay fever medication. I also needed a shower to wash off all the sweat and drink some coconut water to replace all the electrolytes.

I had to visit Dad in San Remo today, but he had a midday appointment and wouldn't be home until one, and I wasn't sure when or where I'd fit in my recovery exercise. I just didn't know where to start.

I sat at the kitchen table, eating my breakfast and crying. For the first time, it registered with Daisy that something was wrong. She asked to be picked up, then looked deep into my eyes, frowning in concern. Then she tried to wipe my tears away. This gesture made me tear up even more.

I felt like all my coping mechanisms had fallen by the wayside. I couldn't listen to uplifting music because Daisy was watching TV. I didn't know what I would even listen to anymore since I'd stopped listening to Lizzo. It had been ages since I'd last used my mental health app, with motivational quotes and checklists that used to help. It hadn't been engaging me for a long time, partly because I hadn't needed it but also because logging everything was time-consuming, and time was something I had less and less of nowadays.

Somehow, I pushed through it all. I started with the dishes, then tackled all the other stuff, bit by bit. Showering and getting dressed was a good mental re-set. When I look good, I feel good. Then I got Daisy dressed, and despite the mild weather, she threw a tantrum and wouldn't stop until I put her warmest winter coat on.

We went outside, and I put her in her little bike, which I could push with a handle, and we went for a brisk walk around the block for 20 minutes.

I timed it perfectly so that we came home, packed a bag, got into the car, and arrived in San Remo at exactly one o'clock. Daisy napped most of the way in the car. She was still drowsy and half asleep when I took her inside to say hi to Dad and his wife, Val.

Dad seemed to be in pretty good shape, considering he'd recently broken ten ribs and one vertebra. Six on one side, four on the other. It would take six weeks to heal, but it would likely take up to three months for him to fully recover.

After a few hours, we made the long drive back home, and Daisy fell asleep in the car again. That meant she was bound to be up late. I was so tired. I thought about my writing and how behind I was. I had written a few pages last night, but not nearly enough. I hoped to wake up early enough to start the day with writing, but we all know how that turned out. I was hungry. I was depressed. I just wanted junk food. I realised, looking at the time, that I'd have to cook dinner as soon as I got home.

When I got in the door, I was carrying a bunch of things and felt totally flustered. I must have looked it too because poor Chris was concerned. Straight away I asked: 'Did you empty the nappy bin?'

'No.'

'Did you empty the kitchen bin?'

'No.'

'Did you at least bring the big bins in?'

'Someone did, but it wasn't me.'

We have good neighbours. Chris could tell I wasn't impressed and rushed around doing the jobs I mentioned before I could blow my top.

Then Chris asked if I'd had dinner. 'Why? Have you?' I asked.

'I had the soup that was in the fridge. I thought you'd be eating at your Dad's house,' he explained.

'That soup was supposed to be for Daisy!' I whined. Then I started getting the ingredients for dinner out of the fridge, oozing stress from every pore.

'Did you want me to cook?' Chris asked. I realised it was probably a polite, rhetorical question, and he was just assuming I'd say no, but I pounced on the offer. I sat on the couch, opened a bag of salt and vinegar chips I'd bought at 7-Eleven, and washed them down with a Pepsi Max while Chris diligently followed the instructions from our last meal kit for the week. I was so grateful.

Tuesday, 19 September 2023
Week 16, Day 2
45-60 Minutes of Strength Training
And...
My 40th Birthday!

I wasn't feeling great this morning, a bit 'blah'. I'd confessed to my mum last night that I'd been quite down yesterday morning and accepted her offer to come and have breakfast at a café to celebrate my birthday. Then, the plan was for her to watch Daisy so I could get in a morning workout and see Margaret in the afternoon. Then we'd head out to an early dinner with Chris's friends, who I'd gotten to know quite well. As I said, that was the plan....

Mum arrived quite a bit later than I expected, and we drove to a café I hadn't been to before that I wanted to check out. It was so-so, boring and standard. I had scrambled eggs with chilli and chorizo, and Mum went with eggs Benny. Daisy refused to sit in a high chair and I had to awkwardly eat with her sitting on my lap.

There were a couple of gentlemen sitting nearby with their dogs, and Mum took Daisy over to say hi and give the dogs a pet. She was a little wary but interested. She was much more comfortable keeping her distance and pointing to the puppies than getting in close enough to stroke their fur. In the end, she summoned the confidence and tentatively reached out and lightly touched the more docile one on the nose before jumping back and hiding behind her grand-mère.

We bid the guys and the dogs farewell and went back home, where Mum set about doing my dishes and washing as I gratefully collapsed on the couch and accepted the help. It was my birthday, after all!

Chris's mum messaged me and asked to come for a visit, and she came over with a card and some money, and we all waited for Chris to get home so we could enjoy the chocolate cake Mum had bought for me. There was no time for a morning workout.

Margaret called, saying she'd been held up at work, and she didn't know how long she'd be. By the time she was available, Daisy was asleep, and I collapsed into a sleep of my own, despite feeling guilty that I should be writing or going to the gym. I was just so tired and worn out by all the birthday attention and another night of night-sweats and disturbing dreams.

I managed to get up, feeling surprisingly refreshed, and got my arse to the gym. Once again, I struggled with the one-legged calf raises, with bent knees and straight knees, and could only manage sets of 15 reps with the lowest weight of 5 kilos. I also had great difficulty tackling my nemesis, the shoulder press, and only managed a few pitiful sets of reps, again on the lowest setting. Everything else went pretty smoothly. I didn't feel resentful or uncomfortable with being there; whingey, whiny Jacqui didn't rear her ugly head!

I got home in plenty of time to shower and make myself pretty, and we got to the pub at 6 p.m. and seated ourselves at the large table with the friendly, oddball group of misfits.

I'd been craving fish and chips for days, so that's what I ordered, and it turned out to be average. I think we've established that I'm a food snob. I had a couple of Aperol spritzes, and it was nice to indulge in a couple of cocktails for my birthday.

How does it feel to be 40? Pretty good, to be honest.

A friend posted on my Facebook page that she hoped all my dreams would come true, and I replied that they already had.

Wednesday, 20 September 2023
Week 16, Day 3
Rest Day

This morning, I had a huge sleep-in. When Daisy woke up, I brought her into bed with me and we just lay there together. She didn't want to be lying down—she felt like playing. I summoned the most playful effort I could—making silly faces and noises. I kept this up for a little while, but then I just couldn't. I closed my eyes and tried to get in magical, restorative micro-rest.

I felt like the worst mother in the world. At one point I even turned my back on Daisy to get more comfortable, which felt like the ultimate Bad Mum moment. Would the memory of me ignoring her in this moment scar her for life? Was this something that would stick with her? Was I severing our mother-daughter bond?

I only lay there for a couple of minutes, and as soon as Daisy started calling out, 'Mum!' I picked her up and took her out into the lounge room. I tried to give her breakfast, but she refused to eat it. She turned down porridge, toast, bananas, and yogurt.

I don't know what to do with this kid.

I felt depressed, exhausted and overwhelmed again this morning. It took me so long to get organised and get going. I'd said to Mum that I was going to meet up with her today to go and buy new summer shoes from her favourite shoe shop. It was her birthday gift to me. The hours ticked by, and she messaged me in concern. *Are you OK?* By then, I was nearly ready to head out, and I assured her that I was fine, even though it wasn't entirely true. I hate worrying my mum.

Eventually, I got a bag together, and we made the drive to Seaford. Mum had given me the wrong address, but I managed to find my way there without too much fuss.

We arrived at the store before Mum, and instantly I could see what she meant about it being her favourite shoe store. It was huge! They had sandals and sneakers in every colour—proper expensive leather ones. Not like the cheap Kmart shoes I was used to wearing.

The plan was to get some comfortable, stylish, orthopaedic sandals in a beige or tan, or perhaps a pair of white sneakers that I could wear in the summer with dresses and shorts. I have white and yellow jeans that I wear a lot, and they look terrible with black sneakers—the only colour I have.

I scanned the shelves and was immediately drawn to a pair of bright-yellow sneakers—my favourite colour. They were on special. When I eventually got the staff's attention I asked if they had them in my size. Unfortunately, they were limited stock and they only came in a 39—way too big for me.

I think I've mentioned that I have extremely small feet. They're a US size 3, which is right on the borderline of kids' and adults' shoes. The only shoes that fit me in Kmart, Target and Big W are the kids' ones. I couldn't see any kids' shoes in this store and wondered if they'd have anything at all that would fit me.

I explained my predicament and asked about the smallest size they stocked. It was a size 35, which sometimes fits me, and is sometimes too big, depending on the brand. I was anxious to try something on to assess whether this whole trip had been a waste of time.

As a kid, I'd had a yearly ritual of attending a particular shoe shop in Cowes to get my school shoes, and Mum said that the staff would always hide in the back when they saw me coming, as finding something to fit my small— and extremely narrow—feet was something of an odyssey.

I'd been eyeing off a white pair of sandshoe-style leather sneakers, with tiny little holes punched in for decorative purposes and breathability. They were lace-up but also had a fashionable and convenient zip on the side. Plus, they had great arch support.

I took a seat and awaited the presentation of the size 35, feeling a bit like Cinderella. The lady brought over a box and pulled out the shoe in question, and I unzipped it and slipped it on. A perfect fit! I stood up. It felt comfortable.

The woman suggested I put on the left shoe as well and have a walk around. I did. Still comfortable. Extremely comfortable. I couldn't believe I'd lucked out with the very first pair of shoes I'd tried on. It was a miracle!

Just then, Mum came in. 'I think I've found "The Ones,"' I exclaimed in wonderment. Mum seemed sceptical. 'Are you sure?' She glanced around at the huge range of shoes and sandals in the shop. 'You don't want to try anything else on?' I think she was disappointed that she'd missed out on sharing most of my shopping experience.

'What did you want to do now?' she asked me. 'I'd kind of been hoping you'd watch Daisy for a little while so that I could get some writing done,' I admitted. It was also lunchtime, so we went to a nearby shopping centre where Daisy could play, and I could wolf down some lunch and get out my laptop and start typing away.

I got a lot done in a short space of time. Something I'm used to doing out of necessity. Mum had an appointment to get to, so I had to be productive and speedy. I don't waste time with my writing. I don't sit and ponder. I don't do little exercises to 'warm up.' I just get into it and plug away. I guess that's just my personality.

I'm the same with exercise. I don't dilly-dally. I can't afford to.

Mum returned with Daisy, and I saved my work and shut down. I'd hoped to get a bit more done, but I was still happy with what I'd produced. I decided I'd get Chris to watch Daisy at home and either go to the library or lock myself in my room and just work.

When I got home my exhaustion had caught up with me. I didn't feel like writing; I felt like having a 'little lie-down.' We all know how that goes. Half an hour turns to three! Today was no different. By the time I emerged from the bedroom, it was time to think about dinner. We had no groceries. I'd asked Chris to pick some up after work, but he'd been hoping to do it in the late afternoon instead. Of course, I'd thrown that plan out the window with my 'Sleeping Beauty' act.

'Did you want to cook, or did you want to get something delivered?' asked Chris. I didn't want either of those two things. I'd had Hungry Jack's for lunch, and we were trying to save money. 'Why are those always the only two options?' I complained. 'Why can't you cook?'

'I can. . . . ' He hesitated. 'I just don't feel like it.' I was so annoyed. I didn't 'feel like it' either. I never 'feel like it.' I rolled my eyes, sighed and went to survey the pantry, fridge and freezer. We had some bolognese in the freezer, and although we had no pasta, there was some gnocchi in the back of the pantry.

I was impressed with myself for scrounging up dinner. It was nice, easy and pleasant. I was glad we hadn't succumbed to the takeaway option. We do that too often, and we'd be eating out most nights soon during our holiday to Magnetic Island.

Thursday, 21 September 2023
Week 16, Day 4
Rest Day

This morning we'd planned to try out a new swimming class with a different company at 9:45 a.m., which meant a bit of a sleep in. Daisy woke up in the early hours of the morning, and I gave her a bottle and brought her into bed with me, and we both quickly fell back asleep.

We were supposed to get up at 8:30 a.m. but I just couldn't. I was flattened. I could barely move. I knew it was the depression, but today I let it win. It didn't help that I'd been unable to sleep for most of the night. I didn't know what to say to Margaret, so I lied. I sent a quick message saying Daisy was sick, then instantly felt terrible about it.

We got out of bed around 9:30 a.m., and I began to feel worse and worse about sleeping in, missing swimming and being too ashamed to admit that it was essentially laziness holding me back. After breakfast and getting Daisy settled, I messaged Margaret telling her to ring me after the swim class to let us know how it went, and I made up my mind to tell her the truth.

When Margaret called, she was excited about the new swim school. It was more expensive, but she felt like it was worth it as it was less play-oriented and more focused on technique and water safety. I wasn't completely sold. For George, Margaret had already made up her mind, and decided to enrol him.

I told her I'd lied about Daisy being sick and apologised profusely, and Margaret was quick to reassure me. 'Don't ever feel like you have to lie to me,' she soothed. 'You can tell me anything.' I knew she meant it.

I couldn't talk for long, as I had to get myself and Daisy ready to go to a pub in Springvale to have lunch with the girls from work. I was excited because I'd be seeing my old colleague, Rachel, for the first time since having a beautiful baby boy, Isaac, whom she was bringing with her. I'd worked with Rachel for two years with the grade preps when I first got my job at the school, and we'd both wanted children for a long time.

I managed to get to the pub a little early, and I was the first one there. I bought myself a beer from the bar and headed over to the big empty table that had been reserved for us, with the two high chairs at either end.

For someone who feels like they're always rushing around and running late, I seem to show up on time, or early, a lot. I've only realised this through writing these journals and reading them over. It's quite a skill of mine.

I think it will always be a source of anxiety for me, though—the fear of running late. The catastrophising as though something terrible will happen if I'm not completely prompt and punctual. I think it's about that mask, and the fear of letting it slip. As though my lateness would be some huge signal to everyone that I'm a mess and I'm falling apart. I'm like a duck furiously paddling away under the water—even though it's completely calm on the surface.

As the ladies started to arrive, I saw that Sally, our old receptionist, had made it out to see us all again! I was so happy to see her! She'd always been such a sunny, happy, cheerful addition to our little team of staff, and I hadn't realised how much I'd missed that friendly face first thing every morning. It was a wonderful reunion!

It was so nice to finally catch up, without our time being limited by allotted breaks and yard duties. Instead of shovelling in food as quickly as possible and trying to have a conversation, only to have it cut short by the bell, we could just take our time and relax. And everyone was in such a good mood because of the school holidays. It was like everyone's shoulders had lowered an inch.

Everyone fussed and fawned over Daisy and Isaac. There were a few at the table who were dying to finally be grandparents, so they couldn't get enough. It was a bit of a game of Pass the Parcel. Daisy was a bit wriggly, wanting to get down and walk/run around, and I had to take her over to the play area a couple of times. Eventually, she got a bit sooky, and I realised it was time to go home for a nap. She fell asleep in the car, and it was easy enough to transfer her to her cot for a proper sleep.

With Daisy down, I lost all the willpower to be upright and functional. I crawled into bed with the realisation that I seemed to be spending half my life lying down these days! It felt pathetic, but I didn't have it in me to fight it. I wanted to be able to make it a short nap so that I could get out for an easy run, but I knew deep down that I was unlikely to be able to summon that sort of energy.

I was right. I lay there for hours. The time for running came and went, and my workout gear and running shoes remained untouched for another day. I was vaguely aware of my phone beeping but had no mental energy for dealing with text messages.

I was thinking about our Magnetic Island holiday. We were leaving tomorrow, and I had to pack. I hated packing for holidays. Just like my fear of being late, I had a terrible paranoia of forgetting things—essential things. I checked my messages. Mum: 'How's the packing going?' I didn't want to answer honestly, 'It's not,' so I started to put some things into the suitcase.

I made a list. A comprehensive list. Things to pack for me, for Daisy, for running, for the beach, and a separate list of things to put in my backpack to take on the plane. Essential items that I couldn't forget were my hydration vest, which went in my suitcase; and my laptop, which would go in my backpack. I laid out my clothes for a Friday morning run, and then something nice and warm, but not too warm, to wear to the airport. Melbourne and Townsville weather are very different. I laid out some clothes for Daisy too.

My anxiety started to alleviate. I felt like I was nailing this. I was organised. I wasn't forgetting anything. Chris just had to pack a few clothes and his bathers. I didn't trust him to handle Daisy's stuff, plus there was just the assumption that I'd do it. Packing the suitcase, I started to feel excited and pumped for tomorrow.

Our yearly family holiday was just a day away!

Friday, 22 September 2023
Week 16, Day 5
45–60-Minute Training Run

All three of us slept in. We were allowed to. For once, we had nowhere to be early in the morning. Mum was coming at 12:30 p.m. to have lunch with us before we all drove to the airport, so all I had to do was get in a quick run, shower and get dressed in the clothes that I'd already laid out.

I was happy to be getting back into a proper training routine. The extra rest yesterday had done me some good, and I was energised and ready to get out there and get my blood pumping. It was a beautiful day, and as I slipped into my singlet and clipped on my bum bag, I realised I couldn't even remember the last time I'd needed to run in a sweater.

I had to cross at the traffic lights twice to get to the corner where my running route began, and as I waited for the lights to change, I enthusiastically loosened up with some leg swings, holding onto the pole. I like the idea of the people in the cars stopped at the lights looking over and noticing me and thinking, *Ah. She must be about to go for a run.* I'm so proud to be a runner.

It took me a few strides to remember I was supposed to be running fast, and after a shaky start I fell into a rhythm. I bounced on the balls of my feet and swished my legs forward, repeatedly, and enjoyed the feeling of pushing myself. I thought of my running coach and his advice to speed things up a bit on Fridays, but also of how he'd relieved me of the burden of those gruelling tempo runs that I'd been doing on a Tuesday. It's often said that a runner should focus on one goal at a time—speed or distance—and Stuart had given me the permission and the freedom to put speed on the backburner for a while.

It was also nice to be focussing on 'time on my feet' instead of striving for a particular distance, which in my earlier days of training used to be 7 or 8 km. This was a lot easier. Stuart's words echoed in my head. 'Anything longer than 60 minutes of running for a shorter run is just junk miles.' I loved the idea of 'junk miles.' The term had a nice ring to it. I was so happy to be shedding those junk miles; the over-training; the burnout. I was happier now. Running had started to feel like work, and now it didn't anymore.

As I traversed the concrete path of the Eastlink trail, I couldn't help but feel disgusted and annoyed at some huge, garish graffiti that had been sprayed onto the footpath. Ugly, red letters spelling out 'VOTE NO!' It was a reference to the impending political referendum, where all Australians were being asked to vote on whether to give Indigenous Australians a Voice to Parliament. It goes without saying that I will be voting YES. I couldn't understand why we were voting at all! Just give the people some rights! It was a repeat debacle of the referendum of a few years earlier, when the right to marriage equality had been put to a public vote. Why? Why vote? Luckily the public had seen sense, and freedom had prevailed on that occasion.

I got back to my starting point—my corner of traffic lights pressed pause on my Garmin and started stretching. Again, I was aware of signalling to everyone that *oh yes, I was a runner.* Look at me stretching! Aren't I disciplined? I'm not at all self-conscious about it. I love being seen.

When I got home, the excitement about our trip was palpable.

The drive in was easy and stress-free. No traffic, no roadwork. No missed turn-offs. Nothing unexpected. We were all so pumped, and even Daisy had the sense that something special was going on. We carted all our stuff out of the boot and onto the little airport shuttle and sang to Daisy 'The Wheels on the Bus.' It's her favourite song, and she was *so* happy to be on a real, live bus for once.

Check-in was quick, efficient, and breezy, and we strolled through security and into the airport's Food Court. Mum and I have a tradition of having celebratory champers before flying anywhere, so we got a couple of glasses and took a selfie for Facebook. Then we sipped away and took in the busy atmosphere of the airport. Then we got on the plane, and we all took another selfie.

Daisy was good as gold on the plane. It's a short flight, only a couple of hours, and she kept herself occupied by pretending to read the safety instructions and the menus, taking them in and out of their little compartments on the back of all three seats in front of us. Once the seatbelt sign was off, Mum also let her walk up and down the aisles. We were there in no time.

We could feel the Queensland heat hit us as soon as we stepped off the plane. *Ah! This was what we were here for!* We wrangled our awkward suitcases from the baggage carousel and picked up Daisy's pram and ambled over to the taxi rank. We were too late to catch the early ferry but had a couple of hours to kill before getting the next one.

The driver dropped us off at the Townsville casino hotel, and they took all our bags at the entry, so we didn't have to cart them around.

We dined on the patio of a trendy bar and shed all our outer layers to better acclimatise to the weather. It was noisy; it was lively, it was /happening/. Chris hated it. It was too much for him. He begged us to go to the much quieter ferry terminal so that we could wait in peace.

Again, we lumbered our suitcases, backpacks and pram down the road and across to the ferry terminal, and before long we were on the boat. This is the part of the trip that excites me. When you're almost there. The lights of Townsville slowly get dimmer and dimmer, until all there is is black. Black, and the stars, and the sound of the ferry engine carving through the water. Then it happens. You see the lights and the outline of the island. It gets bigger and bigger as you get closer and closer, and finally, you're home.

Well, it feels like home, at least to me.

This island has been my annual sanctuary for around 20 years. So many memories, especially of my late stepfather, Ivan, who always came with us, year after year.

Through so many of my episodes, my mania, my craziness, and that unlikely gradual maturity I somehow managed to manifest, Magnetic Island and Ivan had been there for me.

Saturday, 23 September 2023
Week 16, Day 6
Rest Day

It's so nice to be on holiday! Even though it took forever for everyone to get some sleep (Daisy was awake 'til after 1 a.m., thrown out by a completely different daily schedule and an unfamiliar environment), we all managed to have a nice sleep in and woke up feeling refreshed and relaxed. I always worry before a holiday that it might not be relaxing—like the pressure to enjoy it and make the most of it will make the whole experience counter-intuitively stressful, but that hasn't been the case so far.

We ambled about this morning. I sat outside in the courtyard and got some writing done. We watched as skinks darted through the dead leaves on the ground. We took our time having breakfast. Later in the morning we packed a lunch of bread rolls with ham, cheese and salad, got sun-screened up and walked to the nearby Alma Bay—our favourite beach on the island.

It was quite uncharacteristically windy, with white peaks and rough waves, but we found a sheltered spot by some large boulders and settled down with our towels and all our beach gear. Daisy was so cute, deciding she was obsessed with helping Chris rub on his sunscreen, and getting mildly upset when the job was done.

She and I wandered into the shallows, and she squealed in delight as the water rushed over her feet and ankles. Then Mum came to play with her in a tag team as she emerged from the ocean, and I wandered out to dive into the waves and have a glorious little dip in the pleasantly warm water. As the tide came in it created a little pool for Daisy to play in, and she splashed around with some beach toys, and we made dribble castles.

Then we all ate our lunch, and I had another swim. Even Chris got in, and he held onto Daisy and dipped her in and out of the water as the waves crashed in.

After a while we made our way onto the grassy area and dressed Daisy into a dry nappy and clothes, and she ran towards the playground, where we pushed her on the swing. With each swoop of the pendulum she giggled and cried 'Whaaaa!' and every time we asked her if she wanted to get off, she protested, 'No, no, no, no, no!'

Eventually we got her off and headed across the street to where there was a gorgeous little pub and café. We all had ice-cream, and surprise, surprise, suddenly Daisy had an appetite and felt like eating something! I enjoyed a nice cold cider under the shade of the glorious palm trees, surrounded by national park—hills of granite and tall gum trees. We even got offered free fish and chips, as the kitchen had made a surplus and were ready to close for the afternoon!

We made the short walk home to the unit, and Daisy fell asleep. I enjoyed a couple of beers and went for a beautiful swim right across the road at Geoffrey Bay, which was usually quite shallow and rocky, but had turned it out for a stunning high tide.

I watched as a family played beach cricket; the children clumsily fumbling through it and brandishing the bat like it was baseball. Way down the far end of the beach there seemed to be a small wedding going on. Apart from that I was all alone in the water. Even in the school holidays the island is peaceful and never crowded—an undiscovered gem.

Late afternoon crept in, and we wandered back to the pub so Mum could watch the AFL semi-finals. Carlton was playing the Brisbane Lions, which normally wouldn't have been a big deal, but a win for us would mean a Carlton-Collingwood Grand Final—blood in the streets and riots as the bitter rivals battled it out.

I normally don't get invested in football, or any sport for that matter, but this game brought out the Carlton supporter in me—and in every Melbourne tourist in the bar. The locals rooted for their team with equal gusto! I leaned forward in my seat, alternating cheers and boos at every mark and goal. We were thrashed, and it was devastating! I messaged all my Carlton supporter friends and family in commiseration.

I had a couple more drinks and the sun began to set and soon we ordered dinner. A burger for Chris and a steak sandwich for me, chips and nuggets in the shape of dinosaurs for the little one. Mum was content with bar snacks.

Daisy was fascinated by the curlews, the large, strange (but cute), local, flightless birds, with their long necks, stalky legs and huge, beady eyes. They were quite tame and wandered between the outdoor tables as Daisy chased them around, squealing and hollering.

As the night ended, we popped Daisy into the pusher and walked back to our unit and prepared for the rigmarole of trying to get Daisy to calm down and sleep. I also laid out my running clothes, shoes and camelback for the morning, hoping to get up early for my long run.

Sunday, 24 September 2023
Week 16, Day 7
Rest Day

Today was obviously not meant to be a rest day. Sunday is always long run day. Always. I'd planned to beat the Queensland heat by getting up super early, but at 6:30 a.m. I didn't feel up to it. Besides being tired from another night of Daisy's bedtime shenanigans and refusal to go to sleep, I was feeling chesty and asthmatic—in no state for the gruelling 29 kilometres I had planned. I rolled over and went back to sleep.

We all had another lazy morning and eventually got organised for a bus trip to the Horseshoe Bay markets. The bus driver was a lark—a huge personality—pointing out all the sights and attractions and offering cautionary advice to the hikers to drink enough water, and, for those going to the afternoon lorikeet feeding session, to wear a hat to keep off all the bird droppings.

I *love* the Sunday markets. I convinced Chris to let me buy a stunning green and navy tie-dyed slip dress, harking back to the kooky, hippy days of my early 20s. We devoured some Thai street food—curry puffs, pad Thai, satay chicken and papaya salad with prawns. Then we indulged in some *poffertjes* (Dutch mini pancakes) dripping with Nutella for dessert. Daisy was a big fan.

Daisy went to a little pen manned by some local kids and petted and fed their guinea pigs. I got a reflexology foot massage, and Mum relaxed with a head massage while I had a swim. Daisy refused to go in the water, as it was a little muddy and murky. As the markets were packing up, a lady with a dog invited Daisy to come over and say hi and feed her a treat. (The dog, not the lady!)

We crossed the road for some ice cream cones from the famous ice-cream parlour and waited for the bus back to Arcadia, where we'd decided to take Daisy for a swim in the pub's lagoon-style swimming pool. Daisy showed off, walking on tippy toes in water that was much too deep and let me help her float on her back and doggy paddle. She stayed in until her fingers and toes were prune-like, and her little lips were trembling and shivering, then it was time to get dressed, have a quick drink and head back home.

Daisy slept in her pusher while I wrote, and Chris and Mum had an afternoon nap. When she woke up, she played a little, and I continued with my writing until after sundown.

We headed back to the pub for dinner before it got too late and got a bunch of junky, carby food, which I insisted I needed to fuel for tomorrow's make-up run. Once again, Daisy got all excited chasing the curlews and it was hard to keep up with her. We took it in turns chasing her, chasing the birds. Other diners approached us and had to comment on how cute and what a little darling she was—it happens wherever we take her.

Eventually she settled down a bit, and we walked back to the unit, steeling ourselves for another night of tantrums and sleep refusal. True to form, Daisy did not disappoint. I let Chris deal with her and went into Mum's room in the hope of getting some shut-eye. I tossed and turned and couldn't sleep a wink, so I went out in the kitchen to write. A sleepless night before an early morning long run was hardly ideal, but alas, it couldn't be helped. I was determined not to let it phase me and to head out bright and early anyway, after pulling an all-nighter.

Monday, 25 September 2023
Week 17, Day 1
26.4 km Long Run

Today I was hoping to run somewhere between 31 and 33 km, but obviously that didn't happen. At about 5 a.m., I was sitting in the kitchen drinking a Coke Zero, after having 2 Minute noodles for breakfast, when my Mum came out and said, 'You can't expect to go running when you're up at 3 a.m. drinking Coke Zero!' She was pissed off. More likely worried, but it was coming across as pissed off. She probably thought I was manic, which, to be fair, I *have* been a few times during holidays to Magnetic Island.

'It's 5 a.m.!' I protested. 'But you've been up since three!' She had me there. I had literally just been lying awake all night before getting up at three, but I thought it best if she didn't know that. I placated her by going back to bed and lying down, but again, I couldn't sleep. I realised I'd forgotten to take my Olanzapine tablet last night before bed, but it was too late now. It would just make me even more tired all morning.

At around six, or just a bit before, I crept quietly out of bed, got dressed, put on some sunscreen and headed out for the earliest long run I've ever done. At this hour it wasn't yet too hot, but I knew that feeling was only going to last an hour or so before things started to get uncomfortable.

Instead of doing an out-and-back route, I'd just decided to explore the island and run wherever, as Mum would be hiring a car today, and I'd just call her to pick me up when I was done. Magnetic Island is hilly, and unless I was just going to stay close to home and do loops, some major elevation was going to be unavoidable.

After a quick warm-up, I crossed over to the beach side of the road and onto a boardwalk that would take me from Geoffrey Bay, where we were staying, to Nelly Bay, the next town over. It was my first big hill of the day, and it was much bigger than any of the hills back home, but I tackled it OK.

The views were magnificent, turquoise-blue ocean stretching out to the horizon, where the faint outline of Townsville's own hilly landscape could be seen. There were little white peaks, where the waves crashed, along the rocky outcrop of Geoffrey Bay's old ferry terminal. Towering hoop pines dotted the granite coastline, and I even spotted a few sea eagles in the sky.

As I descended into Nelly Bay, I crossed over towards the marina and ran down the canal to the edge of the harbour and back. I enjoyed taking in all the island's unique architecture; with little beach shacks, humble fibro abodes, A-frames, and impressive contemporary designs perched high on the rocks, with steep little steps cut into the granite, hugging the hillsides.

There were a few other runners out, it being the coolest part of the day, and I wondered if they were local or enthusiastic tourists, like me. All of them were much faster and easily overtook me as though it was nothing, and it made me wonder if I would, in fact, come last by a rather large margin on race day.

I made my way to a continuous footpath that would take me all the way from Nelly Bay to Rocky Bay, via the island's most popular backpackers, and up a punishingly steep hill. I ran past a little encampment of vans and four-wheel drives with tents on the rooves and saw a couple of hippies emerging for their morning coffees. We exchanged greetings as I cheerfully jogged past.

As I approached the backpackers, I was flooded with memories, mostly good, but also embarrassing, of my nights spent partying there in my 20s: getting drunk, dancing and picking up guys, skinny-dipping and generally making an ass of myself. A little further up the hill was an old shack, now dilapidated with broken windows, where I'd once spent the night with a tour bus driver I'd only just met. It was a bitter-sweet little pang of nostalgia, seeing it that way. I tried not to think about how worried my folks must have been that night when I didn't come home.

My trips to the island had often coincided with hypomanic and even manic episodes, which brought out an overly confident, hypersexual, wild side—something that must have been a nightmare for my parents to deal with. I would literally stay out all night every night. I'd throw myself at men and ingratiate myself with strangers in a fashion that I thought was charismatic at the time, but which was more likely grating and irritating. I regretted my selfishness and felt that familiar pang of shame that punctuates all my reflections of my unstable youth.

Just past the backpackers was a mammoth hill, I'm talking gargantuan, compared with what we have back home. I've struggled to walk up that hill in the past, feeling like it was absolute torture in the blistering heat. Today, as I weaved back and forth on my route around the island, I managed to run up that hill not one but three times. No wonder I was so tired.

When I got to about 20 km I hit the wall. Big time. I told myself that 20 km wasn't even a half-marathon and pushed on. By then I'd started up my walking and running intervals, and it was getting harder and harder to run for a full four minutes each time. I was constantly glancing at my watch, which seemed to be ticking agonisingly slowly, and landmarks up ahead seemed to get more and more distant. I broke the last part of that run into four-minute chunks, telling myself, *Only four minutes of running, then you can have a break.*

I started to feel my camelback getting lighter and lighter and could barely hear or feel the water sloshing around inside. I'd have to stop somewhere and rehydrate soon—the water I had on me was not going to last the whole run. Not in this punishing heat.

My mouth was dry. My feet were sore. My neck was wet and slippery, and the rest of my body was gritty with the salt of dehydrated sweat. My headphones had died, and it was hard to carry on without the motivation of a good playlist.

For the last six kilometres I was promising myself, *Just one more cycle of running and walking, and then you can give up.* I'd resigned myself to the fact that there was no way I would make the full planned-out distance, and I'd resorted to bargaining with myself to push it as far as possible.

I'd decided to keep the rest of my route flat, even if it meant a lot of repetition. No more hills for me today. At the Nelly Bay shops I turned into Mandalay Avenue—the street where we used to stay in a beautiful resort named Amaroo. My energy was winding further and further down as I passed the resort, and I told myself I'd just run to the end of the street and back, and finally *stop* at Amaroo, where I'd call Mum to come pick me up.

Making it that far was like I'd conquered the impossible. I was staggering, barely holding myself up. I dragged myself into the reception area, and there it was. A miracle! A water cooler and a stack of cups! I filled a cup and gulped down the cool, clear liquid greedily and desperately. Then a second, and a third cup.

I thanked the receptionist and remembered that I hadn't stretched. I forced myself to go through the motions, right there in the reception area, next to the tropical fish tank. I could feel the fishes' eyes on me, judging me, goading me. *Who is this weird woman? Why is she so tired/red/sweaty/exhausted? What's with the backpack and bum-bag?* I felt extremely self-conscious.

I made my way over to the pool area where I told Mum I'd be meeting her and shed myself of all my gear—including my shoes. It felt so good to set those tired feet free! I plopped myself down in the shade on the edge of the baby pool and dunked my feet, swishing them around in the cool water.

I pulled out my phone while I waited for Daisy and Mum and went into my Garmin app to look at my stats. Not good. My average was 9:49 min/km—much too close to that ten-minute pace, which was the slowest I could possibly run and still make cut-off on the day. It was a cause for concern. I was bound to slow down as I approached the 42 km mark, so I needed to shave off quite a few precious seconds to allow for that. I decided to try to fit in another session with my running coach to discuss strategy.

Soon Mum and Daisy arrived with a protein bar and some coconut water, which both went down like absolute heaven. I went to change into my swimsuit, only to realise Mum had accidentally forgotten it. There was nothing for it but to plunge into the pool wearing my shorts and sports bra. It was such a relief! I glided under the cool, clear water to the steps of the pool, where I just collapsed and lounged in the shallows. I was too tired to swim. Mum asked me how far I'd run. When I told her it was 26 km, she exclaimed, 'Very good!'

It didn't feel very good, but her comment was still a nice little boost.

Tuesday, 26 September 2023
Week 17, Day 2
20–30-Minutes of Recovery Exercise

This morning, we decided to take advantage of the car Mum had hired for three days by driving to the other end of the island—to Picnic Bay. I'm not a huge fan of the beach there, but it was nice enough today. The tide was in, which was perfect, as at low tide there's a lot of mud and reef to deal with.

I ran into the water and waded out until I was at waist level, then dived into the waves. Looking after a kid brings your available swimming time down to a minimum, so you must make the most of it. No time to stand, half-in, half-out, building up the nerve to go under!

I looked at my watch: 10:17 a.m. I'd need to swim until 10:37 to get in my minimum 20 minutes of recovery exercise. After doing a few dolphin dives into the shallower waves, I turned over onto my back and kicked my legs, facing the shore and propelling myself out to sea. I went as far as a buoy that was floating in the deeper water, then turned around and headed to shore doing breaststroke. I repeated this little pattern a few times, treading water here and there, and before long I'd been in the water for half an hour.

Meanwhile, on the shore, Daisy was kicking up a fuss. She cried every time Chris brought her down to the water and refused to get in, throwing tantrum after tantrum. She didn't even want to play in the sand. In the end we got back in the car and drove her down to the Nelly Bay foreshore, where there was a little playground. As soon as she saw the swing set, she called out, 'WA!!' and ran over to the swings to be lifted into the little harnessed seat. We always call swings 'Wa' now, as that's the sound she makes as we push her, and she whizzes through the air. 'Whaaa! Whaaa! Whaaa!'

We had agreed to meet some of Mum's friends at our favourite café on the island; Scallywags, a pirate-themed affair run by a family of eccentric hippies. Daisy played on a little ship at the back of the café while the adults sat down to eat.

Mum's friends were happy to see Daisy again; a year had gone by since our last visit. When they'd last seen her, she had still been a baby—not even walking yet. Now she was a big girl! We talked about family, about the local island gossip, and about what had been happening in Mornington, where they had originally lived next-door to Mum and Ivan.

Chris and I checked out the cakes that were on offer and chose a couple to take back to the unit. Then we chilled back at the unit for the rest of the afternoon while Mum went for a walk along Geoffrey Bay. I'd intended for us to eat the cakes that afternoon, but we were so full from lunch, and before long, it was dinner time.

Once again, we thought we'd take advantage of the car and get something from the other side of the island—either Italian from Picnic Bay or fish and chips from Nelly Bay. I checked online to find that the Italian place was closed on a Tuesday, so we ordered the fish and chips, and Mum drove into Nelly Bay to get them.

The food was so-so. I know fish and chips on an island holiday is pretty much a cliché, but I'd been looking forward to it, and was a bit of a letdown.

We had a nice, easy, fuss-free evening, with a bit of TV and playing with some Play-Doh with Daisy, as well as rolling around a little ball that she'd found in one of the cupboards. We scrolled though our Facebook pages, and I got some writing done and messaged back and forth with Christoph. We tried to have an early night, but Daisy decided to make sure *that* wasn't an option.

All in all, I was happy with how the day had gone.

THE BIPOLAR RUNNER

Wednesday, 27 September 2023
Week 17, Day 3
45–60 Minutes of Strength Training

I woke up and had breakfast, then suddenly I didn't feel so great—mentally or physically. I couldn't put my finger on it; I just sort of felt dizzy and exhausted, even though I'd had plenty of sleep, so I went to lie down. I felt kind of lazy and a bit guilty for wasting my time on holiday. Daisy was climbing into her pram and obviously wanting to go outside, so Chris took her for a walk.

Mum wasn't happy. She asked me where Chris was, and then said something along the lines of, 'Whatever. If you're just going to lie around all day, then I'm going for a drive,' then left in a huff.

Now, let me preface this by saying that, in retrospect, my mum is human and was understandably annoyed and a bit anxious because she had to leave for Townsville at 3 p.m. and wanted to get some beach time in before then, but I went into total anxiety mode. In my mind, I was bad at being on holiday, I'd ruined our whole vacation, and my mum was passive-aggressively trying to show that she hated me.

I had a panic attack. I started crying. I was a mess.

I messaged Chris to hurry home, and I frantically whizzed about the unit trying to get ready for the beach as quickly as possible, so as not to incur any more of my mother's (imagined) wrath.

My mother's (imagined) wrath has been a big motif in my life. I spent half of my youth with the vague sense that my mother was constantly frustrated and pissed off about something and assuming that thing was me. She didn't yell, she didn't swear. She wasn't violent or aggressive. I was just overly sensitive to things like her breath and the way she sighed or walked—or the tone of her voice.

She and my father were old-fashioned, and he was always away fishing, while she did all the housework and all the child-rearing of four kids, and I think she resented that. I also had the sense that she was a bit of a martyr and that any offer of help from us would have been rejected—despite all her resentment. In my mind, she was kind of addicted to the burden of all the pent-up anger.

I have all these memories of Mum storming through the house vacuuming, usually wearing thongs. To this day I have anxiety attacks over the sound of a vacuum or thongs slapping on the floor as someone walks from room to room. I even make sure I'm not home whenever Chris is vacuuming. We have a joke that I've made up a lie that I'm 'afraid of the sound of the vacuum' to get out of doing it myself, but as with most jokes, there's an element of truth to it.

So this morning I felt I needed to jump through hoops to try to placate my mother, to mend whatever had been broken by my laziness and selfishness. I did my best to make things right by getting my shit together as quickly as possible to get us all down to the beach in record time.

And it worked. As soon as we got out of the car at Horseshoe Bay and claimed a shady spot on the sand, my mother's mood was lifted. All was forgiven.

Bygones were bygones. Crisis averted.

Unfortunately, Daisy was in a mood of her own. She wasn't interested in the sand; she wasn't interested in the sea. All she wanted to do was cling to her dad. Every time Mum or I tried to engage with her, or if Chris tried to put her down or take her down to the water, she cried and screamed, 'No, no, noooo!'

Eventually we managed to swing her around in little whizzy dizzies in the water without her complaining too much, and she did play in the sand a little, and Chris took her for a walk along the beach.

Mum had packed a picnic lunch of ham, cheese and salad wraps, and we ate under the shade of some banyan trees. Then we took Daisy down the road to the famous ice-cream shop, before heading home so Daisy could have her afternoon nap and Mum could get ready to go sailing in Townsville.

Not having a gym to go to for strength training, I had to improvise. The unit wasn't carpeted, and I didn't have a yoga mat, so I folded a blanket and placed it on the floor to do my bug crawls.

Then I piss-farted around. Then I did 100 wall push-ups, which I'd only just discovered were a thing on YouTube. In between every set of 20, I piss-farted around some more. Then I piss-farted around quite a bit more between five reps of 40 lunges.

It's hard to find the proper motivation to exercise with *any* kind of discipline when you're on holiday. Working out without a gym is kind of like what I imagine working from home is for a lot of people. Too many distractions. Nothing gets done. I'd intended to also do squats and planks, and maybe wander down to some of Geoffrey Bay's outdoor gym equipment, but by the time I was done with my lunges, we had to get ready for dinner.

We'd decided to go to a new restaurant around the corner, before migrating to the pub for the famous weekly toad races, which were held as a fundraiser for the local surf club.

There were a few mix-ups with dinner, and Daisy was still in a weird mood, running around, refusing to sit down, chasing birds, stealing other people's food, and for some reason doggedly attempting, over and over, to get into the door of the shop next-door, which was closed. I think maybe because the door was bright green?

Who knows how a child's mind works?

Anyway, all this made us late for the toad races, or rather—on time—which in terms of securing a spot to watch the action, is definitely *too* late. We tried to find a spot at the back of the crowd where we could get a decent view, but it was pretty hopeless. Also, Daisy didn't seem all that interested.

As I've said, I've been coming to Magnetic Island every year for 20 years, and this was the first time I hadn't sat on the ground right in front of the racing ring. I usually get swept up into the spirit of the auctions and the betting, and cheer and whoop, as the toads hop in random directions, while spectators eagerly wait for the first toad to make it out of the ring.

Tonight, we gave up on the whole thing and just went home. I was more than a little sad but tried to just shrug it off. It had been an anti-climactic night, with a less-than-satisfactory dinner experience and now this. It had been a weird day in general, with Mum, Daisy and me all being a little off, and a vague sense of ennui over the monotony of my training.

Thursday, 28 September 2023
Week 17, Day 4
Rest Day

This morning, while Chris had a sleep in, Mum Daisy and I decided to go for a walk to Alma Bay to see if the sea was rough or calm and whether there was any wind. It was perfect! *So* perfect that Mum decided to pop home and get all our beach things and then come back.

While she was gone, Daisy approached a little girl on the beach, and I politely asked if she could borrow one of her plastic spades. Daisy watched the little girl make sand castles and tried to dig with the spade, but then, disaster struck.

Daisy ran over to the little girl's sandcastle, which she'd been working hard on, and destroyed it with the spade. 'Daisy! No!' I exclaimed, and of course Daisy started crying. She doesn't like being told off. 'Say sorry to the little girl.' I said.

Poor Daisy, who had no idea what she'd done, was getting worked up, so I took her over to the swing set on the foreshore to calm her down.

Once she was on the 'waah,' Daisy calmed down quickly, and as I pushed her, I kept an eye out for Mum.

Before long, she arrived with all the beach stuff, and I went into the bathroom to get changed. Then we changed Daisy and covered ourselves in sunscreen.

Today Daisy was in a much better mood, and much more interested in the beach. Maybe it was the calmness of the ocean and the lack of wind.

It was a beautiful day.

Daisy ran in and out of the shallows of the water; I took her in with me and whizzed her around, carving through the water, leaving splashes in our wake. She was giggling and squealing and having fun! Mum and I took turns playing with her so we could each have a swim, then Chris arrived with some drinks and snacks.

We ate the dips and crackers together; Daisy mostly licking the dip off and just sucking the crackers. Then we went to explore a little tidal river that we saw some other kids playing in.

The water was clear, warm and shallow, and Daisy loved it. She walked in up to her neck, and I had to wade around trying to keep up with her in case she went under.

Eventually she started to look cold, so we got her out, stripped off her bathers, and put her into a clean nappy and fresh clothes. Meanwhile, Mum went to get her an ice-cream. Once she'd finished licking the melting, dripping cone, we headed home so that she could have a nap.

The afternoon rolled along, and we had toasted sandwiches for lunch before heading back out to the pub to swim in the baby pool. Daisy was having the time of her life. Both Chris and I were in the water with her, and we took turns throwing her up in the air, helping her 'swim' and catching her as she jumped off the edge of the pool.

Soon, another little girl arrived, and it turned out she was almost the exact same age as Daisy. They played together, and we chatted to the parents, and Daisy decided she was obsessed with the little girl's mother. She kept reaching out to her and calling, 'Mum! Mum! Uppa! Uppa!' meaning she wanted to be picked up. The woman thought it was sweet and indulged her in some cuddles. I laughed and protested, 'I'm your mum, Daisy!'

We tried three times to get her out of the water, as she was trembling and her little lips were getting blue, but she was having none of it. As long as her friend and her new 'mum' were still in the pool, she wasn't going anywhere! The poor trio were trying to take some family photos, and we tried as best we could to stay out of their way.

Eventually we all got out, got dry, dressed and parted ways, with Daisy reaching out and calling, 'Mum! Mum!' as we pried her away from the woman. I joked to Chris that people probably thought we were kidnapping her!

We ordered some pizza to go, got some drinks from the bottle shop, and headed back to the unit. Daisy managed to eat some pizza, much to our surprise. She'd hardly eaten anything all holiday. The alcoholic ginger beer we'd purchased went down a treat, and it turned out to be a nice evening.

Throughout the day, I'd been messaging back and forth with Stuart, my run coach. I'd contacted him because I was concerned that I'd only managed 26.4 km on Monday and about my average pace. I asked him if he thought a run/walk ratio of 5/2 would be better to increase my pace, but instead, he suggested 3/1. Shorter bursts of faster running would get me across the finish line quicker. He was determined for me to finish the race in under six hours, which sounded to me a little ambitious. There was also one more thing that was worrying me. A cough. A chesty cough. I can't afford to get sick now! Not two weeks out!

Friday, 29 September 2023
Week 17, Day 5
45–60-Minute Training Run

I woke up feeling ordinary. The cough had gotten worse. I felt like there was *no* way I'd be able to go out running and maintain a decent pace for 45 minutes.

But as you can tell, I'm stubborn, and a bit of a stickler for sticking to my training plan, to a fault. I took a couple of puffs of my asthma puffer and decided to give it my best shot.

As I made my way down the driveway, out towards the road, I saw a group of runners getting ready to head out. Proper runners. Athletic, tanned, lithe, muscular. Donned in short shorts and crop tops, looking like something out of a fitness magazine!

I was struck by an astonishing wave of insecurity like I'd never felt before. My mind was flooded with self-doubt. Who was I to call myself a runner? I had no business being a runner! I didn't belong in a race like the Melbourne Marathon. I was pathetic. I was fat, I was slow, and I'd always be fat and slow.

Running with these thoughts in my head, listening to my laboured breathing, I felt like I just couldn't find my rhythm. Where was the lightness in my stride that had always come to me on the Eastlink trail back home? Then I realised—I was running without music! I'd completely forgotten to turn on my headphones and press play!

I rectified the situation and immediately felt a shift. I also decided to shift that damn attitude. *You are a runner. You've trained bloody hard. You've lost so much weight. You've turned your life around*, I told myself.

I envisioned my life as it would be if I hadn't discovered running. By now,

I'd probably be morbidly obese, at risk of diabetes and heart failure. Possibly in need of a walker or a cane, just to support my weight. I'd seen it happen to others. It was where I'd been headed.

I thought about the newspaper articles that had been written about me, about the attention from Beyond Blue and the Marathon PR team. They all saw something in me—something inspirational. I was a beacon of hope for a whole new breed of runners—people defying the odds. People who never thought they'd make it to the start line, let alone the finish line.

I was fat and I was slow, but I was bloody doing it anyway, and that was admirable.

Forty-five minutes felt like *ages*. With what was probably a chest infection, my fitness had been severely impacted. Every kilometre felt like ten.

I plugged on, determined. I avoided hills and ran back and forth close to home so I wouldn't have to do a long cool down walk.

Finally, after counting down the seconds of the last ten minutes, I made it to 45 minutes, pressed stop on my Garmin, and walked home. I'd made it!

Even when I was not feeling the best, I'd put in the work and got it done. And my pace was decent 8:15 minutes per kilometre—much closer to the pace Stuart was hoping for in my marathon.

I'd figured maintaining a faster pace was largely a matter of technique. All of my slow runs had been completely different in terms of motion. My strides were shorter and heavier. I was kind of trudging and shuffling. With bigger, bouncier strides, maybe I could cover more distance, in less time, without expending too much energy. It was worth a try. I decided to experiment with my long run on Sunday, then touch base with Stuart again.

It was a bitter-sweet day today, as it was our last day in Magnetic Island. We went back to Alma Bay, had our last swims and ice-creams, and headed back home to pack our suitcases to be ready for Mum's friend to give us a lift to the 6:00 p.m. ferry.

The trip home was a whole thing. The car ride to the ferry, ferry to Townsville, shuttle to the airport, flight, shuttle to the car park, drive home. Daisy was OK on the plane until it was time to put our seatbelts on for landing, and then she had the biggest tantrum I've ever seen! Kicking and screaming and bucking in spasms, yelling, 'Nooooo! Noo!' Repeatedly. I was so embarrassed and felt so sorry for everyone else on the plane.

When we got home, it was midnight, and my coughing had become serious. I fell into bed and sighed. It was back to reality now. Our week in paradise was over.

Saturday, 30 September 2023
Week 17, Day 6
Rest Day

Today was a relaxing and chilled-out 'nothing' day. We watched some TV, went to the supermarket, and, in the afternoon, I went to the doctor.

Being a Saturday, they only had one doctor on, and it turned out to be the same doctor who had refused to give me a preventative medication for my asthma and who had suggested to me that perhaps I should quit running. I explained that I'd been coughing up a lot of phlegm, that I was pretty sure I had a chest infection, and that I was eager to recover, as I was running a marathon in two weeks.

He was highly unsympathetic. I'd been hoping to get some antibiotics, but he suggested some cough medicine and said I 'should' be better in two weeks. 'Should' wasn't good enough. There was too much riding on this.

I'd been working so hard for the last six months, not just on my training but also on this book and all the fundraising. I'd been in three newspapers, and they discussed putting me on the news.

I left the doctor frustrated and went home after stopping at the chemist to get my bloody cough medicine.

Sunday, 1 October 2023
Week 17, Day 7
Rest Day

I decided not to run today. As usual, I turned to my internet support last night and asked for advice. I detailed my predicament on a couple of Facebook marathon training groups, asking whether I should run, rest, or compromise with a slower pace or shorter distance. Most people advised me to rest. I sent a message to Stuart saying I was thinking of trying my luck with a long run, and when he wrote back, it was a resounding, 'Bad, bad idea!'

So I listened and had another rest day. I also decided to seek a second opinion from a general practitioner who specialised in sports physiology and did some googling. I found a couple who were not too far away and decided to call them first thing in the morning. I'd also decided not to go to work tomorrow. Aside from needing the rest and the doctor's visit, I was probably quite contagious with all that coughing.

Monday, 2 October 2023
Week 18, Day 1
Rest Day

Another rest day. Another day at home. I got a little sleep in, as Daisy hasn't yet adjusted to Daylight Savings Time. To be honest, neither have I. My body clock's out a whole hour, feeling as though it's earlier than it is. For a person who's already fundamentally lazy, it's not a good state to be in! Not sure how I'll adjust, going back to school.

I woke up at 8:30 a.m., and tried calling one of the doctors I'd googled, but I just got the practice's answering machine; then fell back asleep until 10 a.m. In that time, I had constant dreams about calling doctors, looking at Google Maps, and not being able to get an appointment. This happens to me a lot—where my dreams are so close to reality, in real-time—to the point where it's incredibly confusing and anxiety-inducing. I can't tell if I'm dreaming or awake.

At 10 a.m. I was a little freaked out by all the dreams, and I was terrified it was too late in the morning to secure an appointment. Luckily my fears were unfounded, and I managed to get in to a clinic at Rowville at 3:15 p.m.

The doctor was amazing. He took the time to listen to me, listen to my chest, check my temperature, check my oxygen levels and consider thoughtfully what our best course of action was for me to be ready on race day. 'We'll have to hit it hard,' he said. He prescribed some strong steroids and a preventative asthma medication—something I'd been asking my usual doctors for since the start of hay fever season.

Friday, 6 October 2023
Week 18, Day 5
Rest Day

I haven't written in days.

I almost gave up—on this book, on the marathon, the fundraising, everything. My whole life has been falling apart. The only training I've done all week was a 60-minute power walk yesterday. I managed to maintain a sub-ten-minute pace, so if worse comes to worst, in theory, I can just walk as fast as I can for roughly seven hours and make the cut-off on race day!

I honestly don't know if I'm fit enough right now to even keep up a brisk walk for that long though.

I'm depressed. I'm not coping. I'm struggling. This morning, I woke up and vomited in the toilet, then felt sick all day. I spent pretty much the whole day in bed, only getting up to eat a few mouthfuls of sandwich, then finally emerging in the afternoon to attempt to cheer myself up by watching a movie, which I couldn't even get into or focus on at all.

Then I forced myself to make a risotto for Daisy so that I could at least be able to say I'd achieved one small thing in my day. I had a panic attack over making that risotto. My mind drew a blank and I forgot how to make it and it took every ounce of concentration just to get the ingredients out of the fridge and follow the instructions on the packet. Chris put on music, which is usually uplifting for me while I cook, but today it was just noise.

After that, I totally broke down and just spent hours huddled on the couch, crying. Chris didn't know what to do. I didn't know what to do. I didn't know what I needed and who or what would help.

I felt like a failure; like the last six months had just been a complete waste of time. So many hours training for this marathon, so much work put into it, so much mental and physical energy. And now it seemed like it was all for nothing. I have no confidence that I'm going to be able to run, or even walk, 42 kilometres in less than seven hours next Sunday. Such an anti-climax.

If the story has no proper ending, the whole thing was pointless. I haven't been able to write anything lately for several reasons. Nothing's been happening, and I've had nothing to write about. I haven't had the time or the energy.

Why did I ever think I'd be able to write a book? Why did I ever think I'd be able to run a marathon? I've had stupid ideas and delusions in the past, but I've never taken anything this far. Usually, after a couple of months at the most, I realise I've been overly ambitious and sensibly abandon whatever impossible feat I've gotten myself into.

But this time I allowed myself to believe in the dream, and pushed on and on with it, focused on nothing else. I don't know if that's a bad thing or a good thing. People are proud of me. People are rooting for me. I wanted to raise $10,000 and so far, it's a little more than $3,000. I could see that as a huge failure, or a good effort. A third of the way there.

There's a possibility that I'll be too sick on race day to even attempt the race. If that's the case I'll turn up anyway, in my Beyond Blue singlet and hat, and support the other marathoners, cheering them across the finish line. I still want to be involved in the event. I don't want to stay at home feeling bitter. There's also the possibility I'll start the race and won't be able to complete it. I don't even want to think about the kind of devastation and embarrassment that would make me feel.

Saturday, 7 October 2023
Week 18, Day 6
Rest Day

Today, after huddling on the couch again and crying for hours at home, I'm being brave. I went to the library. I opened my laptop. I've 'put on my big girl pants.' I have a back-up plan in case this all goes pear-shaped. I must stop feeling sorry for myself.

After I went to the library, I just didn't feel right. I thought getting back on top of things, writing-wise, would make me feel better, some kind of relief. But it was hard to be happy with what I'd written, to go over it, and to fully concentrate; my mind was just mush.

Not long after I'd closed my laptop and given up, Chris called and said that he was at the shopping centre with Daisy and asked if I wanted to join them for lunch. I said yes, because when I'm like this, it's a relief when decisions are made for me, and I don't have to think about things.

I got into the car and drove to the shopping centre on autopilot, trying to think about what I was going to have from the food court. Decisions, decisions. I settled on lasagne, just because it was what I'd eaten the last time I was there. I couldn't put my finger on what I felt like; in fact, I didn't have much of an appetite at all.

I went through the motions of cutting up my food and gingerly spooning it into my mouth, barely tasting it. Certainly not enjoying it. At one point Chris left Daisy and I to go and get some juice, and she got a bit sooky and restless. I didn't know how to handle it. I was hopeless and useless, like somebody who has never spent time with a kid before. I felt self-conscious like everyone in the food court was looking at me and thinking I was a bad mum.

Sometimes depression and anxiety are not dramatic; not all crying and panic attacks. Sometimes it's just permeating and lingering, like living in a fog. You feel almost like you're floating just above the world and not quite connected to it. Things that people say to you seem far away and go over your head. You're just not present, and you don't know how to be. Just occupying a space with any sort of weight feels difficult.

All day today, I was filled with this all-encompassing feeling of emotional discomfort. I couldn't shake it; it just wouldn't go away. When this feeling descends and takes hold, the time drags by, and you don't know how to fill it. You can't concentrate on things like television or a book. It's as though you're counting down the hours until you can go to bed, fall asleep and surrender to that sweet oblivion.

When it was time for Chris to go to bed, I felt a sense of anguish and grief and hopelessness once again. I just didn't want him to leave my side. I didn't know how I was going to cope with Daisy and how to just be awake and sitting in the lounge without him there. I felt like I was losing my anchor. I put on a brave face, because I knew as his bedtime approached, the minutes ticking by with him just worrying about me was equalling precious lost sleep for him.

With great difficulty, I held it together and managed to do all the little things I had to do to entertain Daisy until it was time to put her to bed. I'd made it through the day, and I could sleep (with the help of medication) and not have to worry about my life and how to cope until tomorrow.

Sunday, 8 October 2023
Week 18, Day 7
10 km Long Run

This morning, I woke up feeling terrible. Physically, I was fine. My chest infection has mostly gone away, and I'm close to feeling back to 100% in that regard. But I can't shake this funk.

This morning, my mum was coming to watch Daisy while I went for my run. I was hoping she'd arrive while we were still in bed so that she could drag me out and handle the morning routine tasks, like changing Daisy and giving her breakfast. I was just lying in bed, feeling flat, praying that Daisy wouldn't wake up just yet and that Mum would get there soon.

In the end, we had to get up and face the day without her, and I did everything I needed to, but I was still a mess. I felt panicky that she wasn't there. I felt like I'd fallen overboard and needed someone to toss me a life raft. I was begging in my head, *Please, please turn up soon, I can't do this without you.*

I wasn't left hanging for long, and when Mum came in the door ready to lend a hand, I had to apologise that we weren't dressed, and I hadn't had my breakfast. When she asked how I was, I said I was 'OK physically . . . ' then let the rest of the sentence hang in the air. I didn't need to say any more.

She was sympathetic, but she was also all about getting down to business. 'I've made you a few containers of fried rice,' she said as she went to the fridge. 'What have you got in here that I can cook for you?' I went over the ingredients from our meal kits and what needed to be done with them.

'What usually makes you feel better when you feel like this?'

I shrugged. I didn't think anything would work. I said, 'Stuff like having a shower, putting on nice clothes, putting on music. It hasn't been helping.'

'Normally you feel a lot better after a short run . . . ' she offered. I agreed with her. It almost always helps—like a reset.

'I'm doing 13 km today,' I said. 'I think I'll feel a bit better after that.'

I was feeling apprehensive as I got ready. Would I be able to run 13 km? Would I be fast, would I be slow? Would I run out of breath? Would I have to walk most of the way, and if so, would I be able to walk fast enough? Would today's run be a confidence boost that I was finally back on track, or just a bad omen that next Sunday was going to be a disaster?

My coach Stuart suggested that I need to get my pace up a bit so that I'm closer to the six-hour mark than the seven-hour mark. This is supposed to allow for things like slowing down or needing to stop for the toilet at an aide station. He suggested three minutes of running and one minute of walking, which was less recovery time than a 4/3 ratio but also less time to keep up a decent pace. It made sense.

Once I was walking into my warm-up with my music on, my troubles were pushed momentarily to the side, and my head was in the game. I was in action mode!

As I started to run, I made a conscious effort not to plod, not to shuffle. It's been a bad habit on all my slow and easy runs, and I'd made the decision to take longer, bouncier strides for better economy of movement. I needed to employ better technique, as sloppy running was slowing me down and using just as much energy.

I was less than a kilometre in when I realised my lungs weren't feeling great. I wasn't having an asthma attack, and I could breathe okay, but my breathing just felt more shallow than usual and a little laboured. There was still something lingering from that chest infection.

I hadn't covered much more than two kilometres when I started to feel worried. If I ran 6.5 km away from home and then turned back, I was worried I might not make it all the way. I'd have to call Mum to come and pick me up. I didn't want to be left stranded.

I turned around and slowed to a walk, still a fast walk, but I'd given up on running. Was this going to just be a four-kilometre run/walk? Was this going to be an epic failure? Less than an hour on my feet?

I thought today was not the day to give up so easily. I decided to run closer to home, then run/walk circles around the block, keeping my pace up as best as I could, and hopefully get a decent length run in. Maybe even the 13 km I had planned. My spirit was weak, and I needed to buck up and find it again.

After a bit of a walking break that I didn't bother to time (as I mentioned, I'd virtually given up), I took a deep breath, set my head straight and picked up my speed to a determined trot. *Bounce, bounce, bounce,* went my ponytail. Big strides. *Pretend this is the marathon.*

As I neared my street, I found myself walking again. Should I just go home? Conserve my energy and hope for the best on the day. Just pack it in? Maybe. I'd see how I felt in a couple of blocks.

I did my best to just snap out of it. This wasn't good enough! I had to try, God-damn it! Where was that spunk and pluckiness I'd had only a few weeks ago? Where was my confidence? Where was the focus? That little light had faded in me somehow, and I had to reignite it.

Once again, I started running, but this time, I looked at my watch. Three minutes. That's all I needed to do—three-minute intervals. Three minutes is not a long time.

In theory.

I took in my surroundings and started marking little milestones along the way. That bush, that tree, that letterbox. *I just need to make it that far, and then I can look down at my watch,* I kept telling myself.

In my one-minute 'breaks', I still powered forward. If I was resorting to intervals this early on, my walk had to be a fast one. My walk had been a virtual crawl when I'd suffered through that dismal long run in Magnetic Island. I couldn't afford to let that happen—not now—and certainly not on race day.

I tried to take in the sunshine and draw some positivity from the weather. It was a beautiful day. The sky was blue, and the people I passed seemed to be in a good mood. I soaked up that positive energy and fed on it to get me through.

I was doing it! I was running at a decent pace! I wasn't collapsing at the end of each three-minute stretch! My walk was swift and energised and not just a lumbering lope. I was beginning to think I might be able to run the freaking Melbourne Marathon!

On Thursday night, I'd met a lovely woman who'd run the Melbourne Marathon twelve times. Her words resounded in my head, 'There's going to come a point where you're going to want to stop. Don't! Walk if you have to, but whatever you do, don't stop. Because once you stop, you won't be able to get going again.'

I decided to adopt those words as a mantra for race day, as if she was running beside me, guiding me on.

I ran a lot further than I expected to. At 9 km I still had a fair bit of energy but decided to call it a day once I hit ten. Today was more about the mental game than anything else. Ten solid kilometres under my belt that I felt confident about would be better than 13 km where I ended up flailing and floundering. I still had a bit of healing and recovery to do, and a whole week to let nature run its course and let my body do its thing.

I had my coconut water and shower and dressed up in my favourite colour—yellow. Accessories and all. Chris asked if I was going somewhere. 'No,' I smiled. 'I just wanted to look nice.'

I made a bit of a plan in my head to get my body and mind ready over the next seven days. Lots of carbs. Lots of water. Watching *Brittany Runs a Marathon* again. Looking over my half-marathon race day photos to get some inspiration. Laying out my outfit, trying it on. Packing my bag. I'd also make a little plan of what to do afterwards—where to go, how to celebrate. Maybe I should book in to get my celebratory tattoo as well. No more failure mindset. No more defeatist attitude.

The countdown is on.

Monday, 9 October 2023
Week 19, Day 1
20-30 Minutes of Recovery Exercise

I had terrible night sweats again last night. I woke up with my pyjamas soaking after intense and vivid dreams. As I slowly came into consciousness, I curled up even further into a ball and clung to the covers. How would I get out of bed? How would I go to work? How would I think? How would I function? I was struggling. I couldn't cope.

I tried to visualise the day ahead, and it just loomed ominously. I'd have to pretend to be OK. I'd have to hold it together. I'd have to breathe, and function, and go through all the motions of planning, teaching, communicating and interacting like a normal human being. I felt like I couldn't do it, but I knew I had no choice. *Be brave, Jacqui*, I tried to tell myself.

I pulled myself out of bed and got dressed without even showering the disgusting sweat off me. I'd slept in too late for a shower, and the idea of having one was too overwhelming anyway. My appetite still hadn't returned, so I forced myself to have a banana and a cup of tea, all the while freaking out and trying to stave off a full-blown panic attack.

I was in a real state. I decided to take a Valium. I would have taken two, but my limit is two per day, and I wanted to save one in case I needed it at school. It's hard to say whether it had an effect or not.

Shortly, Tonia arrived to watch Daisy, and I answered the door with an obvious tear trickling down my cheek. She asked me how I was, and I replied, 'Not good,' and she gave me a huge, tight, long hug. It was hard to appreciate the hug and fully take it in, in case it made me cry even more, so I withdrew from the hug, barely made eye contact, grabbed my things and headed out the door.

I forgot to say goodbye to Daisy, so I popped back in and gave her a hug and a kiss. I felt terrible for that. What kind of a mother am I? So wrapped up in my own bullshit!

On the way to work I listened to the usual breakfast radio and hoped it would cheer me up, but it didn't help at all.

When I reached the traffic lights just around the corner from work, I thought, *Oh God, I'm almost there, and I still haven't pulled myself together.* I envisioned myself just sitting in my car in the car park before work with my head in my hands, crying. I thought how embarrassing it would be if someone saw me and tapped on my window.

Against all odds, I did it. I composed myself and went into work, ready to give whatever the day threw at me my best shot. At recess, one of my colleagues asked how I was going. I replied, 'A bit of a shaky start, but we're getting there.'

She asked if my student was a bit off. I replied honestly that it was me who was a bit off. I admitted that I still haven't gotten back into the swing of things after the school holidays and being ill. She agreed that it was hard getting used to being back.

I sort of feel proud of myself for these little exchanges. For being able to be honest and vulnerable. I hate holding it in, and I hate pretending, but it's the easiest thing to do, and 'Fine, thanks' or 'I'm good, thanks,' extra chirpy is the gut-reaction response I usually come out with. I want to push beyond that etiquette and do my part to forge a path where it's oky and—dare I say it—'normal' to talk about this stuff like it's a sniffly nose or a tickly throat. Baby steps.

My recovery exercise was a quick and simple 20-minute walk.

Tuesday, 10 October 2023
Week 19, Day 2
Rest Day

This morning was like a repeat performance of yesterday. The night sweats were even worse. My pyjamas were dripping wet, the sheets were wet, even the doona cover was wet! At least it was an impetus to get out of bed. I got out of bed a bit earlier than usual and showered for once. My hair was all matted, and I stank to high heaven.

Anxiety was still at an all-time high, that vague feeling of existential dread. Sometimes at times like these it helps to put a post on my bipolar page on Facebook. I posted that I just wanted to crawl into a hole and die, then clarified that by 'hole', I meant 'bed', and by 'die', I meant to lie down for a whole week and not talk to anyone or do anything.

I'm not suicidal. I don't want to self-harm, but I just get hit by the overwhelming sense that I just can't do it all. That I can't do anything.

I feel like these emotions are just so big to bursting inside me, and I need to get them out to unburden myself. I think about my support system in my depression management plan. Friends like Jess and Rob. Margaret. Mum and Chris. They all have a sort of sense and inkling that things aren't quite right, but none of them have any idea of how bad it is. How could they?

I contemplate sending out a group text message to give them the run-down. I'm not sure what I'd say. Something like, 'Hi, all, because I've listed you all as my closest supports in terms of my mental health, I just wanted you all to know that I'm not well. I'm going through a major depressive episode, with features of high anxiety and difficulty functioning. I'm still going to work at this stage and trying to carry on as normal, but I just wanted to touch base with all of you so you're not blindsided if things get any worse.'

That's quite good. I might send out a message in those exact words if I can pluck up the courage.

I also thought about making my colleagues aware of the situation at school. I already disclosed my bipolar disorder to a few colleagues I work closely with, but we now have a new principal and a new teacher in the room next door who are not up to speed. I could send out a quick email to say I'm in a depressive episode or just have a quick talk to my classroom teacher, letting him know.

The problem is, though, there's nothing they can do. They can check in and encourage me, but things that I'd like to do, like duck out of the classroom for a cup of tea or a quick five- to ten-minute meditation when I'm feeling overwhelmed are not practical. I don't know what the solution is.

I got to school and opened the playgroup room, and I was crying and gasping for breath as I set everything up, then just sat there in tears, waiting for everyone to arrive.

Then a strange thing happened. As Mum, Daisy, Margaret, and George came in the door, my mood started to lift. I was able to stop crying and, believe it or not, smile and laugh—genuine smiles and genuine laughter. I didn't feel like I was just barely holding it together; I felt present and relaxed.

A couple of other mums arrived with their kids a bit later and it felt nice to see them, and I felt like I was able to establish a genuine connection and relationship. It didn't feel disconnected and forced like it sometimes does when I'm depressed or anxious.

By the time playgroup was over, I did a bit of an emotional stocktake and realised all the intense negative feelings from the start of the day had basically washed away! Also, the sun had come out, which always helps me feel more positive.

It felt like a miracle. I felt grateful that, even though I'd started feeling depressed and anxious last Wednesday night and had been consistently bad ever since, I was still able to find small moments, like going out with Chris on Thursday night, and then today, where things were basically okay. I wasn't a lost cause.

I got through the working day much better than anticipated, and I didn't have any little 'moments' or need to take any more Valium. I was bloody proud of myself.

Wednesday, 11 October 2023
Week 19, Day 3
30-Minute Run

Last night the night sweats weren't so bad. I did sweat a little, but the bed sheets were spared, and it didn't feel like someone had tipped a bucket of water over me in the night.

It wasn't hard to get out of bed to greet Daisy and Mum or to have breakfast. I left the house feeling okay. It was only as I got into the car and started driving to work that that familiar panic started to hit me. Tears were welling up, and I started feeling more and more anxious the closer I got to work.

Just around the corner from work, I pulled over and just let myself cry, collapsing into an absolute puddle. I couldn't help but think, *What do I even do now if I get sick?* I knew from experience that periods of feeling like this could go on for weeks or even months. I spent the better parts of 2020 and 2021 profoundly depressed, and I'm astonished I got through it.

In the past, if I've been suicidal, I've had stays in the psychiatric ward, or the slightly less extreme precaution has been to stay in a rehabilitation-type centre, called PARC, which stands for Prevention and Recovery Centre. PARC is like hospital, and you usually stay for about a week. There are full-time staff, who facilitate activities, and it's similar to a share house, where you all do the grocery shopping together, and the patients take turns cooking dinner for everyone.

Things would have to be dire to resort to either of those two options, but there has to be some sort of happy medium between admission to the mental health system and just toughing it out and going to work every day.

I think we need to come up with a plan, so I feel like at least I have options for what will happen if I become so unwell that I can't function at all. Maybe option one could be having a week or two off work, and option two (for if I'm too unwell to even look after Daisy) could perhaps look like Mum taking a week off work and coming to stay with us. There's also the option of contacting the CAT, or Crisis Assessment Team, who do home visits, checking in on mental health patients.

In terms of psychiatric hospital admissions, the public health system is extremely stretched, and it's not just a matter of feeling like you need a wee break and checking yourself into hospital. To be hospitalised in a mental health ward, you usually have to be a danger to yourself or to others, and you often have to justify an admission by proving that you don't have adequate support at home. Occasionally, a patient will be hospitalised to observe a change in medication or for something like ECT (electro-convulsive therapy), but those instances are fairly uncommon.

Thinking through all this stuff wasn't helpful, as I'm just so scared of telling people I'm not OK. Maybe I'm scared of them not believing me, not listening to me, or not taking me seriously. I also have this irrational fear that saying I need more help will make people angry with me, which is crazy, as that's never happened in the past.

As I got to work and started preparing for the day, I was still in anxiety mode. My chest felt constricted, and I realised I was only taking the shallowest of breaths. I made a conscious effort to focus on my breathing, like we're always telling the kids to do, and chided myself for not thinking of that sooner. It's so obvious! Then I took a Valium.

By the time the bell went, I had calmed myself sufficiently to begin working in earnest, and I soldiered on through a day that seemed long but was, all in all, surprisingly OK.

Then after work, I got my shit together for a half-hour run. It wasn't a great run, or even a good run, but it was a run nonetheless!

I'm stronger than I give myself credit for.

Thursday, 12 October 2023
Week 19, Day 4
Rest Day

This morning the alarm went off before 8 a.m., and I just rolled over and said to myself, 'No. No sir. Not today. There is no way we're going to that nine o'clock swimming class.' Then I set the alarm for a little before nine, aiming for the ten o'clock class. Nine a.m. rolled around, and my attitude hadn't changed. *Not a chance,* I thought and let out a deep breath of relief that I'd given myself permission to have a real sleep in.

We all slept in—Daisy, Chris (it was his day off) and me. For once I didn't feel guilty. It felt like necessary self-care. For a week I'd basically been in fight-or-flight survival mode, and I needed this. I wasn't a bad mum; I was just putting on my oxygen mask first like the flight attendants always say you should do.

When Daisy finally woke up, Chris offered to feed and change her, and I lay in bed for a little while longer.

'Is there anything you need to do today?' he asked me.

'No,' I replied. 'I have to go into the city to pick up my race bib at some stage either today, tomorrow or Saturday.'

'Why don't you do it now?' he suggested, not in a pushy way, just gently encouraging. 'It'll be good for you to get out of the house.' I thought about it and agreed with him.

I hopped into the car and typed 'MCG' into the GPS. I live in Melbourne. I should know how to get to the MCG (or Melbourne Cricket Ground). It's where most of our major sporting events and mega stadium concerts are held. But I hate driving into the city and have a terrible fear of getting lost and facing the worst-case scenario, one of Melbourne's infamous hook-turns.

So I listened carefully to the GPS instructions and diligently followed them. Soon, the MCG was in my sights, but there was no parking anywhere.

Amazonian men and women in athletic gear were darting in and out of traffic, obvious marathoners, some holding race bibs and some on their way to get them. I'd thought that, with the marathon office being open to the public for three days, the pick-ups would be more spread out, but I was wrong. Even in the middle of a workday, it was an absolute shit show!

I drove around and around until I found something, a bit of a hike away, but good enough. I made a concentrated mental note of exactly where my car was situated and then walked through the Botanical Gardens to the hallowed MCG. When I got there, I was swept up in Marathon Fever. The whole place was decked out with signage and banners heralding the upcoming event, as if it was the Olympics or the Australian Open. I hadn't, up until that moment, realised what a big deal this all was! It was a major sporting event, and I was taking part in it. Little old me!

When I approached the desk and the man handed me my bib and four shiny silver pins, I suddenly felt excited and special! It was like Christmas and Easter and my birthday all rolled into one! I was like a little kid! I was smiling so hard my face hurt!

I strolled over to a big Nike Melbourne Marathon sign and accosted a stranger. 'Can you please take a photo of me in front of this sign?' I asked shyly.

'Are you running the marathon?' he asked.

'Sure am!' I beamed, and he quickly snapped some photos of me holding up my race bib. I thanked him profusely and immediately posted the photos on Instagram.

Friday, 13 October 2023
Week 19, Day 5
Rest Day

Unfortunately, yesterday's excitement didn't last. I was in a funk again. I was feeling flat, and I had no energy. I'd planned on another easy half-hour run, but I just didn't have it in me, so I decided to 'listen to my body.' I knew I was just making excuses, but I didn't care. I was depressed. I just wasn't feeling it.

Dad came to visit, but it didn't lift my spirits. It had been raining for a few days, and Daisy hadn't had a chance to play outside, so she was restless and moody. I felt incredibly embarrassed at how obviously addicted to the iPad she was and felt like my dad must be justifiably judging our parenting choices.

I felt awkward like I didn't have the social skills to entertain my dad or be a proper host. I offered him a cup of coffee, but we didn't have any food in the house. Chris had to run to 7-Eleven to get some sandwiches.

Dad wanted to be there this Sunday, but in the end, he was too worried about being jostled in the crowd and hurting his broken ribs. We agreed it was a bad idea.

I explained that there was an App he could use to track me in real-time as I ran the race, and he was gobsmacked as if I'd mentioned super-intelligent robots or space travel. 'How the hell do they do that?' he marvelled.

'There's a chip in your race bib,' I explained. Dad was sceptical. He didn't trust this kind of 'new-fangled' technology.

I also said he could click on a link and type in his email address to receive all the photos as they were being taken, but I think he found it too overwhelming.

He much preferred to look at the course map Mum had printed out for me and analysed the route. Maps he could handle. Maps he could understand. He was a fisherman. I think he still owns a Melways (a big publication known as a street directory) and keeps it in his car. I'm not sure if it's intended to be a nostalgic relic or if he uses it in place of Google Maps. My dad is the absolute archetypal 'old man,' God bless him.

Saturday, 14 October 2023
Week 19, Day 6
Race Day Eve

The funk continues. This morning, I slept in, then felt incredibly anxious about fitting all my plans into the day. I was supposed to vote in the Referendum, then meet Margaret for a play date, then be at Chris's grandparents' house by 2 p.m. I'd predicted big crowds at the voting booths and thought it'd be a good idea to get there when they opened at 8:30 a.m., but of course, my lazy arse couldn't get moving and make that happen.

I decided to go to the closest voting centre, at Dandenong Stadium. It was pandemonium. The traffic was insane. It took me forever just to turn into the car park. There was a pile-up in both directions. The car park was filled to the brim, and people were driving up onto the curb and parking on the grass, squeezing into every available inch of space. I had to do the same thing. I hadn't experienced anything like it since the COVID vaccinations at Sandown Park a couple of years ago.

I waited in line for more than 45 minutes. The queue was all the way out the door, went around the corner of the building, and was moving at a snail's pace. I had poor Daisy with me, and she was in a bad mood.

I hadn't brought the pram, thinking I could just hold her, but I hadn't anticipated such a long wait, and with how much she'd grown lately, she was just too heavy! I had to keep putting her down, but every time I tried, she cried and gripped onto my hips for dear life, lifting her little legs up into the air so that I wouldn't be able to set her down.

I was in a mood too—not just about the wait and the crowds, but by the 'Vote No' people aggressively trying to convert everybody to their cause, which I viewed as overtly racist. I had to bite my tongue and tune them out.

When we finally got inside, it all made sense. They'd chosen to simultaneously schedule the voting with not one but four basketball games, and the modest little stadium was packed to bursting, way beyond capacity.

When I finally left the door, I looked at my watch and freaked out. Margaret had been messaging me all morning trying to gauge a timeline for when we could meet up, and I'd been vague and unhelpful. I was annoyed, feeling like she was pestering me, and she was annoyed, feeling like I was avoiding her. Neither was true, of course.

I headed to Parkmore, the most convenient local shopping centre, and just messaged her that I was on the way there. I was in a rush and didn't have time to um and ah about where to go and which place would be most appropriate and the least crowded. Luckily for me, Margaret is incredibly flexible and quick to get organised and out the door, and we didn't have to wait long for her and George.

When they arrived, I apologised that I'd be leaving at 1:15 p.m. to get to Chris's grandparents in time. I like to spend time with Margaret and George—proper, quality time. I wanted to wander through Kmart and Big W, buy the kids a Boost juice, talk and catch up! We hadn't had a real chance to do that since before our holiday!

Chris's family lunch was a pleasant enough affair. Everyone is so lovely, and they adore me and Daisy, and the food is always to die for, but just like with Dad, I didn't feel present. I felt uneasy like my heart wasn't in it. I tried to talk about the marathon enthusiastically and excitedly, but my words came out dull and emotionless. At least, that's what it felt like. I'm pretty sure nobody noticed.

Usually, Chris wants to leave, being a tad antisocial by nature, but today, I hurried things along. I wanted to get home. I couldn't handle people anymore.

I spent the afternoon lying down like an invalid or a moody teenager and couldn't shake the feeling of being glum. I can't think of another word for it. I was like a colourless version of myself. Even pepperoni pizza didn't cheer me up. My mood wasn't even lifted by a movie about a team of underdog disabled basketballers triumphing against all odds. Usually, that kind of thing is right up my alley.

I should be excited, pumped, and buzzing. I'm not. Instead, I've been wandering from room to room with the vague sense that I was forgetting some essential piece of the preparation puzzle and agonising over what to wear: bright-pink long sleeves and leggings, like I wore for my half, or my new bright-yellow shorts and singlet.

Neither seemed right. I felt like I'd be too cold in one and too hot in the other. Rain is predicted, but I haven't needed to train in long sleeves for months. There are also the photos to consider. If I wear pink again, I won't be able to tell my marathon and half-marathon photos apart.

I even turned to social media for advice. The mixed suggestions just made everything more confusing and added to my already throbbing headache. One person would say, 'Pink! Definitely pink!' Another would insist, 'Yellow for sure!'

Others offered the possibility of a mix-and-match type option. I think I've mentioned before that I hate making decisions, especially when I'm depressed or anxious.

I've laid out both outfits next to my bed in the hope that the solution will suddenly and magically dawn on me in the morning. I plan to go to bed early, but I'm terrible at falling asleep, so I've got no chance of drifting off before at least 10 p.m.

I'm not looking forward to the piercing sound of my alarm jolting me awake at 4:45 a.m. tomorrow.

Sunday, 15 October 2023
Melbourne Marathon Day!!!!

I was worried I wouldn't be able to get enough sleep last night and that it'd be hard to wake up and drag myself out of bed at 4:45 this morning, but in the end, that wasn't a problem. I woke up feeling well-rested and full of energy, feeling excited and mentally prepared! I decided to wear my pink outfit but packed the yellow one just in case.

I ate Stuart's recommended breakfast of banana bread, double-checked that I had everything and was out the door right on schedule. I popped the location of the car park I'd booked into the GPS and didn't get lost (a miracle for me)!

That early in the morning, the car park was virtually empty, and I parked in the same spot I'd parked in for the half-marathon so it'd be easy to find my car. I have a horrible memory and an even more horrible sense of direction, so I've had issues in the past of not remembering where I parked my car more times than I can count. It's a real first-world problem.

There were a few other runners in the same car park, so I just followed them, trusting that they knew where to go.

As soon as I got to the MCG, I saw a toilet and popped in to do my business. Nervous peeing. While I was in the ladies' room, I had a sudden change of heart and quickly changed into my yellow outfit. Lots of other people were in shorts and singlets, and it wasn't that cold. I wanted my marathon photos to stand out from my half-marathon photos, where I was in pink.

The next step was to go to the bag drop, and once again, I just followed everyone else. Then, I did the same thing with my walk to the start line. I saw a couple of rows of Portaloos with huge lines, and I thought, Lucky for me, I don't need to go. Then, when I was warming up at the back of the crowd, I had that nervous urge to do so and thought, *Oh no! Will I miss the start of the race?*

While I was waiting, I did a stupid, stupid thing. I don't know why I did it. I looked down at my feet, thought, *My shoes feel a bit loose*, and tightened the laces so that they were snugger around my feet. I have never tightened my shoelaces before. I have never run with them 'snug around my feet.' I should have known better. I think I just felt nervous and wanted to feel more comfortable. I was also looking for something to do with all that nervous energy—something to fiddle with. It would later come back to bite me in the arse.

Despite my worries about the minutes ticking by, I made it to the start line on time. There was a commentary over the loudspeaker, talking about the 'Spartans,' the old guys who had done more than 30 Melbourne Marathons! They had special dark green singlets that said 'Spartan, 30' and were dotted through the crowd. There were even some people who had run every Melbourne Marathon since its inception, and this was their 45th time! They looked positively ancient. But I had a strong suspicion they were a lot fitter than me.

The loudspeaker guy welcomed all the 'marathon debutantes'—the first-time racers. Being at the back of the crowd, I was hoping to see a few other debutantes; people with the same goal as me just to bloody finish the thing before the seven-hour cut-off, without dying!

I nervously looked around and introduced myself to a couple of girls I overheard talking about the race. They confirmed that they, too, were first-timers, incredibly nervous, and had no idea if they would be able to make it or not. I was in good company and relieved I wasn't the only one.

Then I heard the voice over the loudspeaker say, 'These guys have been training for months—some of them have been training for years!'

Years . . . Yes, years. This hit home, and I was swept up in a wave of emotion. I reflected on the four years I'd been running, some of them tough years, especially 2020 and 2021. The 'lockdown' years.

It was like my life was flashing before my eyes, but, more specifically, my running life. Right from those early days of plugging away at the Couch to 5 K. I teared up a little. I thought I'd feel emotional at some point, but I had no idea when it would hit me.

Then it was time.

The countdown, and then the horn, and the slow, nudging and shuffling forward as the front-runners began to take off. I had my Garmin ready to go, and pressed start at the exact moment I crossed the start line.

The race had begun! I was doing it! It wasn't a dream!

The first step of the journey was to run down Flinders Street, past Federation Square, making a turn at St Kilda Road—the famous intersection of Flinders Street Station. On the opposite corner was the iconic St. Paul's Cathedral. I didn't notice any of these beautiful landmarks. I was just focused on the running. We ran past the Arts Centre and the National Gallery of Victoria. Again, I didn't even notice.

I was running at a steady pace—faster than I had in most of my long-run training. I was a bit worried about being too slow, thinking of Stuart's advice to run faster in my running intervals to get a time closer to the six-hour mark, rather than the seven-hour mark. At the same time, I was also worried I was running too fast—the classic marathoner mistake that everyone talks about. Being swept up in the excitement at the start and then running out of steam later.

About 8 km in, as we were running past the Albert Park Lake, I realised that I had gone out too fast. I was running out of energy, and I wasn't even a quarter of the way through! My feet were also starting to hurt. I cursed myself over that tight lacing mistake, but thought, *There's no way I have time to stop and re-lace.*

It was at this point that I started with my 3/1 intervals. Every three minutes felt like an age, and my feet were becoming more and more painful. They were throbbing—they felt like they were on fire. I could feel the blisters forming with every stride. I seriously thought about quitting, then I realised that all the roads were closed, and I'd have to walk all the way back to the MCG anyway.

When I got to the 10 km mark, I expected to feel relieved. A quarter of the way through, right? I did not feel relieved. I felt gutted. How could I be so exhausted after 10 km? I'd felt so much fitter when I'd done my half-marathon. How could my fitness level have declined so much in that time with so much training? What had I been doing wrong?

Running along the St. Kilda esplanade by the water, I started to feel a bit better, emotionally at least. There were plenty of photographers, and I smiled or made a silly face every time I saw one. I was also falling into the rhythm of my intervals with a sense of determination.

By then, some other runners had started to walk/run, and it made me feel like less of a loser. I also finally started to take in the surroundings—the palm trees and the ocean. At one point, this magical sea breeze just wafted in and whooshed right through me, and it felt like absolute heaven.

Soon, we got to the point where the slower runners were redirected, skipping the section that went all the way to Elwood and back. They gave us slow runners a fluoro green wristband so that they'd know to redirect us again near the end. At this time, a swarm of faster runners started to weave through us. The runners who had done a shit-tonne more kilometres than us, with seemingly no effort at all!

From that point onwards, all the kilometre markers on the roadside were a big fat lie. A big fat tease. No, we had not run anywhere that far; only the 'real' runners had, not us. I had to rely on my Garmin to tell me how far we'd come, or (more importantly), how far we had left to go.

Running up Fitzroy Street, back towards the city, I saw the spectators starting to show up in droves: people with signs, people dressed up as cheerleaders, waving pom-poms, people handing out snake lollies to everyone, and little kids wanting to give all the runners a high-five.

It made a big difference to my spirits. I acknowledged all of them. They all pointed out my bright yellow outfit, cheering, waving, smiling and wishing me luck. One person held a big sign that said, 'You got this!' then as I ran past, he flipped it around, and it said, 'There goes a hero!' I felt like a hero!

After that, we started heading back down St Kilda Road in the direction we'd come, back towards the MCG. At that point, I thought, *Fuck it. Fuck these intervals. Fuck you, Coach Stuart!* (If you're reading this, sorry, Stuart; it's not personal!)

I just gave up and started walking. Fast walking but walking all the same. Instead of looking at my watch, I just listened to my body, waiting for little surges of energy. When I felt like I could manage it, I'd say to myself, *OK, I'm just going to run as far as that traffic light, then I'll start walking again.* I repeated this over and over again, all the way back through the city and into the Botanical Gardens.

My walking breaks were getting longer and longer, and my running stints were shorter and few and far between. By this time, all the green wristband people around me were basically just walking. I looked at my watch. Twelve kilometres to go. Twelve kilometres is a long way when each foot feels like one big giant blister and you're basically stumbling.

But I also looked at the time. We had two and a half hours until 2:00 p.m., the dreaded cut-off. I could power-walk 12 km in two and a half hours easily! Heck, I could crawl 12 km in two and a half hours! Every now and then, I'd fall in step with a couple of other walkers, and we'd all chatter excitedly. 'We're going to make it! We're going to make the cut-off, even if we walk the entire way!'

I can't describe what a relief it was to have that realisation dawn on me! It felt surreal! What had I been worried about? Instead of worrying I wouldn't finish, I should have been worried about the torture I'd have to endure to finish. And it was torture. I couldn't believe so many people chose to do this on purpose. I couldn't believe so many people did it more than once!

When we got back to the MCG, the faster runners and the green wristband people filed off in a different direction and parted ways, once again. They were heading in to the stadium for one last victory lap, while we headed into seven laps of shame.

I'd read in the guideline that we'd have to do seven laps, but I'd pictured some decent-sized loop. It was just a big stretch of straight, ugly road with a sharp U-turn at either end.

The idea was that after each 'lap,' they'd put a little mark on our wristband until we had seven marks and could finally enter the hallowed grounds of the MCG. Those seven laps were the hardest seven-odd kilometres I've ever done in my life!

It was agonising to know that we were *so* close and yet still so far!

Along this stretch, there were a lot of spectators. People handing out slices of watermelon and oranges, icy-poles and chips, plus a water and Gatorade station. Through every aide station so far, I'd refused the Gatorade and only taken the water. The reasoning behind this was the adage 'nothing new on race day.' I hadn't trained with Gatorade, so I didn't know how my body (or more specifically, my bowels) would handle it.

Once again, I found myself rejecting all advice, and thinking, *Fuck it! Fuck the stupid running books, and fuck you, Coach Stuart!* (Again, Stuart, I'm terribly sorry). Over those last seven laps, I drank enough Gatorade to kill a horse. Maybe two horses. Every single lap, 'Yes, please!' down the hatch. Down the hatch with the melon slices, the orange slices, the icy poles and the chips. Anything they could give me. Gimme, gimme, gimme!

Most people were totally resigned to walking at this point. We were all going to finish, so what did it matter? It mattered to me. I'd expected to see my family on the sidelines for the seven laps, but they were nowhere in sight. With every lap, I scoured the side of the road, desperately seeking a familiar face. Nothing. I texted Chris. I texted Mum. 'WHERE R U??'

After waiting for what seemed like an eternity for a response, Chris rang me. 'Where the hell are you?' I demanded. 'I'm at the Beyond Blue tent with Daisy, and your Mum's at the finish line.'

'You were supposed to come to Brunton Road for my seven laps!' I panted into the phone. He seemed a bit taken aback by how pissed off I sounded. He fumbled through an excuse about them getting lost and not being able to find it and thinking I was finished, judging by the tracking app. I explained that I still had a heap more laps to go, then hung up on him.

I was too exhausted to talk.

In the middle of the 'lap area' was a large cowbell with a sign that said, 'Ring if this is your last lap.' Every now and then, someone would ring the bell enthusiastically, and a huge roar would erupt from the volunteers, spectators and runners alike.

I wanted so badly to ring that fricking bell!

For about the first three laps I did a mixture of run/walk, despite the fact that running had become incredibly painful and excruciating on the balls of my feet, but then I gave up. I walked, I walked fast, and I smiled and waved at the spectators and volunteers, and just thought, *Let's get this done!*

I'd given everything I had to give. I couldn't run anymore.

When I came to my last lap, I could hardly believe it. It felt much longer than any of the other laps before it—of course it did! When I got to that bell, I rang it like my life depended on it. A huge cheer went up, and I felt like a rock star! As I got to the people marking off our wristbands, I grinned and held up seven fingers; then they waved me into the MCG.

Suddenly I could run. Not just trudging along like I had in my weak little bursts over the last two hours, but a full-blown run. I didn't care how much it hurt; I was seizing this moment of glory! I looked up into the stands, which were mostly empty by this stage, but I didn't care.

I was on top of the world! Nothing could bring me down! All around the stadium were huge balls of fire being shot up into the air, heralding the auspiciousness of the event.

Suddenly, I heard my name! Not just being called out, but over the loudspeaker! *Was I imagining things? How did they know my name?* In amazement, I heard my victory lap being commentated, 'That there is Jacqui in the yellow! Jacqui's running for Beyond Blue, a wonderful charity, and this is her first ever marathon! Jacqui, if you look to your right, you'll see your mum right there in the stands. . . . '

I looked over, and there she was, waving proudly like it was the bloody Olympics. To be honest, it felt like the Olympics. I felt like a superstar athlete!

I felt a tap on my left shoulder and turned to see a man handing me a big bouquet of yellow flowers, matching my outfit exactly, and a yellow sign saying, 'Go Jacs!' 'These are from your mum,' he quickly explained as I ran by. I was grinning from ear to ear as I crossed the finish line, bouquet and sign in hand.

I stumbled over in a daze to retrieve my medal and disappeared into the bowels of the stadium.

I was disoriented. I think I was in shock and my brain wasn't working. I saw a sign saying 'Massages' with an arrow and started to shuffle in that direction. It felt like a long, agonising walk, through a dark concrete tunnel, to the massage area, and I thought, *Are they doing this to fuck with us?*

Finally, I ended up in an enclave full of massage tables and volunteers, and they told me to shed my bags, flowers, sign, and medal. I was reluctant to take off my hard-earned, coveted medal, but I was more desperate for a massage.

I was genuinely fearful that if I lay down, I'd never get back up again, but I climbed onto the table and got the gentlest, lamest massage of my life. It was a bit of a disappointment, but I hadn't been expecting much.

After my massage, I felt dazed and disoriented once again. I was back in the concrete tunnel, just wandering around past various ambulance vehicles and asking for directions. Somehow, I found my way to the bag drop, and there were only a few bags sparsely scattered around, so I found mine easily.

After that, I got lost and confused again, trying to find my way to the race village. When I found it, it was quiet; just a few stragglers eating and drinking at picnic tables. I called Chris. I tried to describe where I was, and he did the same, and we both got totally confused.

I was hungry. I was thirsty. I needed a wee. 'Just find Mum and ask someone where the race village is!' I demanded—bossy and curt. Then I looked at the various food trucks, all unappetising, and settled on a pathetic little chicken wrap, just because it was already made.

I sat down at a free table, and before long, Chris appeared and I waved him over, with Mum and Daisy in the pram in tow. Daisy was fast asleep. She'd missed all the action. There were huge hugs all around, and Mum and Chris both told me how proud they were.

Mum made me promise never ever to run a marathon again, and I assured her my marathon days were over. It was a bucket list thing, and I'd ticked it off!

We took some photos of me with my medal and my flowers, and I tried to shovel some nutrients into my mouth. It was hard to chew and swallow. It felt like an effort. Of course, my body was hungry—but at the same time, I had no appetite. I think I was in shock. So many things were happening at once, text and Facebook messages pouring in, questions from Mum and Chris, Daisy waking up, and my fried brain was having trouble processing!

I had an idealised vision of how the aftermath of my marathon would go. I romanticised eating the best meal and drinking the best beer I'd ever tasted. I had imagined an afternoon of basically pigging out and getting drunk into the early evening—a celebration.

I asked Mum to get me a beer, but after the effort of eating my pathetic little wrap and drinking a soft drink, it was hard to even get it down, let alone savour the taste. There was no party atmosphere. The place was deserted. Most people had just finished the race and then gone home. It was all a bit of an anti-climax.

One thing that wasn't anti-climactic was the social media blow-up. So much attention! So much praise! The word 'inspirational' was thrown around a lot. Getting all the photos from the race was so cool. I don't want to toot my own horn, but the camera loves me. You would never guess how gruelling the race had been from the big grin on my face in every shot—plus a couple of silly ones.

My official time was 6:21:39, which is pretty good, considering my goal time was 7 hours. According to my Garmin, I did it in 6:17:15. Of course, I'd like to think the Garmin was more accurate. Speaking of Garmin stats, I got personal bests for my 10 km and half-marathon distances! I may have gone out too fast, but I did it in spectacular style! Who needs negative splits?

Mum and Chris said they were surprised how fast I was going as they were tracking me at the start of the race. When I looked at my Garmin, the first 11 km were all under eight minutes, even though I'd already begun my intervals at around the 8 km mark.

I was much more interested in burying my head in my phone and checking out my photos and stats than I was in partying. And in terms of social energy, I was just done! Kaput! I just wanted to take off my shoes, go get a proper massage, have an Epsom salt bath, and then lance all my gigantic blisters—in that order.

So that's exactly what I did. I went to bed early because I was tired. Strike that, exhausted. But I wasn't sleepy. My head was buzzing. I was wired. I was on a high. After a proper dinner and a bath, the brain fuzz had lifted, and mentally, I was firing on all cylinders.

From the comfort of my warm bed, I went on a frenzied social media free-for-all!

Facebook! Instagram! Running groups! Bipolar groups! This photo with that caption, that photo with this caption. Hitting 'Like' on hundreds of comments. Congratulating everyone else on all their marathon, half, 10 km and 5 km efforts! After all, Sunday is race day all around the world—and the online running community is a global one.

I started to think about what was next for me. Some 5 km races and 5 km PB? A 10 km PB? Maybe even a half-marathon PB? In my madness, I even considered running next year's marathon!

The possibilities were endless, except for the possibility of sleep. I was way too excited for that! I was still in disbelief that it had all finally happened!

EPILOGUE

In the days and weeks after the Melbourne Marathon I was extremely proud—proud is an understatement, but I can't come up with a better adjective. For the first couple of days, I wouldn't even take my medal off, thrusting it in everybody's face like a kid with their show and tell—everyone at work, choir, family, friends, and even Chris's friends. I was walking on air!

My feet were killing me for the first few days. I was hobbling around like a woman nine months pregnant with triplets. Our school receptionist took pity on me and assigned my yard duties to someone else. Thanks, Fiona!

I didn't run at all for a few weeks. I was totally over it and felt I more than deserved a little break. It was an extremely weird feeling not running. I didn't know what to do with myself and felt a bit like a ship without a rudder, lost at sea.

On marathon day, the results of the Referendum came in, but in all the excitement, I didn't realise until the day after. Australia had voted 'No' to an Aboriginal Voice to Parliament. I couldn't help but wonder what the rest of the world thought of us.

Two days after the marathon, a very significant thing happened. Significant for me, anyway. I was diagnosed with borderline personality disorder and generalised anxiety disorder, along with my bipolar. I'm still getting my head around it.

I got my semi-colon tattoo on my right wrist, as well as the bipolar symbol :) : on my right hand.

I continued to hustle and spruik my Beyond Blue campaign, getting sponsors from nights out, choir, and through a couple more newspaper articles. In the end, I raised more than $4,500, fourth on the leader board for the marathon's Beyond Blue fundraisers. The 2023 Melbourne Marathon campaign for Beyond Blue, with 3,316 fundraisers, raised over $220,000!

After saying 'Never again' and 'This was just a bucket-list thing,' I'm already considering running another marathon, once Daisy's old enough to get her head around what a marathon is and she can come and cheer for me.

I have a niggling, itching desire to beat my time and get a new PB.

ACKNOWLEDGEMENTS

I'd like to thank my family. My mum, for keeping me sane, looking after Daisy, cooking numerous meals and keeping my house from looking like a bomb site. My partner, Chris, for putting up with me—probably the most amazing and patient man on the planet. My mother-in-law, Tonia, my father-in-law, Emilio, Tia Faviola, and my cousin Michelle, for all the babysitting. My daughter, Daisy, for making me smile and laugh even on the worst of days.

My Parkrun Family—Stuart, Hung, Charles, Knowles, Prue, Garry, Tanya, Joe, Susan, Tania, Dale, Kathleen, Paul, Rosalind, Rolf, Ruba, Megan, Rebekah, Abi, Peter, Andrea and Michael.

To Brent Adcock, Julie Jones, and Justin Fitzpatrick—Melbourne Marathon veterans who gave me tonnes of reassuring advice.

My running coach, Stuart Marshall, who is largely responsible for getting me across the finish line.

My psychiatrist, Lucinda Smith, and my psychologist, Stuart Cheverton, for working so hard to help me manage my mental health.

Thank you to *The Dandenong Star Journal*, *The Sentinel Times*, and *The Advertiser* for running my story and helping me promote my Beyond Blue fundraising campaign.

Tristan and Natalie at Beyond Blue.

All the staff and volunteers, and sponsors at Run Melbourne and the Melbourne Marathon.

Christoph Bartlett and Jess Rae Allie, for reading my pages and guiding me through my writer's block and Imposter Syndrome every day. Judith Rochecouste, for all your editing skills.

Catherine Deveny, a goddess and a mentor from the Gunna's writing retreat. What a great weekend!

To Bonita Mersiades, and everyone from Pepper Press (Fair Play Publishing), for taking a chance on this first-time author.

My best friend Margaret, for all the support and for a beautiful friendship, and lastly, all the sponsors who generously donated to my Beyond Blue Campaign.

ABOUT THE AUTHOR

Jacqui Louise Swallow is a dedicated mum and teacher's aide who has lived with bipolar disorder since her teenage years and more recently has also been diagnosed with borderline personality disorder and generalised anxiety disorder.

Now in her 40s, she has found running to be the most effective way to manage her symptoms. An enthusiastic park runner, in 2023 she took on the challenge of the Melbourne Marathon, embracing the 6+ hour endurance run at her own pace.

* * * * *

If you or anyone you know needs help or advice about matters raised in this book, please contact one of the following organisations, or a medical doctor or other professional healthcare provider.

Beyond Blue
1300 224 636
www.beyondblue.org.au

Mensline Australia
1300 789 978
www.mensline.org.au

headspace
1800 650 890
www.headspace.org.au

Suicide Call Back Service
1300 659 467
www.suicidecallbackservice.org.au

Lifeline
13 11 14
www.lifeline.org.au

More really good books from Fair Play Publishing

My Business is Now North
By Anthony Sobb

Turning the Tide
By Michelle Ford-Eriksson

Woman Offside - A year with Lise Klaveness as she tries to reform football
By Marius Lien

Tales of South American Football – Passion, Revolution and Glory
By Jorge Knijnik

Ladies First - The Story of Australia's First Olympic Hockey Gold Medal
By Ashley Morrison

Shirley's Story - A tale of strength, courage, and hope
By Emily Eklund Power

Just Because - Love Loss Renewal
By Lisa Gallate

George Best Down Under
By George Best

Available from
fairplaypublishing.com.au
and all good bookstores

FAIRPLAY

www.ingramcontent.com/pod-product-compliance
Lightning Source LLC
Chambersburg PA
CBHW070658120526
44590CB00013BA/1010